D1506592

The Last Days

A Catholic Analysis of the Apocalypse and the Second Coming of Jesus Christ

By Shane Schaetzel

Regnum Dei Press
MMXXII

March 25, 2022
Feast of the Annunciation of Our Lord
First Edition

Edited by Michael Hartung

Unless otherwise indicated, all Scripture references are taken from the World English Bible (Catholic), WEBC, 2020 Stable Text Edition, Public Domain, www.worldenglish.bible

Cover Art
Woman of the Apocalypse
By Jacopo Palma il Giovane
16th century
Public Domain

**To my parents:
Stephen & Tricia**

Thank you for a good Christian upbringing.

I want to thank Mr. Michael Hartung for his editing assistance. I also want to thank Fr. Christopher Phillips, Fr. Kenneth Bolin, Fr. Chori Seraiah and Fr. Jeffery Fasching for their valuable reviews and suggestions.

Woman of the Apocalypse
By Jacopo Palma il Giovane
16th century
Public Domain

CONTENTS

Foreword by Fr. Kenneth Bolin

Did you know that Satan hates the first two and last two chapters of Scripture (Genesis 1-2, and Apocalypse 21-22)? Do you know why? Because he isn't in them. He wasn't the Adversary in the Beginning, and he won't be there in the End. Between those two, though, he perverts God's Creation, turning order into chaos.

Dispensations or covenants? Pre, Post, or A-millennialist? Pre, Mid, or Post-Tribulation? Eschatology, the study of the End Times, makes for big theological business. It is the equivalent of religious clickbait. Is prophecy "Thus saith the Lord," or a prediction of when the end will come, and how can we know for sure? Have we forgotten that Our Lord Jesus Christ Himself stated in the Gospels that no one knows, not even the Son (referring to Himself), but only the Father?

These are issues that I, personally, thought were left behind (forgive the allusion) when I became Catholic. Like Shane, I passed through various non-Catholic systems of belief: raised Lutheran, attended Methodist, Presbyterian, United Church of Christ, Baptist, Gospel, and non-denominational evangelical communities; exposed to eastern mysticism and western pagan practices; studied Arabic and read the Koran in its original language. I ended up as a non-denominational minister who became an Anglican priest, whom God finally called home to the Catholic Church. Yes, there was a senior protestant cleric, someone I served alongside in Iraq, who said the word most appropriate to describe me at the time (I was on my way into Anglicanism) was "confused." There was much relief, though, in setting aside certain theological issues, not feeling as though I had to try to figure them out myself, and trusting the authority and wisdom of Holy Mother Church. This isn't being stupid or setting aside logic or reason. On the contrary, the Summary of the Law, as given to us by Our Lord, is a reflection of the Shema of Deuteronomy 6, in that we are to love the Lord our God with all our heart, soul, **mind**, and strength (emphasis added). Our Lord is the Divine Logos of John 1:1; He is reason, order. Thus, there is a call to trust His Body, His Bride, the Church. The reality is, though, nearly a decade into this priesthood, that such discussions continue to abide within the Catholic Church Herself, sometimes as though the Church had never spoken on the issues.

Knowing where Shane is coming from in writing this book, I want to affirm some things. — Aside: Another Evangelical Anglican clerical convert, Fr. Dwight Longenecker, once quoted, quite profoundly, British philosopher F.D. Maurice, in that "a man is most often right in what he affirms, and wrong in what he denies." — First, there are some people who are "so heavenly minded that they are of no earthly good." You live in this world for now; God put you here, so be here. As author Scott Hahn said at a conference I attended with him in 2021, "this is a great time to be Catholic." If God is truly God, then you are here, in this time and place, and there is no other place or time for you to be that is most glorifying to Him, or that will assist you more in growing in holiness (otherwise that's where you'd be). Second, God put you here, but to learn and prepare for Eternity, so don't focus so much on here and now that you forget about the future. There are lessons you must learn as the Lord gives you the opportunity to grow in holiness and virtue, to grow toward perfection. You have a teleology, a divinely inspired end-state, so don't think of your mission as making a utopia here in this fallen creation. Third, prophecy, the way the culture thinks of it, as in predictions of the future and focus on the End Times, does little for the firm believer in Christ. Its main focus is to get the attention of those who don't believe, who have truly lost their way and need something to call them back and put them on the path toward salvation. Finally, for the believer, the one earnestly trying to follow Christ, albeit with setbacks, sins, trials, and temptations, be ready and live. I am not saying that this is all easy, but it is quite simple.

Are we living in the End Times, the Last Days? Yes, we are, and humanity has been for nearly 2,000 years! When it comes to Biblical prophecy, we see the metaphorical wave tops, really knowing neither the amplitude nor the frequency of the waves of time that we reside upon. When we keep the reality of eternity in mind as our context, even 2,000 years is nothing, which is reminiscent of the Psalmist.

Reflecting on the Psalmist, and on Christ, I was reminded of our Jewish heritage as followers of Christ, Himself a Jew. I pondered this while looking at the different perspectives between Catholics and Protestants about the End Times. Shane does a very good job of laying out a lot of historical perspective. The Catholic Church understands its roots, historically, liturgically, religiously, as being the New Covenant Body of Believers, just as the nation of Israel is the Old Covenant Body of Believers. As baptism is to circumcision, laid out for us by St. Paul, so is the Church to Israel. Yet, we are still one body, one faith, one Kingdom, fulfilled in Christ. Incorporated into that is a respect for where we've come from. As so many separated themselves from the Church Catholic, though, a new connection to Israel had to be understood, and hence an inordinate emphasis on the continuation of contemporary Israel as God's chosen nation and people. Unfortunately, within both *eschatology* and *soteriology* (theology of redemption or salvation), this created a dual-covenant understanding, in that Jews would have one way to be saved in the end, by virtue of their being members of Israel, and the Gentiles, becoming Christians, would have a different way of being saved. This has never been and can never be right. As St. Paul reminds us, all have sinned and fallen short of the glory of God, and that we are all saved by grace through faith in Christ (excluding the word "alone," which Martin Luther inserted).

All people are called to Christ, and all people are made in the image of God, Jew and Gentile. All are called to conversion and holiness. The universal call to holiness has been an ongoing emphasis of the Catholic Church. While respecting cultural differences, the Church has always maintained core beliefs and embraced some sense of diversity across all of God's children. Cult is the root of culture, and religion, particularly religious expression, as you may see in liturgy, is what drives culture. God's children, while all possessing His Divine Image, look different in different places at different times. Yet, the Kingdom of God has been established. A Kingdom, to be a Kingdom, needs a King, a people, and a place. Christ is King, and just as surely as King David and his successors had prime ministers (Matthew 16, referring to Isaiah 22), so the Pope is the prime minister of Christ on earth. While the nation of Israel was the ruled people of God under the Old Covenant, this was expanded by Christ to all people, even to the ends of the earth (Acts 1). Rather than bringing people to the place that was ruled, the boundaries of the Nation of Israel, Christ commanded that the nation, the place to be ruled, expand out to include all places and all peoples. This is why the Church is Catholic, as in universal. This Church is the fulfillment of Christ's call to His Jewish Apostles, the Great Commission of Matthew 28.

Thus, in the end, both literally and metaphorically, both individually and corporately, our charge is the same: the fulfillment of the Great Commission, based on the Great Commandment, and the second, like unto it, while maintaining true religion (James 1). Our call is not to test the Lord, to discern when "the End" is going to come, but to live each day now, seeking virtue, holiness, and perfection. As the Baltimore Catechism asked and answered, God made man to know, love, and serve Him in this life so that we might enjoy Eternity with Him forever. If you think of those whom you love the most, they are those whom you have spent a great deal of time with. You talk with them, listen to them, open your heart up to them. In the process of truly knowing them, you first open yourself emotionally, until you realize that you have made a choice in their favor. You are committed to them in some way. The reality of that choice drives service to them, seeking out what is best for them, which is the true meaning of love, Christian charity. The same thing is true in our relationship with God. Our study of God, which has a specific end or telos attached to it, is oriented toward Love, the choice of what is best for "the other," as Pope St. John Paul II stated. What is best in life? Those of you familiar with Conan the Barbarian would answer, "to crush your enemies, to see them driven before you, and to hear the lamentations of their women." This is an abbreviation of something the pagan Genghis Khan was reputed to have said, but it is the opposite of what is best, in that it is a rejection of love. What is best is union with God for eternity.

You possess an immortal soul, even while you live now in a mortal body. Stop worrying about what may or may not happen to the mortal body, and really start living now in a way that prepares that immortal soul for eternity. Eschatology has driven many to fear the future, just as much as fear of disease and death has driven many to fear over the last couple of years. God tells us not to be afraid; anything that drives this unhealthy fear is not of God, period. If this book helps you to live without fear now in light of eternity, then thanks be to God (Deo Gratias). It is because of the unhealthy preoccupations out there that I typically do not recommend eschatological books or writings. I know and believe in Shane, though, and am reassured in his treatment of the topic. May God fill you with faith, hope, and love.

Fr. Kenneth M. Bolin
Pastor, St. Thomas Becket Catholic Church
Fort Worth, Texas
Chaplain, U.S. Army (Retired)
Ordinariate of the Chair of St. Peter
ThM, Dallas Theological Seminary
M.A., Catholic University of America

Chapter 1
Last Days Craze

In 1980, I was a young fellow in the fifth grade of my elementary school in West Covina, Southern California. It was a rough year for me. I was dealing with some bullies in my class and having problems academically. During this difficult year, I made just one close friend. He was a classmate. For this book, I'll call him John. He and I both struggled with the same group of bullies, and so we tried to watch each other's backs as well as we could. I'm pleased to report that one of those bullies got his just-deserts in the sixth grade, which left him and his comrades unable to bother me again, but that was the sixth grade. In the fifth grade, I was much smaller. So John and I spent a lot of time together, and during this time he decided to share his religious faith with me.

You see, I was born a Lutheran (LCMS)[1] but raised in the American Baptist Church (ABC). It was Baptist in doctrine, like the Southern Baptists. However, the particular church we attended[2] was more liturgical in practice, almost Methodist in character. Our pastor wore some black liturgical robes and a stole. We sang hymns and offered some liturgical responses. Overall, it was a pleasant religious upbringing, and I am grateful for it. By the fifth grade[3] however, my family wasn't going to church that often anymore. I could probably count on one hand the number of times we

---

[1] LCMS - Lutheran Church Missouri Synod, a conservative Lutheran denomination in North America

[2] First Baptist Church of West Covina, California no longer exists.

[3] 1980-81 school year

showed up in a year, so I was religiously hungry and didn't know it yet. That's the funny thing about spiritual hunger. You can be starving, and not even know it for a long time.

Even though our church attendance waned during those years, I was never in want of a Bible, religious books and articles of faith (crosses, statues, pictures, etc.). My parents made sure of that. I also knew that I could attend church any time I wanted. Not only would my parents take me there upon request, but I could have easily ridden my bicycle there on my own. Most importantly, I knew I could talk to my parents about religious matters whenever I desired, and I occasionally took advantage of that.

My friend, John, was part of a large religious movement called *Evangelicalism*.[4] I'm not sure which church specifically he was a member of, but that doesn't matter. I remember him speaking to me quite a bit about the televangelist, Jim Bakker, and some religious television network. I had the feeling that whatever church group he was part of, it was obscure. Members of this group frequently watched Jim Bakker, but I don't think they were affiliated with him in any official way.

---

[4] Wikipedia, as of the date of this publication, presents probably the best definition of Evangelicalism, which reads as follows: "*Evangelicalism, also called evangelical Christianity, or evangelical Protestantism, is a worldwide trans-denominational movement within Protestant Christianity that maintains the belief that the essence of the Gospel consists of the doctrine of salvation by grace alone, solely through faith in Jesus' atonement. Evangelicals believe in the centrality of the conversion or 'born again, experience in receiving salvation, in the authority of the Bible as God's revelation to humanity, and in spreading the Christian message. The movement has long had a presence in the Anglosphere before spreading further afield in the 19th, 20th and early 21st centuries.*"

John told me about this thing called "The Rapture" and how we are living in the Last Days of the world. He told me that Ronald Reagan was the Antichrist because the letters of his name add up to 666 and that Pope John Paul II was the False Prophet spoken of in the Book of Revelation. He assured me that we were just a couple of years away from the Rapture of the Church, and the beginning of the Great Tribulation, which would see Ronald Reagan and Pope John Paul II rule the world by a global tyranny. Christians, who weren't taken in the Rapture, would be persecuted to death. In fact, he pegged the Rapture to happen in 1982, which was why it was so imperative that we all be prepared as soon as possible. The year 1982 was a fairly popular Rapture date among Evangelicals at that time. This was in part due to a prediction by a popular Baptist minister named Pat Robertson. So, a great many Evangelical preachers latched on to that date.

John was apparently a member of a group run by one such Evangelical preacher. He was worried about me, and I think he believed I wasn't "prepared" for the Rapture. He asked me to say the "sinner's prayer," which I was reluctant to do because I mistakenly thought it would mean that I would have to join his church. I didn't want to do that. Because I refused to say the prayer, he thought I might be one of the souls who would be lost. So, John took me under his wing as his "disciple."

The bullying he and I endured that year only made things worse. It solidified his belief that these were the Last Days, and he was sure that the reason why we were bullied was that we were Christians and they were not. Or at the very least, he was a Christian, and I was his disciple. Either way, it was a persecution complex, validated in his mind by a group of punks who thought they were so tough. They were just bullies, nothing more, who enjoyed being creeps and beating up smaller boys. I think if they knew what kind of persecution complex they were creating in John, they would have enjoyed it even more. We kept all that to ourselves though. They were never the wiser.

The fifth grade came and went. I moved on to the sixth grade at the same school, while John moved away to someplace far east of the Los Angeles valley. He told me his parents were moving away from the city to escape any potential chaos that might soon unfold, and prepare for the Rapture. I got the feeling they weren't alone. I think they moved with a group of people.

That was the last time I ever saw John, but I did hear his voice once more. He called me on New Year's Day in 1982 to remind me that the end was near, the Rapture was coming, and to say "goodbye" just in case I wasn't ready. By this time, I had already spoken to my parents about the whole thing and felt assured that he was wrong and would soon find out the hard way. We chatted for a bit, exchanged some pleasantries, and then said our goodbyes. On my end, I figured he would call back in a year or so, and we would both laugh about it later. On his end, there was a solemn tone of sadness. I think he believed I wasn't ready and would be "Left Behind" to face the horrors of the Ronald Reagan Antichrist and his Papal False Prophet. He never did call back. I tried to call him a couple of times, but the phone number had changed. I never heard from John again.

John was an *Evangelical*, who subscribed to an end-times belief system called *Dispensationalism*. Basically, John had a very literal understanding of the Bible, and most especially the Book of Revelation, which he believed foretold future events that would unfold during his lifetime. It's actually a very common belief system. Granted, John's version of it was a little wacky: identifying Ronald Reagan as the Antichrist, Pope John Paul II as the False Prophet, and 1982 as the year of the Rapture. This was the early 1980s, however, and at that time there were many wacky things going on in American Evangelicalism.

John certainly wasn't my only friend who believed in the Rapture. There was another who lived across the street from me. I'll call him Roger. He was a good kid who accepted my Christianity and never pressured me to subscribe to his Evangelical beliefs. He was also part of another obscure Evangelical church which he invited me to once, and they gave me my first adult Bible. It was the NASB[5] version. I spent a lot of time reading it and have many fond memories of my friendship with Roger. I also had some extended family members who believed in the Rapture. At that time, they too were part of an Evangelical church called Calvary Chapel, which taught the Rapture and Dispensationalism as a matter of religious dogma. Again, their views were much more reasonable, tamed, and they never made me feel uncomfortable about it. In fact, I always felt a sense of warmth and affection at their house. Years later, my own parents joined Calvary Chapel, and they now believe the same thing. Both of my sisters are likewise part of similar Evangelical churches that teach the Rapture. So, I want to avoid leaving you with the impression that all Rapture Dispensationalists hold to bizarre teachings like that of my fifth-grade friend John. In fact, most are really toned down, speak more in generalities, and never set dates.

Rather, I bring up my experience with John to give you some of my background and illustrate how

---

[5] NASB - New American Standard Bible, a popular Protestant translation

bad it can get. My exposure to John's beliefs, at a time in my life when I endured a lot of stress caused by schoolyard bullying, led me to eventually develop a profound interest in this subject. That interest manifested in a virtual obsession with Dispensationalism after I became an Evangelical myself in my early adult years. After my conversion to Anglicanism, and later to Catholicism, that obsession chilled to an academic pursuit focused on developing a healthier Christian understanding of the Book of Revelation and the Church's teachings on the Last Days.

One thing that's true about many Protestants is that they move around a lot. It's very common for Protestants to hop from one type of denomination to another, as many as four or five times during their lives. Such was the case with me. I started out as a Lutheran (from birth to age 5) but was raised as an American Baptist (from age 5 to 19). That was my parent's choice, not mine. Then as a young adult (from age 20 to 27), I decided to attend Calvary Chapel like my extended family. So, I went from Lutheran to Baptist to Evangelical. That's three denominations so far. There I met my wife, who was baptized into the Methodist church as a baby but attended many denominations during her childhood. Later in my adult years, my wife and I became Anglicans (from age 27 to 29). That's four denominations for me now. It was only after spending some time as Anglicans that we decided to join the Catholic Church (from age 29 to present), and here we have stayed for over two decades. We finally found our way home.

It was during our time as Evangelicals at Calvary Chapel, from 1990 to 1997, that we too subscribed to the doctrine of the Rapture and Dispensationalism. It was drilled into us every Sunday morning and Wednesday night. (Yes, we often attended services twice a week.) My own obsession with the topic made me a bit of a sponge, absorbing every bit of information that I could, and spending countless hours reading books, commentaries, and journals on the subject. Every week at Calvary Chapel, Bible studies were interpreted in one particular way -- Dispensationalism -- to the point where we started to think there really is no other way to interpret those passages of Scripture. When we ran across Christians who didn't interpret the Bible that way, we started to think there was something wrong with them. I'm not talking about a difference of opinion here. I'm talking about questioning the legitimacy of their Christian faith. Specifically, I remember wondering if people who didn't believe in the Rapture were even Christians at all. I was becoming like my childhood friend John, minus the date setting and other peculiarities.

After becoming Anglican, and eventually Catholic, my wife and I were able to leave the Rapture thing behind us. Now and then, however, I still run across Evangelicals who are devout Dispensational Rapturists. I remember having conversations with them in the early years following our conversion to Catholicism, and I remember how disturbed they became when I said I no longer believed in the pre-tribulation Rapture. By the way they reacted, you would think that I had just told them that I no longer believed in Jesus Christ!

We are living in an age of confusion, especially about the End Times and the Last Days. I've run across many Catholics who are confused about these things, and a good number of them have even adopted the Rapture theories of Evangelical Dispensationalists. Part of it has to do with the times we're living in. Indeed, we may be living in a prophetic time, but I don't think it's prophecies of the Last Days we're dealing with. I'm speaking more of Marian prophecies here, dealing with the Church's struggle with political Marxism in the East and cultural Marxism here in the West.

I should make a clear distinction here in terminology. The "End Times" are not the same as the "Last Days." In Christian eschatology, the phrase "End Times" can mean the time leading up to the destruction of the Second Temple in Jerusalem (A.D. 70), or it can mean the time following the First Coming of Jesus Christ 2,000 years ago, all the way up to the present day. Yes, according to this latter definition, we are now living in the "End Times," and we have been living in the "End Times" for two millennia. I tend to prefer this latter definition and will use it in this book. As for the term “Last Days,” that’s different. For this book, the term "Last Days" pertains strictly to the time just before the end of history, at the end of the world.

This is where the confusion lies. I think it's safe to say that most Western Christians, particularly Evangelicals, believe we are living in the Last Days and this is because of all the radical changes over the 20th century, combined with the increase in violence and political upheaval in the early 21st century. While the technology is new, many of the problems are not. The world has been here before. The world is at the end of something, but it's probably not the end of the world.

Rather, I think what we are facing, right now, is the end of an era. By that, I mean the end of the era following the Second World War, which was defined as a stalemate between the two superpowers of the Cold War. I also think we are approaching the end of the era of large democratic republics, as our system of national government becomes increasingly unmanageable.

Along with that, I think we are approaching the end of the Age of Enlightenment ideas, as the promise of individual liberty and religious pluralism has left us in a state of social upheaval. Finally, I think we are approaching the end of the era of Protestantism, as we witness the collapse of mainstream Protestant denominations and an impending bigger collapse of mainstream Evangelicalism which may come within our lifetime. That's a lot of endings coming all at once. It's no wonder people would think it's the end of the world. Indeed, it probably is the end of the only kind of world our generation has ever known. That doesn't mean it's the end of the planet though. The planet will go on, and so will humanity, with or without these things, just as it did in the past. We can't imagine it right now because the thought of losing this way of life is unfathomable to us.

When the Roman Empire fell, the Romans thought it was the end of the world. When Jerusalem fell, the Jews thought it was the end of the world. When the Aztec Empire fell, the Aztecs thought it was the end of the world. Indeed, to all of these people, it was the end of *their* world, the only world they had ever known. Yet, the planet went on, and so did humanity. So it will be with us. We are facing the collapse of the largest civilization in history -- modern Western Civilization, which is rooted in European Christendom. However, when it falls, it won't disappear into a black hole. It will simply be reshaped into something else. That's just how these things work, and the human race will go on.

As a Christian, I still believe in the Last Days and the Second Coming of Jesus Christ. I embrace these beliefs as an integral part of my faith. As a Catholic Christian, I accept all the teachings of the Catechism about these things, and as a student of the Bible, I embrace them even more. I just no longer accept the common narrative that is promoted by Evangelicalism and Dispensationalism.

In the pages of this book, I hope to explain some problems associated with Protestant beliefs about the last things (eschatology), paying particular attention to the Evangelical phenomenon of Dispensationalism and how that interacts with Catholics living in predominantly Protestant nations. Then I hope to explain a proper Catholic understanding of last things (eschatology), focusing particularly on the Book of Revelation (Apocalypse), the Augustinian approach to the Last Days, and the message of Church-approved Marian apparitions. So sit down, grab a nice cup of tea, and buckle up, because unless you're used to this kind of stuff, it's going to be a wild ride.

Chapter 2
Whore of Babylon

I hate to break this to you. It's pretty tough news. I hope you're sitting down. The pope is the Antichrist, and the Catholic Church is the Great Whore of Babylon from the Book of Revelation. And if you remain a Catholic, in good standing with the Church, then you are part of the problem. ***Or at least, that's what Martin Luther and his contemporaries wanted us to believe back in the sixteenth century.***

That's the eschatological message of the Protestant Revolution (Reformation). I know some people will find this offensive, but it is the truth. For all the talk about "faith alone" and the “Bible alone,” the real message of the Protestant Revolution (in an eschatological sense) was that salvation cannot be found in the Catholic Church because the Catholic Church is a false religious system controlled by the devil. It's an old heresy, pushing five centuries to be exact, and throughout these centuries, millions of Protestants believed it. More than a few Protestants still do.

It all began with Martin Luther in the early 16th century. Luther needed to justify his schism with Rome, and in doing so, he needed to persuade as many people as possible to follow him. Yet, Luther was faced with a pretty big problem. How do you get a Catholic country to turn against the Catholic Church? His answer was to persuade these Catholics that the Book of Revelation (Apocalypse) was being fulfilled in their time and that the pope himself was none other than the foretold Antichrist! Therefore, a more pure and authentic Christianity would demand a clean break with the pope, and with Rome, for the sake of preserving the one true faith of Jesus Christ. It's a pretty clever tactic. It was so effective that it's been used at least a dozen more times ever since, by various Protestant groups seeking to carve out their niche in Western Christianity.

Martin Luther was born in Eisleben, Saxony of the Holy Roman Empire, back on the 10th of November in A.D. 1483. (This would be a part of modern-day Germany, about 120 miles southwest of Berlin.) After receiving a master's degree from the University of Erfurt in the year 1505, he entered law school in accord with his father's wishes. However, he dropped out that same year and entered Saint Augustine's Monastery in Erfurt on the 17th of July. His decision to do this was curious. He claimed that upon returning to the university earlier that month by horseback, he found himself in the middle of a thunderstorm. A bolt of lightning struck a tree near him, and fearing God's judgment, he called upon Saint Anna to intercede on his behalf, promising to become a monk if his life was spared. According to Luther, he was just keeping his end of the bargain.

However, one of Luther's friends attributed this decision to a bout of depression following the untimely deaths of his two closest friends. According to witnesses at the time, Luther was visibly distressed at his farewell party. His father was furious with him as well, seeing his entry into religious orders as a waste of his education and life. Luther was dedicated to the Augustinian Order and plunged himself into intense penance and frequent confession. His depression seemed to worsen, and he described his time at the monastery as follows…

> *"I lost touch with Christ the Savior and Comforter, and made him the jailer and hangman of my poor soul."*

His religious superior, Father Johann von Staupitz, was worried about Luther and tried to help him by redirecting his mind away from his sins and toward the merits of Jesus Christ. Luther was eventually ordained a priest by the Bishop of Brandenburg two years later in 1507. In the year 1512, he was awarded a doctorate in theology from the University of Wittenberg and received into the faculty there a few days later. He remained in this position for the rest of his life. He was also made provincial vicar of Saxony and Thuringia by his religious order in the year 1515. This meant he would oversee eleven monasteries in his province. Thus, Martin Luther was given a considerable amount of influence and control over religious institutions and academia at the age of thirty-two.

Corruption and Abuse of Doctrine

Wittenberg is about 60 miles southwest of Berlin in modern-day Germany. Back then, Germany didn't exist as an independent state, and the whole region was part of the Holy Roman Empire. This was, at the time, the heart of Christendom. However, this part of Europe had a serious problem with the sale of indulgences. The sale of indulgences was an abuse of the Church's teaching on the doctrines of Purgatory and indulgences. What was intended to be a holy and pious practice, that encouraged people to make small sacrifices following an ancient Jewish custom recorded in the Old Testament,[6] was perverted into a money-making racket that misrepresented the teachings of the Church.

At the center of this scandal was a figure by the name of Johann Tetzel, a Dominican friar and preacher, who also served as the Grand Inquisitor of Heresy in Poland. He was appointed Grand Commissioner for indulgences in Germany and was well-known for taking large monetary donations in exchange for indulgences. An indulgence is not a forgiveness of sin. That's a common misunderstanding. It is rather a remission of the temporal punishment due to sin.

For example, when one sins in this life, he may repent and go to confession, thus receiving forgiveness from God. However, even though sins are forgiven, sometimes sins carry temporal consequences to be experienced either in this life or the next (Purgatory). An indulgence remits the consequences of those sins, primarily in the next life (Purgatory).

As I said, it's an old Jewish custom that's recorded in the twelfth chapter of the second Old Testament book of Maccabees and applied in the New Testament under the teachings of Saint Paul.[7] Officially speaking, the Catholic Church only teaches two things about Purgatory and indulgences. One, Purgatory exists. Two, our prayers and sacrifices help those souls who go there. All of this can be found in the Catechism.[8] Some misconceptions about Purgatory need to be dispelled here. Purgatory is not a "second

[6] 2 Maccabees 12:44-46
[7] 1 Corinthians 3:11-15
[8] Catechism of the Catholic Church 1030-1032; Baltimore Catechism 231-237, 414-416; Catechism of Trent Part I Article 5 *Different Abodes Called Hell* & *To Liberate the Just*, Part 4 *The Dead* & *What Do We Pray For*

chance" for unrepentant sinners. The only souls who go to Purgatory are those already on their way to Heaven, and nothing can stop their eventual entry into Heaven. It can be likened to Heaven's front gate, where the impurities of this life are burned away so that only that which is pure enters the glory of Heaven. The practice of dispensing indulgences is backed by the authority given by Christ to the ministers of the Church to "bind and loose" not only things in this life, but in the afterlife as well.[9]

Tetzel was accused of "selling" indulgences in advance for future sins, a clear violation of the intent behind indulgences, so the rich would "stock up" on indulgences by making large monetary donations anticipating any future sins they might commit.

Tetzel greatly overstated the Church's teaching on Purgatory to make it appear as if the dead could be bought out of Purgatory with enough money. Though he never said it himself, this saying is often attributed to Tetzel's ministry...

"As soon as the gold in the casket rings, the rescued soul to heaven springs."

Martin Luther was rightly scandalized by this and countered it with his Ninety-Five Theses in the year 1517. He was 33 years old when he nailed his Ninety-Five Theses to the chapel door at Wittenberg University, where he served on the faculty. Though commonly portrayed in religious art as some great act of defiance, the door was merely a community bulletin board and was regularly covered with flyers and notices of various sorts. Some say he never actually did this. Whether he nailed it to the door or not is

---

[9] Matthew 16:18-19; Matthew 18:18-20; John 20:23; 2 Timothy 1:16-18, James 5:16

unimportant. What's important is the content of the document itself.

The Protestant Revolution

The Ninety-Five Theses was a challenge to the practice of indulgences in the area, commonly attributed to Tetzel's preaching, and Luther sent a copy to the Archbishop of Mainz, as was the proper protocol in situations like this. This happened on the 31st of October in 1517, which is now attributed as the beginning of the Protestant Revolution (or "Reformation" as it is commonly called). The official response came from a papal bull in the year 1520 entitled *Exsurge Domine* (Latin: "Rise Up O' Lord"), which overtly rejected six of Luther's Ninety-Five Theses, but didn't explicitly state why. Based on interviews with Martin Luther, and things he said in defense of these theses, Rome was able to formulate 41 rejected propositions that demanded his repentance. That's when things started to go downhill fast.

Luther responded by publicly burning the papal bull and declaring that unless he himself was convinced by Scripture alone (*Sola Scriptura*), he would not accept the correction of the pope. Luther was excommunicated from the Catholic Church on the 2nd of January in 1521.

At this time in history, Northern Europe was primed for revolution. Politically speaking, European rulers were interested in massive decentralization of the continent, both on political and economic levels. If Northern Europe was a tinderbox for revolution, then Martin Luther was the poor soul unfortunate enough to strike the first match. Immediately, his resistance to Rome was seen as the spiritual catalyst needed to start the process which ended, of course, in much unnecessary bloodshed.

Quickly thereafter, other religious revolutionaries entered the scene. Chiefly, these included John Calvin of Geneva and Ulrich Zwingli of Zurich. Later, King Henry VIII of England would throw his crown into the ring of Protestant revolutionaries. While he hated Luther, Calvin, Zwingli, and everything they stood for, Henry needed to break with Rome to set himself up as the "head" of the Church of England, so he could give himself an annulment from his first wife. This was an attempt to secure a male heir to the throne. Henry's break with Rome was highly political in nature, but that was actually true for all of Northern Europe. The only difference is that on the main continent, the teachings of Luther, Calvin, and Zwingli (German Reformation) were used as religious cover for the political and financial revolution of European rulers and politicians. In truth, England was a latecomer to the "Reformation" bandwagon. It wouldn't be until Henry's second daughter, Elizabeth I, ascended to the throne in 1558, that England's Revolution (or English Reformation) would take on a more theological tone, mirroring what was happening in the German regions of the main continent.

Luther's excommunication apparently took a great toll on him, both spiritually and mentally. He continued to spiral downward into more heresy and exotic interpretations of Scripture, particularly his interpretation of the Book of Revelation (Apocalypse) which he apparently rejected as canonical and removed it from his list of divinely inspired books, along with the New Testament books of Hebrews, James, and Jude, in addition to the seven Deuterocanonical books he rejected from the Old Testament. For Luther to attribute so much of his eschatological beliefs to a book that he canonically rejected is very peculiar. Nevertheless, he did it, and he did it with great enthusiasm.

Luther's New Approach to Eschatology

Up to that point, most Biblical scholars followed the Augustinian approach to interpreting the Book of Revelation (Apocalypse), which I will explain later in Chapter Six of this book. For now, it will suffice to say that the Augustinian approach is commonly known in eschatological circles as *amillennial*. That is to say the thousand-year millennium, in the twentieth chapter of the Book of Revelation[10], is not to be taken literally. This effectively changes the entire outlook of the Book of Revelation (Apocalypse) to a more non-literal interpretation and moves us away from a linear (or timeline) method of reading it.

Martin Luther, formerly an Augustinian monk (ironically), now an excommunicated heretic, took it upon himself to change all that. He rejected some aspects of the Augustinian approach to the Book of Revelation, while retaining the core of Augustine's amillennial teaching. Luther introduced what later became known as the *Historicist* interpretation or *Historicism*.

Historicism works on the premise that the Book of Revelation is an allegorical timeline spanning from the first century until the Second Coming of Christ. Thus, the Historicist approach would be able to find certain figures and events in history allegorically represented in the Book of Revelation. Luther connected passages from the Book of Revelation to

---

[10] Revelation 20:1-10

certain persons and events in history, even certain persons and events in his own time.

Luther was particularly interested in the time in which he lived and what he believed to be the Book of Revelation's foretelling of it in chapters 13 through 17. He believed the Second Coming of Christ was not far away from his own time, and he stated as much, claiming that he could not imagine the Lord tarrying longer than the end of his century (so Christ would return no later than 1600 according to Martin Luther).[11]

To understand this, we have to look at the time in which Luther lived. His work in the Protestant Revolution spanned the period from 1517 to when he died in 1546. During this time, the New World (Americas) was rapidly colonized by Catholic, European powers. Meanwhile, the Ottoman Turks (an Islamic empire) rapidly conquered new territories in Eastern Europe and around the Mediterranean Sea. They were preparing for a naval advance into Western Europe which, if successful, would have likely led to the fall of the Holy Roman Empire and Christendom in general.

In his exotic Historicist interpretation of Revelation, Luther considered the pope to be the Antichrist,[12] which he assumed to be depicted as the Beast with seven heads and ten horns in the thirteenth chapter of the book. He also interpreted the Catholic Church, headquartered in Rome, as the "Whore of Babylon," represented in the seventeenth chapter. Likewise, Luther interpreted the Ottoman Turks as

---

[11] Weber, Eugen (1999). Apocalypses. Cambridge MA: Harvard University Press

[12] Luther's Papal Antichrist: "Already I feel greater liberty in my heart; for at last I know that the pope is the Antichrist, and that his throne is that of Satan himself." (Martin Luther, as quoted in D'Aubigné, book 6, chapter 9)

represented by "Gog and Magog" from Revelation chapter twenty. Luther apparently believed that Europe would soon end in a bloodbath between the Antichrist (pope) and his whore (the Catholic Church), fighting Gog and Magog (the Ottoman Turks). This would lead to the Second Coming of Christ, all within Luther's generation (no later than A.D. 1600).

What Luther couldn't foresee is what would happen on the 7th of October, in A.D. 1571, twenty-five years after his death, when a fleet of Catholic warships, led by Spain, crushed the Ottoman Turks in an historic naval victory called the Battle of Lepanto. This prevented any further advance of the Islamic empire and secured the future of Christianity in Europe for the next four centuries. Luther was wrong, but that's the problem with Historicism. Actual history rarely ever conforms to the Historicist's interpretations of the Book of Revelation.

It is worthy to note that not a single Protestant warship was present at the Battle of Lepanto. Catholics alone saved Europe from an Islamic invasion, while Protestants sat idle and did nothing. Why? Martin Luther's popular interpretation of Revelation might have played a significant role in some places.

The Birth of Anti-Catholicism

It would appear the European Protestants, mainly in Northern Europe, were content to let the Ottoman Turks invade Southern (Catholic) Europe and wipe out the pope and as many Catholics as possible. It is likely that these Protestants simply believed that God would save them from the Muslims with the return of Jesus Christ, or at the very least, the Turks' war with Catholics would weaken them enough to later be dealt with by the Protestants. Whatever the case, not a single Protestant was present at the Battle of Lepanto, and that would set a precedent. Protestant and Catholic nobility had been at war with each other since 1522, almost immediately following Luther's excommunication, and they would remain at war with each other until 1712. Almost two hundred years of sporadic conflict left a state of enmity between Catholics and Protestants that is still felt in some circles to this very day. There was no way the original Protestants would ally with Catholics on anything, not even to prevent an Islamic invasion of Europe.

The Historicist interpretation of the Book of Revelation prevailed in Protestant Europe and North America until the early twentieth century. This meant that anti-Catholicism remained the norm in Protestant countries for almost as long. The English Penal Laws kept Catholicism technically illegal in the United Kingdom until the nineteenth century.

In North America, hostilities toward Catholics began immediately following the English colonization of the North American East Coast in the early 17th century. Much of the problems between English colonists and Indian "heathens" (Native American tribes) had to do with the fact that French Catholics had already converted many American Natives to Catholicism before the arrival of English Protestants. For example, the Abenaki Nation, a large and powerful Native American tribe, located in what is now Maine and southern Quebec, had been converted to Catholicism peacefully, the way Christians are supposed to evangelize people. The Abenaki refused to accept Protestantism when the English banned Catholics from all the English colonies (including what is now Maine). The English colonists put a bounty on the heads of all Catholic priests who dared to minister to them, and one of them was martyred by the

Mohawks in a raid on the Abenaki. It wasn't until General George Washington offered to give them a French Catholic priest, during the American Revolution, that the Abenaki agreed to work with English-speaking Protestants.

Indeed, the entire French-Indian War was merely an extension of the Seven Years' War, primarily between Catholic France and Protestant England. Admittedly, the war was more political than religious, as Catholics and Protestants fought on both sides of the conflict. Nevertheless, religion still played a big role in how the war was fought and its aftermath. English Protestant enmity toward French Catholics played out in the Quebec Act. This was seen as one of the "Intolerable Acts" cited by the colonists as a cause for the American Revolution. The Quebec Act allowed Catholics, in conquered French Quebec, to continue to practice Catholicism within Quebec after the English won the French-Indian War. The Protestant-English colonists could not tolerate such a large Catholic province within the English Imperial Realm, so they cited this act as "intolerable" and one of the eventual causes for independence from (and war with) England.

Ironically, to win the war against England, the colonists had to ally with the Catholic French, and General George Washington's magnanimous overtures toward Catholics did much to end extreme Catholic-Protestant enmity in North America. Negative religious sentiments remained, appearing in early American politics and public acts of distrust all the way up to the twentieth century, but nothing on the scale seen before the American Revolution.

In all of this, Historicism played a major role, wherein the pope was seen as the Antichrist and the Catholic Church as the "Great Whore of Babylon" written in the Book of Revelation. The Protestant mind was deeply affected by this manner of interpretation, and some Protestants still think this way even today!

Historicism just doesn't work in the discipline of Biblical interpretation (hermeneutics). The most important rule of Biblical interpretation is the rule of context. *"Context rules!"* This means that every passage of Scripture must be interpreted in the context of the surrounding passages. Likewise, every chapter of Scripture must be interpreted in the context of surrounding chapters. So likewise, each book of Scripture must be interpreted in the context of the entire Bible, as well as the historical, cultural and traditional context in which it was written. Historicism doesn't follow this rule because it operates on the premise that the Book of Revelation is an allegorical history book (or timeline) written over a thousand years *in advance* of the history it's supposed to be predicting. The context of the rest of Scripture, as well as the times, culture, and traditions of first-century Jews, is not taken into consideration.

In truth, the Book of Revelation was a book written by a Hebrew Christian (Saint John the Apostle), primarily for other Hebrew Christians in the first century, relating to the fate of the Hebrew nation (The Holy Land) at that time, as well as the future of the Church, which at the time was still run primarily by Hebrew Christians. It's a highly first-century *Jewish* book, and it must be interpreted in that context alone. It's not a crystal ball looking into the future of European Gentiles.

Inevitably, the Historicist is forced to jump all over the text to find the historical parallels he's looking for. So, he's constantly adjusting and re-adjusting his interpretation as history marches on. Had Martin Luther lived long enough, he would have had to completely reformulate his entire eschatological model. Had he done this, it makes one wonder if he would still assign the role of the Antichrist to the papacy.

The Antichrist and the Papacy

On the subject of the Antichrist, it is logically impossible for any pope to fulfill that role. Here's the reason why. The Bible has very specific parameters for who qualifies as antichrist. The term "antichrist" itself simply means "a false Christ" or "an imposter Christ." Throughout history, many people have been "antichrist" in one way or another. We see it every time a person claims to be the promised Jewish Messiah.

Near the time of Jesus' ministry, there were two great antichrists. The first was Judas of Galilee, who led an armed insurrection in A.D. 6 against Rome over the imperial census which was ordered and carried out some years prior. Jesus of Nazareth would have been just a child at this time. We read about Judas of Galilee in a reference made in Acts 5:37. He was an antichrist (anti-messiah) in that he claimed to be the promised Jewish Messiah but failed to deliver anything other than death and destruction to the Jewish people.

The same thing happened about a century later, long after the ministry of Jesus of Nazareth, with the Simon bar Kokhba revolt. From A.D. 132 to 135, a Jew by the name of Simon bar Kosevah led a rebellion against the Roman Empire and actually managed to successfully rule a large portion of the Holy Land as its "king" for about three and a half years. He was claimed to be the promised Messiah by some Jewish authorities at the time, and his surname was changed to "bar Kokhba" because of this. The name means "son of a star." This false messiah treated local Christians with the highest level of contempt. He persecuted them severely if they failed to reject Jesus Christ and follow him. He was eventually conquered by the Romans, which led to the slaughter of more Jews and their eventual exile from the Holy Land. The point here is that the word "antichrist" (or "anti-messiah") is a wholly Jewish concept that only makes sense in a Jewish context. It means "a false christ" or "a false messiah."

The New Testament tells us that in the Last Days there will come a great and final Antichrist, who will be the ultimate false messiah primarily for the Jewish people but also the rest of the world as well. The New Testament tells us that all future antichrists (especially the last one) will take on some very specific religious characteristics. If one doesn't have these characteristics, then one cannot be considered Antichrist. What are these characteristics? Let's see what the Scriptures tell us.

The word "Antichrist" is mentioned exactly four times in the New Testament, and each time it is mentioned by the same author who gave us the Book of Revelation...

> *"Little children, these are the end times, and as you heard that the Antichrist is coming, even now many antichrists have arisen. By this we know that it is the final hour."* (1 John 2:18)[13]

> *"Who is the liar but he who denies that Jesus is the Christ? This is the Antichrist, he who denies the Father and the Son."* (1 John 2:22)

---

[13] World English Bible Catholic (WEBC): Unless otherwise indicated, all Scripture references will be from this translation of the Bible, which is in the public domain.

> *"...and every spirit who doesn't confess that Jesus Christ has come in the flesh is not of God, and this is the spirit of the Antichrist, of whom you have heard that it comes. Now it is in the world already."* (1 John 4:3)

> *"For many deceivers have gone out into the world, those who don't confess that Jesus Christ came in the flesh. This is the deceiver and the Antichrist."* (2 John 1:7)

As you can see, the very author, who is believed to have given us the Book of Revelation, had some very specific parameters for what he considered "Antichrist." According to the Apostle John, the Antichrist must (1) deny that Jesus of Nazareth is the promised Messiah or Christ, and (2) disavow Jesus Christ entirely, especially his divinity.

According to the man who gave us the Book of Revelation in the first place, the primary qualification of Antichrist is to deny Jesus Christ. A pope cannot do this. For his very office as the Bishop of Rome gives testimony that Jesus is the Christ. For a pope to deny Christ would simultaneously mean he denies his own papacy. He's effectively saying, "Jesus is not the Christ, and therefore I am not the pope." It's absurd! The office of the papacy, the Bishop of Rome, is *built* on Saint Peter and his declaration that Jesus is the Christ…

> *"Simon Peter answered, 'You are the Christ, the Son of the living God.'"*

"Jesus answered him, 'Blessed are you, Simon Bar Jonah, for flesh and blood has not revealed this to you, but my Father who is in heaven. I also tell you that you are Peter, and on this rock I will build my assembly, and the gates of Hades will not prevail against it. I will give to you the keys of the Kingdom of Heaven, and whatever you bind on earth will have been bound in heaven; and whatever you release on earth will have been released in heaven.'"

(Matthew 16:16-19)

The papacy is built on apostolic succession from Saint Peter. The idea here is that Peter appointed successors to take his place in apostolic ministry, who in turn appointed successors to replace them, down to this present day. If Jesus is not the Christ, then his words making Peter the "rock" are absolutely meaningless, and the symbolic "keys" he gave him have no value whatsoever. If Jesus is not the Christ, then Peter was not the first pope, and if Peter was not the first pope, then the office of the papacy never existed, and the man who occupies that office today isn't anything. He's just a guy in a white cassock.

Any pope, who wants to be a pope, has to affirm Jesus as the Christ or else he is not the pope. And if he affirms Jesus as the Christ, according to the parameters established by Saint John (the man who gave us the Book of Revelation and the word "Antichrist" in the first place), he cannot be the Antichrist. It's logically impossible because it denies the standard and definition of what the word means. It's sort of like having an American president who denies the existence of the United States of America. If there is no United States, then he cannot be the President of the United States. It's as simple as that. If he claims to be the president, then he must affirm the existence of the United States, or else he denies his own office!

I find it rather amazing that Martin Luther couldn't see this with all his theological education. Perhaps he was blinded by the sad events of his life and the way his rebellion against Rome was used by civil rulers as a power grab. In a very real sense, the path Martin Luther took locked him down a course that others made sure he saw through. Luther was a powerful tool for the political elite in the German region of the Holy Roman Empire, and they weren't about to let him go. He relied on them for his physical safety and couldn't afford to disappoint them. To Martin Luther, the pope had to be the Antichrist because if he wasn't, Luther would have to face the awful truth of what he had done. The papal-Antichrist cabal was necessary for Luther to retain some level of sanity. Though some think he even lost that, as Luther's later writings have given them just cause to doubt.

By the twentieth century, Historicism was on its way out of mainstream Protestant thinking. The seeds for its demise were planted in the early nineteenth century by none other than an Anglican clergyman. While Historicism became mostly obsolete in the 20th century, the anti-Catholicism that resulted from it remains with us to this very day. Thankfully, this no longer takes on the political and legal manifestations it used to. Yet, it is, nevertheless, a big part of the Protestant psyche. By the end of the twentieth century, the Protestant understanding of Historicism would be culturally replaced by a radically different approach to the Book of Revelation. This particular approach is called *Futurism*, and more specifically, a brand of

Futurism called *Dispensationalism*. We could call it the English rebuttal to German Eschatology.

Chapter 3
Rapture Ready

The dawn of the nineteenth century saw tremendous changes, both in Europe and North America. The United States had just attained independence from the English crown, steam locomotives were spanning the landscape of both continents, the seeds of the industrial revolution had been firmly planted, and the so-called "Enlightenment" had gutted traditional religious beliefs in the Protestant world.

John Nelson Darby was born at the very beginning of this age, in Westminster, London in the year 1800. He was the youngest of six sons to an Anglican family, and they were wealthy landowners in Ireland. His family owned a castle in what is the central county of the Irish Isle. Like Martin Luther, he initially studied law in college, but eventually felt called to the Anglican priesthood. He was ordained in 1826 and assigned to an Anglican parish in Delgany, County Wicklow on the east coast of Ireland. There he claimed to have converted hundreds of Roman Catholic peasants to Anglicanism. He allegedly did this by promising that conversion to the Anglican Church of Ireland would not be tantamount to swearing allegiance to the King of England, which was something that most Irish would never voluntarily do. However, all that ended when the Anglican Archbishop of Dublin ruled that converts were obliged to swear allegiance to George IV as rightful King of Ireland.

Darby was blindsided! He couldn't believe what happened and what an awful situation he had unintentionally put all those converts in. He resigned his curacy in disgust, leaving the Anglican priesthood behind in 1827.

Shortly thereafter, he fell from his horse and was seriously injured. While recovering from his injuries, he began thinking about the Old Testament Kingdom of Israel, and how that seemed so different from the Anglican concept of church. Over the next five years, following the Protestant tradition of reinventing *ecclesiology*[14] and *eschatology*,[15] Darby formulated a whole new belief system. One particular belief he postulated was the rejection of ordained clergy because he surmised that the notion was limiting the Holy Spirit. During this time, he joined an interdenominational group of Christians who met to informally "break bread" together in Dublin as a symbol of their unity in Christ. There was no distinction of clergy and laity between them. By 1832 this group had grown significantly in size and set up multiple houses of worship in England and Ireland. They eventually came to be called the Plymouth Brethren.

By the year 1831, Darby officially and formally left the Anglican Church of Ireland. From that year forward, he was no longer an Anglican. Darby had become something else. It was the beginning of a Protestant movement we identify today as *Evangelicalism*. From 1831 to 1833, Darby participated in a series of conferences organized by a wealthy widow, Lady Powerscourt. It was here, at these conferences, that John Nelson Darby began preaching a Futurist interpretation of the Book of Revelation.

Futurism, as opposed to the Historicism of Martin Luther, sees the Book of Revelation

---

14 Ecclesiology: The branch of theology that is concerned with the nature, constitution, and functions of a church.
15 Eschatology: The branch of theology that is concerned with the end of the world or of humankind.

(Apocalypse) as foretelling events that are entirely in the future. In other words, it presupposes that none of the events of the Book of Revelation happened yet. It's a clean break with Martin Luther's Historicism, wherein he saw the events described in the Book of Revelation as an allegorical timeline of church history including the present day. Darby rejected that notion outright and went with a complete Futurist interpretation.

His version of it, however, was very peculiar. It is what we know today as *Dispensationalism*. It is a belief system that God divides history into segments of time that are called "dispensations." In each dispensation, he deals with humanity differently, and in each dispensation, the way to salvation is a little different as well. The most common version of this teaching proposes seven dispensations from creation to the end of the world. The fifth dispensation was the Old Testament Kingdom of Israel. The sixth dispensation is the current Church Age. And the seventh dispensation comes after the Return of Jesus Christ, wherein he sets up a literal kingdom on earth to last a thousand years (*Millennialism* or *Millenarianism*) just before the end of time. According to this theory, we are now living in the sixth dispensation, called the "Church Age," and we are nearing the seventh.

However, Darby's Dispensational teachings included a “hiccup” between the sixth and seventh dispensations. It's a seven-year span of time, in which the earth transitions from the sixth dispensation to the seventh. It's a time of hell on earth, wherein millions of Christians and Jews will be slaughtered by a figure called the Antichrist. This seven-year hiccup is what Dispensationalists call the "Great Tribulation." The seven-year Tribulation is seen as the time in which most of the events written in the Book of Revelation (Apocalypse) will unfold. So, the Book of Revelation is seen as a text that predicts purely future events, in a timeline, having little to do with church history or the present time.

Included in this seven-year hiccup of transition, between the sixth and seventh dispensations, is an event called "The Rapture." The word Rapture comes from the Latin word *rapio.* This is a translation of the Greek word *harpazo* (ἁρπάζω) which means to be "snatched up" and "carried away." It comes from this passage of the New Testament...

> *"For this we tell you by the word of the Lord, that we who are alive, who are left until the coming of the Lord, will in no way precede those who have fallen asleep. For the Lord himself will descend from heaven with a shout, with the voice of the archangel and with God's trumpet. The dead in Christ will rise first, then we who are alive, who are left, will be* ***caught up*** [harpazo, rapio or 'rapture'] *together with them in the clouds, to meet the Lord in the air. So we will be with the Lord forever."* (1 Thessalonians 4:15-17, emphasis and brackets mine)

Rapture and Parousia are the Same Event

As you can see, the Scriptures teach that there is a "catching up" (*harpazo* or *rapio*) when Jesus Christ returns, but a plain reading of the passage tells us this happens at his Second Coming at the end of the world. Look it over carefully. You will see there is no indication in this passage that being "caught up" (*harpazo* or *rapio*) happens at any other time than at the end of history. The plain reading of the passage seems to indicate that these are all one and the same event, happening in rapid succession. (1) Jesus Christ descends from heaven with a shout. (2) The dead in Christ rise incorruptible. (3) Those Christians still alive at this time are immediately transformed and "caught up" (*harpazo* or *rapio*) together with the risen dead and meet Christ in the air to be with him forever. Let's take a closer look at this using some other passages.

> *"Behold, I tell you a mystery. We will not all sleep, but we will all be changed, in a moment, in the twinkling of an eye, at the last trumpet. For the trumpet will sound and the dead will be raised incorruptible, and we will be changed. For this perishable body must become imperishable, and this mortal must put on immortality. But when this perishable body will have become imperishable, and this mortal will have put on immortality, then what is written will happen: 'Death is swallowed up in victory. Death, where is your sting? Hades, where is your victory?'"* (1 Corinthians 15:51-55)

> *"But immediately after the suffering of those days, the sun will be darkened, the moon will not give its light, the stars will fall from the sky, and the powers of the heavens will be shaken; and then the sign of the Son of Man will appear in the sky. Then all the tribes of the earth will mourn, and they will see the Son of*

> *Man coming on the clouds of the sky with power and great glory. He will send out his angels with a great sound of a trumpet, and they will gather together his chosen ones from the four winds, from one end of the sky to the other... But no one knows of that day and hour, not even the angels of heaven, but my Father only."* (Matthew 24:29-31, 36)

> *"But you watch. Behold, I have told you all things beforehand. But in those days, after that oppression, the sun will be darkened, the moon will not give its light, the stars will be falling from the sky, and the powers that are in the heavens will be shaken. Then they will see the Son of Man coming in clouds with great power and glory. Then he will send out his angels, and will gather together his chosen ones from the four winds, from the ends of the earth to the ends of the sky... But of that day or that hour no one knows, not even the angels in heaven, nor the Son, but only the Father."* (Mark 13:23-27, 32)

In all of these passages, we see the same theme unfold. Jesus Christ returns. The dead rise (both the saved and the damned). The saved are gathered together with Christ, along with those saved who are still living. The damned are judged. The Greek word *Parousia* (παρουσία), meaning "arrival" or "presence," is a Catholic reference to the Second Coming of Jesus Christ. The Parousia includes everything: the resurrection of the dead (both saved and damned), rising up to meet the Lord, the Last Judgment, the end of the earth, and the beginning of eternity. It's a comprehensive term because in the Catholic view, the traditional Christian view, these events are all wrapped up together into one Day, not spread out over time, nor is there an injection of the tribulation of Antichrist in between. It just all happens at once.

First, there comes the Antichrist, with all his mischief and hardships. Then follows Parousia. The end. That's the Catholic, and traditional Christian, understanding of the Last Days and the Second Coming of Jesus Christ, in a nutshell. Again, take a good look at those passages I just cited. Do you see anything to indicate there is a long space of time between the Rapture and the Second Coming? Is there anything in there, anything at all, that indicates the Rapture will happen first, then there will be a long period of seven years before Christ returns? No. There is nothing. The plain-sense reading of Scripture tells us these events are simultaneous or happening in close proximity to one another. There is no long expanse of time in between.

There is nothing all that complicated about it. For almost two millennia, this is what Christians believed and were taught. These things will happen at the end of time when Christ returns. They will happen simultaneously, or in close proximity to each other, and are often referred to as "The Day." Catholics are still obliged to believe this. When we say in the Creed, *"He shall come again in glory to judge the living and the dead,"* this is what is meant. He will separate them. Those in Christ will be raised and "caught up" (*harpazo* or *rapio*) to be with him forever. Those who are opposed to Christ will be raised and sent away for all eternity. Even the Protestants believed this for centuries.

The biblical imagery depicts the arrival of a conquering king in ancient times. It was common for a king, upon liberating one of his cities from enemy control, to be greeted by throngs of civilians, rushing out of the city to meet him on the road, and escorting him back into the city, while singing his praises.

This was the type of greeting Jesus Christ received on Palm Sunday.[16] He was greeted by the civilians of Jerusalem, rushing out to meet him on the road. They laid their coats and palm branches on the ground for his donkey to trod over, as he entered the city. This is commonly called a “king’s greeting,” and that's why the religious leaders were so incredibly upset upon his arrival into Jerusalem. They were afraid this would upset the Roman authorities. It didn’t, but that’s a different story.

The imagery of the Second Coming is like this. Jesus appears in the sky. The dead in Christ rise incorruptible. Christians who are still alive are transformed into incorruptible bodies. All of us rise together to meet Christ in the sky, and like those civilians of Jerusalem long ago, we escort him back to earth, where he commences the final judgment and the remaking of the universe.

Darby’s New Teaching

John Nelson Darby changed all that. In 1831, he proposed in his teachings that there is a separation between Christians being “caught up” (*harpazo*, *rapio* or “rapture”) and the Second Coming of Jesus Christ

---

[16] Matthew 21:1-11; Mark 11:1-11; Luke 19:28-44; John 12:12-19

(Parousia).[17] He placed these events as bookends marking the beginning and end of that seven-year transition hiccup between the sixth and seventh dispensations.

Under his teaching, the sixth dispensation (the Church Age) comes to an end with an event called *The Rapture,* which is authentic Christians being "caught up" (*harpazo* or *rapio*). This signifies the end of the sixth dispensation (Church Age) and the beginning of the seven-year, transition time (hiccup) before the seventh dispensation. The end of that seven-year transition (hiccup) is marked by the Second Coming of Jesus Christ, who returns with those who had been raptured seven years prior.

I use the word "hiccup" here to explain why this seven-year transition time is so different from all others. It appears to be a kind of temporary regurgitation of the fifth dispensation, or a return to the Old Testament understanding of Biblical Israel. Dispensationalists will tell you that it is during this time, God is no longer focused on the Church throughout the world because the Church is gone. It's been raptured. So instead, during this seven-year Tribulation, God is exclusively focused on the State of Israel in the Middle East. This seven-year Tribulation time is kind of like a "no man's land" between dispensations when the principles of the sixth and seventh dispensations no

---

[17] Darby was not the first Protestant to propose this teaching. Another Protestant minister, by the name of Morgan Edwards, proposed a similar theory in a short essay for Bristol Baptist College in 1744. It was later published in Philadelphia in 1788 (Millennium, Last-Novelties, Morgan Edwards, 1744, 1788). However, it failed to gain any traction. It was John Nelson Darby who popularized this theory, and later claimed he had no influence from, or knowledge of, Edwards' prior theory.

longer apply. Instead, salvation can be obtained only by avoiding the Mark of the Beast.

So according to Darby, the church age ends with the Rapture, or believers being "caught up" (*harpazo* or *rapio*). What follows is seven years of hell on earth, while those who were raptured feast in heaven for that same period. After this seven-year Great Tribulation (hiccup) on earth is over, Jesus and his raptured saints return to earth in his Second Coming to set up the seventh dispensation, which is called the Kingdom Age and is believed to last about a thousand years, according to the Book of Revelation. During this Kingdom Age, Jesus Christ will rule the world from Jerusalem with an iron rod. His raptured saints will rule with him as immortal governors all over the earth. The rest of humanity, who were not taken in the Rapture and survived the seven-year Great Tribulation, must prove their worthiness for heaven by being obedient to King Jesus and his immortal governors (raptured saints).

At the end of this thousand-year Millennium of the Kingdom Age, the earth will be seduced by Satan once again and a rebellion will break out. At that point, God will end the world, and Jesus Christ will judge between the faithful and the rebels before creating a new heaven and a new earth.

Dispensational Eschatology

I. Seven Dispensations (long periods) divide world history
    A. God deals with humanity differently in each dispensation (period)...
        1. ***Innocence:*** from Adam and Eve until the Fall

2. ***Conscience:*** from the Fall until the Flood of Noah
3. ***Government:*** from after the Flood until Abraham
4. ***Promise:*** from Abraham to Moses on Mt. Sinai
5. ***Law:*** from Moses to the crucifixion of Christ
6. ***Grace:*** from the crucifixion of Christ until the Rapture of the Church
7. ***Kingdom:*** from the Second Coming of Christ until the Third Coming of Christ after a thousand years.

B. There is a "hiccup" between the sixth and seventh dispensation, which is a transition time lasting seven years...
    1. It starts with ***The Rapture*** of the Church (the Second Coming of Jesus Christ *in secret*)...
        a) The bodies of true believers who died are resurrected.
        b) The bodies of true believers still alive are transformed.
        c) The resurrected bodies and transformed bodies of true believers disappear, vanish, and are taken to heaven.
        d) The bodies of non-believers who died remain dead.

e) The bodies of non-believers, who are still alive, remain as they are, unchanged and still on earth.

2. The chaos of the Rapture causes the world to go into crisis…
   a) Buggies (cars today) without drivers careen off the roads.
   b) Ships (airlines today) are suddenly without pilots.
   c) Surgeons disappear from operating rooms.
   d) Babies disappear from their mothers' breasts.
   e) Children vanish in playgrounds.
   f) Around the world, key people in government and business are gone.
   g) The only people who remain are adult non-believers.
   h) A worldwide emergency is declared.
3. After the chaos of the Rapture, in a worldwide emergency, a man rises to power and takes over as the world's dictator. This is ***The Antichrist***. Following this, most of the prophecies of the Book of Revelation begin to unfold.
   a) Antichrist will be a man of peace at first, who will

calm the world during its greatest crisis.

b) Antichrist will rebuild the Jewish Temple in Jerusalem.

c) Antichrist will merge all religions into one.

d) Antichrist, and his False Prophet, will force everyone to receive a "mark" (microchip today) that works as currency and demonstrates one's allegiance to Antichrist and his New World Order.

e) Antichrist will then declare himself the promised Jewish Messiah and demand to be worshiped as God.

f) Antichrist will then persecute anyone who adopts the Christian faith after the Rapture.

4. After the revelation of the Antichrist, the great plagues from the Book of Revelation will be unleashed upon the earth.

C. The "hiccup" between the sixth and seventh dispensation comes to an end when Christ returns (for the third time) after this seven-year transition time, bringing his raptured saints back with him.

1. Christ destroys the Antichrist and False Prophet.

2. All those who received the "mark" of the Antichrist go straight to Hell.
3. Those who survived the Great Tribulation, without taking the "mark" of the Antichrist, are allowed to live and enter the next dispensation.

II. The Seventh Dispensation (the Kingdom of God) is instituted, with Christ as King over the whole world, reigning physically from Jerusalem for a thousand years.

A. All those who were raptured before the Antichrist and Tribulation are set up as rulers over the earth, each according to his faithfulness in this life.

1. Some will be kings and queens (or presidents and chancellors).
2. Some will be regional governors.
3. Some will be counts and countesses (or county commissioners).
4. Some will be mayors.
5. Some will be advisors and administrators at all levels.

B. Those who were not taken in the Rapture, but survived the Tribulation without taking the Mark of the Beast, will become subjects under this new global government with Christ as King of kings.

III. After the thousand years are complete, Satan will be released from Hell to tempt the world for the last time. This results in a military rebellion against Jesus Christ in Jerusalem. When that happens, the world ends, the Last Judgment commences, the rebels are damned, the faithful are rewarded, and we go into eternity.

As you can see, this is a pretty elaborate eschatology. Yet, this is what Darby preached, starting in 1831, and it was the first time the world had ever heard it.[18] His views were considered exotic, unorthodox and bizarre. Yet, he was a dynamic preacher, and he preached this eschatology with gusto for the rest of his life. Thousands turned to his ministry and his eschatology, but it never hit the mainstream during his lifetime. Throughout the remainder of the nineteenth century, his teachings were considered the obscure belief system of a former Anglican priest and his small Evangelical denomination.

Then, in the year 1909, at the dawn of the twentieth century, the Scofield Reference Bible was published. Cyrus I. Scofield was a lawyer and politician by trade, but he was also a devout student of the Bible and devotee of the teachings of John Nelson Darby. Scofield published an annotated edition of the King James Version (KJV) of the Bible that was filled with thousands of cross-references and notes in the margins. Because of this, Scofield's Bible became the most popular Bible used in Evangelical seminaries both in the United Kingdom and North America. Contained

---

[18] That is with the exception of Morgan Edwards (see prior footnote), who proposed a similar theory nearly 100 years prior, but almost nobody heard about it, because it never gained traction. John Nelson Darby was the man who brought this theory to the world during the 1800s. *"Until brought to the fore through the writings and preaching and teaching of a distinguished ex-clergyman, Mr J. N. Darby, in the early part of the last century, it* [rapture doctrine] *is scarcely to be found in a single book or sermon through a period of sixteen hundred years."* (Harry Ironside, The Mysteries of God, 1908).

within these margin notes were the teachings of John Nelson Darby on Dispensationalism and the Rapture. So over the twentieth century, Dispensationalism became intertwined with Evangelicalism, as Evangelical pastors were schooled in the teachings of John Nelson Darby, built right into the Bibles they used for study in their seminaries. By the end of the twentieth century, Evangelicalism and Dispensationalism were nearly one and the same thing. The overwhelming majority of Evangelical pastors became Darby-Dispensationalists.

The Great Protestant Re-Alignment

Meanwhile, something else was happening simultaneously. Mainstream Protestant denominations were becoming more liberal in their approach to Christian morality and biblical interpretation. This caused a massive exodus, as the bulk of Protestants moved out of their traditional mainstream denominations and into Evangelical churches, which were seen as more conservative on moral and social issues. Evangelicalism thus became the dominant force in Protestantism by the end of the twentieth century. However, because of what was happening in the Evangelical seminaries, Dispensationalism and the Rapture moved to the forefront of the Protestant psyche.

My own family was part of this exodus. My father was raised Lutheran, and my mother was raised Southern Baptist. They compromised and raised my sisters and me as American Baptists.[19] My wife was raised Methodist. However, by the early 1990s, we

---

[19] American Baptist Church (ABC), sometimes called "Northern Baptists"

were all non-denominational Evangelicals. Granted, we were latecomers to this great migration, from mainstream Protestantism to Evangelicalism, but we made the transition. My parents and sisters remain Evangelicals to this day. Only my wife and I eventually returned to our ancestral home in the Catholic Church.

This was the case with the majority of Protestants in North America toward the end of the twentieth century. Most of them became Evangelicals, and only a small few returned to Catholicism. With that transition, "Rapture" became a household word, and Last Days' eschatology became a multi-million dollar industry.

The Rapture was sensationalized in the 1970s by the writings of Dr Hal Lindsey. Lindsey took Darby's doctrines, promoted by Scofield's Bible, and plugged them into the latest news headlines of his time. His best-selling work, entitled The Late Great Planet Earth, published by Zondervan in 1970, sold over 20 million copies. He wrote many similar books thereafter.

Lindsey was not the only one to capitalize on Darby's Rapture doctrine. In 1995, Evangelical minister Tim LaHaye teamed up with Christian novelist Jerry B. Jenkins to create what is known today as the Left Behind book series. It consisted of sixteen fictional novels, written between 1995 and 2007, that chronicle the imaginary events of the Last Days as told from a Dispensationalist perspective. Since then, the series has been translated into three minor motion pictures: *Left Behind: The Movie* in 2000, *Left Behind II: Tribulation Force* in 2002, and *Left Behind: World at War* in 2005. In 2014, there was a cinematic reboot with a major motion picture simply called *Left Behind* starring celebrity actor Nicolas Cage. There is even a video game series called *Left Behind: Eternal Forces,* with many sequels.

Today, the Rapture doctrine is taken for granted as a staple of Protestant eschatology. Some Protestants don't believe it, indeed some never did, but they are the minority now. What was once an obscure and bizarre teaching of a former Anglican priest, less than 200 years ago, is now the dominant eschatological view of the entire Evangelical Protestant world. Back when I was an Evangelical in the 1990s, the phrase "Rapture Ready" was used quite a bit. It means that one believes in the Rapture, hopes for the Rapture, and is living each day according to the teachings of Christ, so he will be ready to be taken in the Rapture when it happens.

After becoming Catholic, I was frequently asked what my views on the Rapture were. When I told my Evangelical friends that I no longer believe in the pre-tribulation Rapture, and that I think the Rapture and Second Coming are the same events, the most common response was: *"I feel sorry for you."* I was told that I had lost all hope and that Christ would never allow us to suffer through the Great Tribulation. One Evangelical friend chastised me for "blasphemy" because, according to her, I was *"slapping Christ in the face by not believing he would rescue us from the persecution of the Antichrist."* I was told to "*repent of your heresy*" as soon as possible, lest I miss the Rapture when it comes. This is how deeply the pre-tribulation Rapture doctrine is ingrained into the Evangelical psyche. For many, it is considered an integral part of the gospel, on par with the Resurrection of Jesus Christ. That's not true for every Evangelical, but it is true for many.

My personal experience with the Rapture doctrine is an interesting one. At first, I was skeptical, especially when my childhood friend (John) told me about it in the fifth grade, along with the Ronald

Reagan Antichrist, even going so far as to set a date for when he believed it would happen (1982). Then, as a young adult, I embraced it fully, minus the date-setting and Antichrist naming, of course. Later, upon becoming Catholic, I rejected it. In my thirties and forties, I was considered a "heretic" by many Evangelicals for even daring to question it. I live in the Bible Belt. So, you should hear the silence it brings to a room when the subject of the Rapture is brought up, and I say: *"I don't believe in it anymore."*

Dispensationalism and the Catholic Church

The Dispensationalist perspective on the Book of Revelation is likewise just as complicated as it is fascinating. Dispensationalists are Futurists when it comes to interpreting the Book of Revelation (Apocalypse). This means they believe most of the contents in the book take place in the future. When attempting to decode the book, they often jump back and forth between literal and symbolic readings of the text. There is no rationale or rule to their process. The text is simply interpreted literally when it's convenient to do so, and symbolically when interpreting it literally is too difficult or sounds ridiculous. This violates multiple rules of Biblical interpretation (hermeneutics).

The Dispensationalist interpretation of the thirteenth chapter of Revelation is not nearly as anti-Catholic as the Historicist interpretation, which I discussed in the last chapter. There are two symbolic beasts described in Revelation 13. One beast comes out of the sea, and the other comes from the land. The sea beast is interpreted as the papal-Antichrist by Luther's Protestant Historicism. While Dispensationalists also interpret this sea beast as the

Antichrist, they tend to see the Antichrist as some ambiguous world leader in the future, not necessarily associated with any particular church or religion. The second beast is the land beast, often associated with the "false prophet," and this one has more of a religious connection. Some Dispensationalists associate this land beast with a future pope who comes after the Rapture. Others see no specific connection to the papacy at all.

Revelation 17 is just as interesting from the Dispensationalist perspective. There is a virtually unanimous consensus among them that "Mystery Babylon" represents Rome, but there is some disagreement among Dispensationalists as to what that means. Some take it to mean a future apostasy of the Catholic Church. Others think it is the pope and Vatican specifically. Still, others think it may be a reference to an entirely new religious entity that will be stationed in Rome and have nothing to do with the Catholic Church. In short, the connection to Lutheran-Historicist anti-Catholicism is still there, but Evangelicals tend to water it down considerably. Some cling to the anti-Catholicism of the Protestant tradition. Others branch out into more imaginative possibilities.

As heavily influential as Dispensationalism has been on Evangelicals, their relationship with Catholics has been tenuous at best. It's infinitely better than the earlier relationship between Protestants and Catholics. When you consider that Evangelicals never started any wars with Catholics, nor did they ever try to outlaw the practice of Catholicism, we could say things got off to a much better start than they did with mainstream Protestants. Dispensationalism doesn't dispel Protestant suspicion of the pope or the Catholic Church, but it does dampen it a little, especially when we consider the rabid anti-Catholicism of Martin

Luther's Historicism. On the flip side, however, Darby's eschatology does create an entirely different understanding of the church in the Evangelical psyche that is impossible to reconcile with the Catholic understanding of the Church. This plays out not only in religion, but also in politics, as we shall see in the next chapter.

Chapter 4
Christian Zionism

Theodore Herzl was born to Jewish parents in Pest, Hungary within the Austrian Empire in 1860. This would be the eastern part of Budapest in the modern State of Hungary. He was a journalist, playwright, and political activist by trade. He is also considered the father of modern Zionism.

Now, Zionism is a political ideology, not a religion. (The word "Zionist" is not a negative epithet toward Jews, though some have misused it that way. Technically, there are more Christian Zionists than Jewish Zionists anyway.) Zionism, properly understood, is the political ideology that Jewish people should return to their ancestral homeland in Palestine and establish their own country there. That was eventually accomplished in 1948. Since then, Zionism has been amended to include the expansion of Israel into the West Bank, Golan Heights, and Gaza. Some dreamers would even go so far as to say it should include more territories spanning from the Nile River in Egypt, to the Euphrates River in Iraq. Thankfully, there is no evidence of the Israeli government including such grandiose plans into its political agenda.

Included within Zionism is a religious component, which asserts that the ancient Jewish priesthood should be restored, and the ancient Jewish Temple should be rebuilt. In other words, Zionism is a political ideology of restoration, which includes the religious restoration of ancient Judaism, the land of ancient Israel, its culture, its sovereignty, and to some extent even its government. Zionism itself is a political ideology because to accomplish its religious and social goals, certain political hurdles must be overcome. It's the idea that an old nation from the ancient world should be restored and rebuilt into a new nation in the modern world.

Historically speaking, what began as one man's dream, becoming what it is today, is quite remarkable. The first European Jewish settlements of Palestine began in the 1870s. These gradually increased over the decades. By 1948 the Israeli Republic was born. By the dawn of the twenty-first century, Israel was the undisputed, supreme, military power of the Middle East. In the history of the world, never has an entire nation come back to life after nearly 2,000 years of non-existence. Some have called it miraculous, but when we closely examine the history behind it, we start to see it was the result of good timing and numerous cooperative players.

The public call for the re-establishment of the Zionist State (the Israeli Republic) came during a time when Britain occupied most of the Middle East. Britain was a global Empire at the time, and following World War I, the British gained control of the entire Middle East. It was during this time that Herzl's dream of a Jewish homeland was fully realized. For decades, Jews were encouraged to immigrate to British-Mandate Palestine (as it was called). Zionists encouraged Jews to move there, and the British government was agreeable to the idea. Due to rising sentiments of antisemitism in Europe, one could say that most Europeans liked the idea of Jews leaving the European continent to go back to the Middle East "where they belong" according to Europeans at the time. Even the Nazi Third Reich reluctantly supported the idea from 1933 to the onset of World War II in 1939.

Yet, it was World War II that ultimately accelerated the immigration of Jews to British-Mandate

Palestine. Following the horrors of the Nazi Holocaust, and lingering sentiments of antisemitism in Europe, many Jews believed their only option for future safety was to return to their ancestral homeland in the Middle East. Then, on the 14th of May, in 1948, when the British Mandate expired, the Zionist leadership in Palestine declared themselves the independent Israeli Republic.

Arab forces immediately responded with three wars over a twenty-two-year span. Their stated goal was to crush the Israeli Republic and drive the Zionists into the Mediterranean Sea. All of them failed. Many attribute this to miracles. Maybe so, but a well-funded and well-trained military, backed by Western powers (including the United States), may have had something to do with it too. This was during the height of the Cold War, and the last thing the United States wanted to see was a Soviet beachhead in the Middle East. The Israeli Republic (basically a European settlement) served America's purposes well during the Cold War. That's not to say that God couldn't have a hand in the matter, but it's important to remember that the Israeli Republic always had a little covert help from Uncle Sam.

As I discussed in the previous chapters, a religious demographic shift was underway in North America following the Second World War, and this was felt most profoundly in the United States. Mainline Protestant denominations were gradually becoming more liberal on moral and theological issues. This caused a large segment of mainline Protestants to leave their ancestral denominations and migrate over to morally conservative, Evangelical churches. Thus, Evangelicalism experienced a boom of growth, while mainline Protestantism experienced a collapse. My own family was part of this migration. Upon entering

Evangelicalism, we were all introduced to the world of Darby's Dispensationalism and the Rapture doctrine.

Dispensationalist teachers were quick to take note of the establishment of the Israeli Republic and marked this as a fulfillment of Bible prophecy. They pulled up Old Testament prophecies in the books of Isaiah and Ezekiel,[20] both foretelling Israel's re-establishment after the Babylonian Captivity in 598 to 538 B.C.

This is how Christian Zionism operates. These prophecies were already fulfilled when the order was given by King Darius to rebuild the Jewish Temple in 558 B.C., and later when King Artaxerxes gave the order to re-establish the Jewish State in 457 B.C. It's not good Biblical interpretation (hermeneutics) to pull these fulfilled prophecies out of context from the Old Testament and then reuse them as a proof text that God supports modern-day Zionism. It's a little intellectually dishonest if you ask me. Nevertheless, that is exactly what they did. I remember my years as an Evangelical hearing, over and over again, how God has his hand on the Israeli Republic, and if we want God to continue to bless the United States, we need to support the Israeli Republic. On more than one occasion, I've heard it said by Christian Zionists that *"Israel is America's key to survival,"* as if to say the United States cannot survive unless the Israeli Republic does.

In the 1980s, the Republican Party quickly picked up on how useful this new ideology would be. By showing support for the Israeli Republic, they could count on the Evangelical vote. In exchange, Republican politicians need only swear their unwavering and unconditional support to the Israeli

---

[20] Isaiah 66:8, Ezekiel 37

Republic, and this is expected of them in their political-stumping speeches before Evangelical crowds. It is peculiar that an American politician would swear unwavering and unconditional support to a foreign state, but this is often what it takes to be elected in the Republican Party these days. It's not uncommon to see Republican politicians with both an American and an Israeli flag on their desks, as well as on their lapel pins. We do see a little of this in the Democratic Party as well, but it's most prevalent in the Republican Party, mainly because most Evangelicals vote Republican these days, and there are good reasons for this.[21]

Antisemitism and Christianity

Within Protestantism, there has always been some support for the idea of sending Jews back to their ancestral homeland. We don't see this in Catholicism at all, as the Catholic Church has always considered the presence of Jews to be an important component to Christendom, and Catholics have always been encouraged by the Church hierarchy to treat Jews with respect and charity. That's not to say it was always done, and Church history is replete with failures to live up to this standard, sometimes epic failures, but the standard exists and always has. That cannot be denied and deserves a spotlight, not just for the Catholic Church's reputation, but also for reclaiming Europe's humanity.

---

[21] Evangelicals, in the United States, primarily vote Republican because the Democratic Party has embraced sexual liberation, abortion-on-demand, and Marxist economics. Republicans countered this by adopting traditional Christian postures on these issues. Zionism was later added as an additional component to further keep Evangelicals loyal to the Republican Party.

Pope Gregory the Great (A.D. 540–604) penned a papal bull, which became official Church teaching, making it obligatory for Catholics to defend Jews against unjust persecution and to regard them as an essential part of Christian civilization. In A.D. 1120, Pope Callixtus II issued *Sicut Judaeis*,[22] which served as a papal charter protecting Jews, particularly those in Europe, but also as a guide for Catholics around the world. This papal bull was subsequently backed by no less than 18 popes in the following centuries,[23] and forbade Catholics, under pain of excommunication, from bringing harm to Jews or interfering in their religious practices in any way.

That doesn't mean that people always listened to the pope. Episodes of flagrant violations of papal teaching can be found in the massacre of two thousand Jews in Strasbourg, France, in February 1349, upon a decision by the city council to eliminate them because they believed Jews caused the Black Death (Bubonic Plague). Similar events happened in Germany during this time. Jews were forbidden from owning land in Europe during the Middle Ages because normally this required a pledge of political loyalty that was Christian

---

[22] Sicut Judaeis: (Latin: As the Jews) was a papal bull setting out the official position of the Catholic Church regarding the treatment of Jews. It was issued in A.D. 1120 by Calixtus II and was intended to protect Jews, following the First Crusade, during which over five thousand Jews were unlawfully slaughtered in Europe.

[23] Alexander III (A.D. 1159-1181), Celestine III (A.D. 1191-1198), Innocent III (A.D. 1199), Honorius III (A.D. 1216), Gregory IX (A.D. 1235), Innocent IV (A.D. 1246), Alexander IV (A.D. 1255), Urban IV (A.D. 1262), Gregory X (A.D. 1272-1274), Nicholas III (A.D. 1277-1280), Martin IV (A.D. 1281), Honorius IV (A.D. 1285-1287), Nicholas IV (A.D. 1288-1292), Clement VI (A.D. 1348), Urban V (A.D. 1365), Boniface IX (A.D. 1389), Martin V (A.D. 1422), and Nicholas V (A.D. 1447)

in nature. (There were some exceptions to this rule, and it was not universal.)

So, most Jews simply moved to the cities, leaving farming and ranching to the Christians, while becoming bankers, retailers, lawyers, doctors, and tradesmen instead. This resulted in higher education for them, as well as good networks that allowed them to thrive in urban environments. Because of their success in banking, medicine, law, and business, brought about by their expulsion from the European countryside, Jews became increasingly associated with money, banks, and highly paid professions. This is why they're often maligned as "greedy," a claim no more true of them than any other ethnicity, but that's part of the whole mistreatment they endured in Europe.

More violations of papal teaching included Jews that were expelled in areas across Western Europe: England 1290, France 1306 and 1394. The greatest expulsions of Jews were in Spain in 1492 and Portugal in 1496, where Jews were ordered to convert to Christianity or leave the country within a year. The Spanish Inquisition, which was originally directed toward crypto-Muslims in Spain, had this effect on the Spanish peninsula. However, what is little known about the Spanish Inquisition was that it was forbidden by Rome. It was run entirely by the Spanish monarchy, against the Vatican's permission. All of these are examples illustrating when and how the official Catholic teaching on Jews was either ignored or purposefully violated.

As bad as these events were, they were somewhat isolated and technically forbidden under Catholic teaching. Anti-Judaism didn't begin to foment in Europe until regions started breaking away from the Catholic Church in the Protestant Revolution (Reformation). Once freed from the pope's restraining hand, European Protestants were able to persecute Jews much more freely. This happened almost instantaneously. Thus, the emphasis in Northern Europe went from grudgingly tolerating Jews, only because the pope says so, to looking for ways to get rid of them because Protestant ministers demanded it.

During the Protestant Revolution (Reformation), the idea was put forward that Jews would be better off back in their ancestral homeland, but how to get rid of them was the trick. The most common "solution" put forward was to just make life so miserable for them in Europe that they would want to leave. Martin Luther was the first to do this. While initially friendly toward the local Jewish population early after his excommunication (1521), he later developed significant hostility toward them when they refused to convert to his new brand of Christianity (German Protestantism or "Lutheranism"). Martin Luther eventually recommended the following actions be taken against the Jews in Northern Europe...

1. Burn down their synagogues,
2. Destroy their houses,
3. Confiscate their religious books and items,
4. Forbid their rabbis from ministering on penalty of death or torture,
5. Harass, rob, and beat them if they should venture outside their ghettos,
6. Confiscate all their money and material possessions,
7. Force them to work hard labor,
8. Or else eject them from Europe.

He wrote this in the year 1543 in a document entitled *Von den Jüden und iren Lügen*: (German: "On the Jews and their Lies") which was a 65,000-word, anti-Jewish treatise. One need not imagine the downward anti-Jewish spiral this put Europe on because history tells us the rest of the story.

By the nineteenth century, Europe and North America were deeply influenced by racial politics, and what was once a purely religious prejudice against Jews developed into racial prejudice. Jews were classified racially as "Semites" (even though most Jews are European genetically speaking), and thus Anti-Judaism devolved into antisemitism. By the 20th century, Hitler and the Nazi Third Reich were using Martin Luther's writings as religious justification for their ethnic cleansing of all "Semites" (which consisted mainly of Jews) from Nazi Germany. Approximate estimates place the death toll of Jews in the Holocaust at about six million.

Jews suffered greatly under the hand of the Nazis, and unlike previous persecutions, conversion to Christianity would not spare them. This is because the racial eugenics of the Nazi Reich classified Jews as a race, not a religion. Therefore, conversion to another religion made no difference. Saint Edith Stein is one such example. She was a Jew who converted to Catholicism and became a nun. Her conversion to Catholicism, and enrollment into the Carmelite Order, made no difference. She was rounded up by the Nazis and died in Auschwitz. She is just one example of many. One can only imagine what would have happened had the Nazis won the war and gained the modern medical advances of DNA testing. Even people with the slightest Jewish DNA, coming from families that haven't been Jewish in centuries (including me), might find themselves imprisoned, enslaved, and even exterminated today.

I would be negligent if I failed to mention the Soviet propaganda that was circulated about Pope Pius XII (1939-1958) in the 1960s after his death. The Soviets sought to undermine the moral authority of the Catholic Church during the Cold War, and this was done (in part) by circulating a rumor that Pope Pius XII cooperated with Hitler during the Nazi Holocaust, or was, at the very least, negligent in trying to stop him. This propaganda circulated in European and American colleges for decades before being picked up by the mainstream media.

The book Hitler's Pope, written by John Cornwell, and published in 1999, was a bestseller for some years. It was a rehash of Cold War Soviet propaganda. The book was debunked by University of Mississippi law professor Ronald J. Rychlak in his book, Hitler, the War, and the Pope, published in 2000. Rychlak also charged that Cornwell even manipulated the photograph on the front cover of the American edition of Hitler's Pope to create a more scandalous image. In 2005, Hitler's Pope was debunked again by historian and rabbi, David G. Dalin, in his book entitled The Myth of Hitler's Pope. Dalin called Cornwell's conclusions "unverified" and "strongly anti-religious." Eugene Fisher, a doctor in Hebrew culture and education, said it was a *"sad commentary on the secular media that this anti-Catholic screed was ever published."* Even the Encyclopedia Britannica disavowed Cornwell's claims.

It would appear officials at the Vatican must have thought Soviet propaganda would disappear after the fall of the Soviet Union, and so all Rome needed to do was wait for its collapse. After all, it was Cardinal Eugenio Pacelli (later Pope Pius XII) who penned *Mit brennender Sorge* (German: "with burning concern") for Pope Pius XI in 1937. This was the only papal encyclical ever written in German, and it was ordered to be read from all Catholic pulpits in Nazi Germany on Palm Sunday of that year. The encyclical was a blatant and direct attack on Nazi racism and the Third Reich. Who would have thought that the man who penned this written assault on Hitler, would later be (falsely) accused of helping Hitler commit the very acts it condemned?

The Soviet propaganda was ridiculous on the face of it, but the resurrection of these old communist lies, in the Western media, likely caught Rome by surprise and forced the Vatican to open its secret archives. It should be noted these Vatican archives are only kept secret for 100 years to protect the personal information contained on figures therein. However, because of the new veracity of old communist propaganda, playing out in the European and American press at the turn of the twenty-first century, the Vatican was forced to open its secret archives early.

The result of this not only cleared Pius XII's name, but also demonstrated that Pope Pius XII was directly responsible for saving nearly one million Jews during the Holocaust and may have very well played an essential role in a plot to assassinate Adolf Hitler as part of a *coup d'état* to overthrow the Nazis. The plot was named *Operation Valkyrie*, and it would have been successful had the assassination attempt on Hitler not failed. The story was retold in the 2008 film entitled *Valkyrie*, starring celebrity actor Tom Cruise. Pope Pius XII's probable role in *Operation Valkyrie* is documented in Mark Riebling's 2015 book entitled: Church of Spies: The Pope's Secret War Against Hitler.

It should be noted that the author of Hitler's Pope, John Cornwell, has since recanted many of the claims he made in the book. What is telling, however, is how quickly the secular media jumped onboard

Cornwell's initial claims disparaging Pope Pius XII, and then how muted their voices became when he walked back on them. The books that counter Cornwell's initial claims never received a fraction of the press that Hitler's Pope did. To this very day, most Americans and Europeans are still under the false impression that Pope Pius XII was complicit in Hitler's slaughter of the Jews. Hopefully, time will remedy the tragic slander of this very holy man who did everything he could to save the Jews and Germany during Europe's darkest hour.

At the Second Vatican Council, the Catholic bishops of the world issued a pastoral statement[24] that dispelled all ambiguity on the Catholic Church's sentiment toward Jewish people. The Church has always, and ever shall, condemn hatred of Jews as a crime against Jesus Christ and the Catholic Faith. Catholics in the past, who perpetrated crimes against Jews, did so against the edicts of Rome, and if ever Catholics perpetrate the same crimes again, they do so in direct violation of Catholic teaching agreed to by all the bishops assembled in Rome during Vatican II, in addition to the commands of popes in ages past.

The Birth of Christian Zionism

While many Protestants had flirted with the idea of relocating Jews to the Holy Land,[25] it was only in the aftermath of World War II that a major realignment of Evangelical thinking took place, changing to the outright promotion and unconditional support. To give credit where credit is due, Evangelicals managed to successfully wipe most antisemitism from their ranks,

---

[24] *Nostra aetate* (Latin: In our Time) chapters 4 & 5

[25] Wesley's Zionist Hymn 1762; Murray, Stephen J. Stein, editor, "Introduction," *Jonathan Edwards, Works, Apocalyptic Writings*, V. 8, pp.17-19; etc.

but in so doing, they created a new error that threatens the very integrity of the gospel they claim to preach.

While many traditional Protestant denominations have issued statements rightly condemning antisemitism and anti-Judaism, many Evangelicals took it a step further by supporting the work of Zionists as a matter of confessional faith. As for why they did this, the answer is likely twofold...

1. It's a way of distinguishing themselves from their Protestant heritage. The history of Protestantism is virulently anti-Jewish, and this is particularly the case in Germany. The very founder of Protestantism, Martin Luther, became rabidly anti-Jewish toward the end of his life. Evangelicalism came from Protestantism. They use the Protestant version of the Old Testament (just 39 books) recommended by Martin Luther, and they subscribe to Martin Luther's core teachings of *Sola Scriptura* (Latin: Scripture alone) and *Sola Fide* (Latin: faith alone). However, in making a clean break with Luther's antisemitism, they went in the opposite direction (overcompensation), becoming pro-Jewish and pro-Zionist. This sends a clear message that Evangelicals are distinct among Protestants. The original Protestants hated the Jews, but Evangelicals love them - maybe a little too much?
2. There is an eschatological motivation behind it as well. The biggest promoters of Christian Zionism are Evangelical *Eschatologists* (Bible prophecy experts) who tell us the State of Israel's restoration signals the coming of the Last Days and hastens the Second Coming of

Jesus Christ. Therefore, in their estimation, Christian support of Israel will help to hasten the Rapture and the eventual return of our Lord.

Dr. Martin Luther King, an American Baptist minister and political activist, was among the first outspoken Christian Zionists. Hal Lindsey, author of The Late Great Planet Earth, likewise demonstrated strong Christian Zionist leanings, as did prominent Evangelical leaders in America like Jerry Falwell and Pat Robertson. Falwell said in 1981: *"To stand against Israel is to stand against God. We believe that history and Scripture prove that God deals with nations in relation to how they deal with Israel."* Sadly, this teaching is based on a poor interpretation of the blessing of Isaac in Genesis 27:29. That blessing reads...

"Let peoples serve you,
and nations bow down to you.
Be lord over your brothers.
Let your mother's sons bow down to you.
Cursed be everyone who curses you.
Blessed be everyone who blesses you."
(Genesis 27:29)

This passage is misused by Christian Zionists to support the idea that God will unconditionally support those who support the modern Israeli Republic unconditionally. Nations that do the same will likewise be blessed. However, a proper interpretation of the passage is a blessing between the Biblical patriarchs, from Isaac to his son Jacob, concerning who would carry the blessing of Abraham to deliver the promised Messiah -- Jesus Christ -- into the world. The promise has nothing to do with national boundaries or political agendas, especially not those of the twentieth and twenty-first centuries!

The Third International Christian Zionist Congress, held in Jerusalem in February 1996, issued a proclamation which said the following...

> *"God the Father, Almighty, chose the ancient nation and people of Israel, the descendants of Abraham, Isaac and Jacob, to reveal His plan of redemption for the world. They remain elect of God, and without the Jewish nation, His redemptive purposes for the world will not be completed.*
>
> *"Jesus of Nazareth is the Messiah and has promised to return to Jerusalem, to Israel and to the world.*
>
> *"It is reprehensible that generations of Jewish peoples have been killed and persecuted in the name of our Lord, and we challenge the Church to repent of any sins of commission or omission against them.*
>
> *"The modern Ingathering of the Jewish People to Eretz Israel and the rebirth of the nation of Israel are in fulfillment of biblical prophecies, as written in both Old and New Testaments.*
>
> *"Christian believers are instructed by Scripture to acknowledge the Hebraic roots of their faith and to actively assist and participate in the plan of God for the*

ingathering of the Jewish People and the Restoration of the nation of Israel in our day."

Please take particular note of the last statement. To prove their repentance for their sins against Jews in ages past, and to prove their fidelity to Scripture, Christians should *"actively assist and participate in... the ingathering of the Jewish People and the Restoration of the nation of Israel."* One would think the proper way to repent of sin and show fidelity to Scripture would be to exemplify Christian charity toward Jews wherever they live, and treat them as our neighbors, rather than support a political ideology that seeks to relocate them into a war-zone filled with people hell-bent on their destruction (the Islamic Middle East).

The frightening consequences of Christian Zionism are twofold. The first frightening consequence is the violence it does to the gospel of Jesus Christ. The gospel specifically commands Christians to show reasonable charity toward all people so that they may know the truth of the gospel and be persuaded (by our works of love) to convert to Christianity. Our practice of the gospel affirms the truth of the gospel, which provides no other way by which we must be saved. The main reason why so many Jews have relocated to the Israeli Republic is because of the failure of Christians to show this charity toward them in ages past. Christian Zionism, on the other hand, asserts that charity means putting our Jewish neighbors in harm's way, by supporting an eschatological belief system that uses them as pawns to hasten the Second Coming of Jesus Christ.

The second frightening consequence of Christian Zionism is the danger it presents to American foreign policy. All that political pandering by Republican politicians to Evangelical voters has its consequences. Once elected, these politicians are expected to deliver on their promises, or potentially lose their re-election campaigns. This means that the United States will effectively turn a blind eye to any humanitarian violations the Israeli government might be committing, as well as turn a blind eye to Israeli expansion into territories not recognized as Israel proper, in addition to ignoring (or even justifying) Israeli military operations against their Arab neighbors in the Middle East. The real danger in all of this is war, and by that, I mean a real shooting war in the Middle East, which America may be drawn into in the interest of supporting new Zionist goals. I'm not saying it *will* happen. I'm just saying it *could* happen.

As an American, I am compelled to support the existence of Israel because of the valuable service it provided during the Cold War in keeping the Soviets out of the Middle East. That valuable service continues until now in the West's war against Islamic jihadism. As a Christian, I desire the Jewish people to have the freedom to live wherever they want in peace. As far as I'm concerned, Israel has just as much a right to exist as Canada or Mexico, and how they govern their affairs is their business, except when it violates international law. However, as a Catholic, I am concerned that there is a greater danger from Christian Zionism than there is from the Israeli government, and that Christian Zionism may soon give the Israeli Republic a proverbial "blank check" to do whatever they want at America's expense and the expense of our fellow Christians in the Middle East.

Christian Reaction to Christian Zionism

Non-Evangelical Christians are not amused by Christian Zionism, especially those who live in the Middle East. It's not popular outside the Evangelical world, which may come as a shock to many Evangelicals. The following statement is an excerpt from *The Jerusalem Declaration on Christian Zionism,* released on the 22nd of August in 2006. The statement was written by Latin Patriarch Michel Sabbah of Jerusalem and other local heads of churches in Jerusalem...

> *"We categorically reject Christian Zionist doctrines as false teaching that corrupts the biblical message of love, justice and reconciliation.*
>
> *"We further reject the contemporary alliance of Christian Zionist leaders and organizations with elements in the governments of Israel and the United States that are presently imposing their unilateral preemptive borders and domination over Palestine.*
>
> *"This inevitably leads to unending cycles of violence that undermine the security of all peoples of the Middle East and the rest of the world.*
>
> *"We reject the teachings of Christian Zionism that facilitate and support these policies as they advance racial exclusivity and perpetual war rather than*

the gospel of universal love, redemption and reconciliation taught by Jesus Christ."

The Christians most significantly affected by the precepts of Christian Zionism have utterly rejected it. These are the Christians who live in Israel and Palestine. They have suffered much from the Israeli occupation of the West Bank. Such a statement is shocking to many Evangelicals who simply don't understand it, and equate it to the only thing they are familiar with in European history -- antisemitism.

On the 10th of September in 2014, U.S. Senator (and then future Republican presidential candidate) Ted Cruz found himself booed off a stage at a Christian event. Moments earlier, Cruz ascended to the podium thinking this was a typical Evangelical event, but what he failed to realize was that while some Evangelicals were in attendance, the event was mainly sponsored in support of Eastern Christians, and was heavily attended by Eastern Christian guests in the audience. Most Eastern Christians are Eastern Orthodox, along with some Catholics and Copts. Naturally, in Evangelical form, Cruz started spouting Christian Zionist rhetoric, singing the praises of Zionism and the Israeli Republic. To his shock, he was immediately heckled and booed. Cruz then compounded his error by assuming (so it appeared) that their negative reaction was due to leftover Protestant anti-Jewish sentiments. So, he doubled down and condemned their apparent antisemitic hatred. This incited more heckling from the crowd, with shouts of anger. Cruz then left the stage.

Senator Ted Cruz, a conservative Christian by American standards, appeared to have made the common Evangelical mistake of equating anti-Zionism with antisemitism and anti-Jewish sentiment. It's sort of like saying that hatred of Nazism is the same as hating all Germans, or hatred of Communism is the same as hating all Russians and Chinese. It seems like a very elementary error, but when it comes to Zionism, Evangelicals have a blind spot.

Hatred of a political ideology is not the same as hatred of a particular race or religion. These were Eastern Christians he addressed. I suspect he either didn't know that, or else he miscalculated how his speech would be received. They had no historical connection to the anti-Judaism of European history. These Christians had lived in relative peace alongside Jews and Muslim Arabs for centuries. Their problems didn't start until the political aims of Zionism were fulfilled with the creation of the Israeli Republic and subsequent occupation of Gaza and Jordan's West Bank. They've had nothing but difficulties in their own countries ever since. It appeared to be a blind spot in Cruz's polished Evangelical image, but I don't blame him for it. It's not unique to him. The same blind spot is common to most Evangelicals. Poor Senator Cruz just got blindsided by it on stage, which later went viral on the Internet.

The Evangelical problem with Christian Zionism goes back to Darby's Dispensationalism. It comes from a profound misunderstanding of the nature of the Church as the Kingdom of God. This leads not only to a distorted eschatology, but also a warped understanding of the Church's relationship with the Jewish people. In the next chapter, I'll explain a proper understanding of Israel from a biblical and Catholic perspective. This may seem like a digression from the topic of eschatology, but I assure you it's integral to it, especially in the wake of Protestant and Evangelical errors.

Chapter 5
Kingdom Come

Jacob Friedman was born into a South African Jewish family in 1916. His friends and family knew him as "Jackie." He graduated from the University of Cape Town in 1938 and went on to become a medical doctor. During the Great World War II, he served in the Medical Brigade, which led to his conversion to the Catholic Church in 1943. By 1947, he became a Discalced Carmelite friar and wrote his first book: The Redemption of Israel. Ten years later, in 1953, he was ordained a Catholic priest and took the name Elias. A year after that, he entered the Stella Maris Monastery of Mount Carmel in Haifa, Israel, where he remained until his death in 1999.

Father Elias Friedman OCD[26] was a Jewish convert to the Catholic Church, a priest, friar, author, historian, linguist, translator, public speaker, musician, and poet. He founded the *Association of Hebrew Catholics*,[27] which became an organization of Jewish converts (like himself) to meet, share experiences, and preserve their Hebrew identity within the Catholic Church. Father Elias was 100% dedicated to the mission of the Catholic Church and the Jewish people. His position was that it is possible, even ideal, for Jews to convert to the Catholic Church, and maintain their Hebrew identity, heritage, and customs, provided it is done so with the understanding that the means of

---

[26] Latin: *Ordo Carmelitarum Discalceatorum* (O.C.D.), meaning "Order of Discalced Carmelites"

[27] Association of Hebrew Catholics (AHC), 4120 W Pine Blvd, Saint Louis, Missouri 63108-2802, Website: www.hebrewcatholic.net

salvation only come through Jesus Christ as administered through the teaching and sacraments of the Catholic Church. Father Elias was adamant that while the Old Covenant of Moses has been superseded (fulfilled) by the New Covenant in Jesus Christ, the Jewish people (by virtue of their prior election) have not been superseded (replaced). He put it this way in his groundbreaking book Jewish Identity.

> ***"The Church is Israel, under the New Law, as Mosaic Judaism was Israel under the Old Law.*** *Israel has extended its titles to the Gentiles by way of communication, not by way of transfer of privileges. It is in this light that we should understand the following text:*
>
> *'Once you were no people, but now you are God's people.'* (1 Peter 1:10)
>
> *'You, however, are a chosen race, a royal priesthood, a holy nation, a people He claims for His own.'* (1 Peter 2:9)
>
> *'You are God's chosen ones.'* (Colossians 2:12)
>
> *"Post-Christic Jewry is a section of Israel, and as such, shares its privileges."*
>
> (Father Elias Friedman OCD, Jewish Identity, page 96, emphasis mine)

The *Association of Hebrew Catholics* (AHC) enjoys the support of Cardinal Raymond Burke,

Archbishop Robert Carlson, Bishop Carl Meneling and received the Apostolic Blessing of Pope Saint John Paul II. While simply an apostolate within the Catholic Church at this time, political circumstances in the Israeli Republic may force the creation of a prelature or ordinariate for Hebrew Catholics at some future date. If this happens, we may see the emergence of a jurisdiction within the Catholic Church that focuses on preserving Hebrew culture and tradition, but most importantly, Hebrew identity as a people called by God.

In some ways, this is similar to what we have seen recently with the creation of ordinariate jurisdictions for the preservation of English (Anglican) Patrimony. However, there is a deeper dimension as well, in that with Hebrew identity we're talking about the people originally chosen by God to bring forth the Messiah (Jesus Christ) for the blessing of the whole world. In the past, joining the Church has amounted to assimilation with Gentile culture. Such a prelature or ordinariate structure would ensure that cannot happen again. The *Association of Hebrew Catholics* may assume a support role at that time, or simply fold into the larger prelature or ordinariate jurisdiction. Whatever happens, Father Elias' association is restoring a more "first-century approach" to the subject of Jewish converts within the Catholic Church.

A small sampling of traditions common to the AHC include the promotion of celebrating the Passover Seder, observance of biblical holy days, a preservation of the Hebrew and Yiddish languages, as well as general reflections on the nature of Hebrew heritage and identity, both as a unique people in the world, and a community within the Catholic Church.

Judaizing

The AHC is adamantly opposed to Judaizing. The definition of Judaizing is imposing Jewish customs and traditions upon non-Jews (Gentiles) with the idea of convincing them that these Jewish things are necessary for their faith as Christians. The AHC opposes this, and strictly adheres to the orthodox Catholic teaching that salvation and holiness come through the ministry of Christ, his Church, and the sacraments. Jewish traditions and customs, on the other hand, are designed to preserve the identity and heritage of Jews who have converted to the Catholic Church and their descendants. By the same token, however, the AHC holds that these things are optional even for Jews who convert to Catholicism. What is necessary for salvation already exists in Jesus Christ and the sacraments of his Catholic Church.

The rites and rituals of Judaism, having once served as sacraments under the Old Covenant in Moses,[28] now serve as sacramentals[29] for Catholics under the New Covenant in Jesus Christ. This does not imply that they've been downgraded, but rather that something infinitely more efficacious has arrived. The purpose of the Old Covenant sacraments under the Law of Moses was to produce faith in the coming Messiah, which in turn merited grace. This is different from how New Covenant sacraments work, which are a

---

[28] This position was held by Saint Thomas Aquinas, though he opposed the observance of these rites by Christians in his own time.

[29] A sacramental is not a sacrament. It is a lesser thing. In the Catholic understanding, a sacramental is a material object or action, often blessed by a priest or approved by the Church (for example; a cross necklace, a rosary, or holy water) to signal its association with the sacraments and so to incite reverence during acts of worship.

means of grace themselves, coming directly from the Messiah (Jesus of Nazareth), operating through the ministers of his Church by the work of the Holy Spirit. This relegates the Old Covenant sacraments to sacramentals, not because they've been downgraded, but because what has arrived under the New Covenant is far more efficacious and powerful.

The Catholic Church is not a monolith and never was. Within the Catholic Church one can easily find a plethora of different cultures, customs, and ways of being Catholic. Irish Catholicism looks nothing like Mexican Catholicism. Yet, they are both equally Catholic. The Eastern Catholic rites bear little resemblance to the Western Roman Rite. Yet, they are both equally Catholic. All of them are *united, but not assimilated* into the greater communion of the Catholic Church. What Christ's Catholic Church has always required of various peoples and cultures is adherence to the doctrine and sacraments of the Church. Culture, traditions, heritage, and even liturgy have always had a certain degree of flexibility to them. The traditionalism that drives many Roman Rite Catholics to request the traditional Latin mass (*Vetus Ordo*, *Extraordinary Form of the Roman Rite,* or *Missal of 1962*) is similar to the traditionalism that led to the creation of *Divine Worship*, which is the official liturgy of the personal ordinariates for former Anglicans. This is similar to the traditionalism that leads Eastern Catholics to continue to celebrate their liturgies and customs in the ways they have always done. All of these are aimed at preserving a certain identity, heritage, tradition, and way of worshiping God. The AHC seeks a similar kind of traditionalism for Hebrew Catholics.

The focus of the AHC is "togetherness" with other Catholics. This often stands in stark contrast to the "separateness" of the Messianic Jewish Movement outside the Catholic Church. Originally started by Evangelical Christians, the Messianic Jewish Movement has a tendency to form its own denominations and affiliations (which they typically call "synagogues"), each with their own doctrinal understanding of their place in Christianity. Gentile Christians who join these Messianic congregations (synagogues) feel a tremendous pressure to adopt Jewish practices, language, and even identity. This is not the case with the AHC, and it will be avoided if a Hebrew Catholic prelature or ordinariate is ever created.

As we have learned from the English Patrimony ordinariates, for former Anglicans, any regular Catholic can join an ordinariate parish regardless of his (or her) background, and no parishioner is required to adopt personal customs of the English Patrimony. For example, Anglican converts to Catholicism (and their descendants) tend to pray in sacred English (thee, thy, and thou), while using prayer forms common to the English Patrimony. Furthermore, the recitation of the Daily Office, according to the norms of the Book of Common Prayer, is also commonplace among the laity, as are certain Anglican devotions, and even veneration of Our Lady of Walsingham in the home. Regular Catholics, not connected to the English Patrimony, might join these parishes and worship with Catholics who are connected to the English Patrimony. When they go home, however, they might not observe the other things associated with the English Patrimony. They may if they want to, but nobody expects it of them. So it would be with any parishioner who joins a hypothetical prelature or ordinariate parish for Hebrew Patrimony. The liturgy might have both a traditional Catholic and traditional Jewish feel to it, but parishioners would never be required to wear a kippah, speak in Hebrew or Yiddish, or celebrate the Passover Seder, unless they want to.

For example, I am a member of the *Association of Hebrew Catholics* (AHC),[30] namely because I have a small amount of Ashkenazi Jewish heritage on my mother's side. So, I see the AHC as important to Jewish converts, if they're interested in it, and I want to maintain some connection to fellow Catholics of Jewish heritage. That said, my family disconnected from its Jewish heritage long ago. We don't celebrate Passover or the Sabbath. I can count on one hand the number of Passover Seders I've attended during my lifetime. I don't wear a *kippah* (yarmulke), and I don't keep kosher. I recognize that some Catholics of Jewish heritage do, and it's okay for them to do so for identity reasons, just so long as they understand that none of this is connected to salvation.

Supersessionism

The Catholic Church teaches the doctrine of supersessionism regarding the old Mosaic Law (Torah), but this has got to be one of the most misunderstood teachings in Catholic history. It is, tragically, a misunderstanding that has led to the slaughter of many Jews, and the unfair mistreatment of countless more. The founder of Protestantism, Martin Luther, so grossly misunderstood supersessionism that his teachings against the Jews in the sixteenth century eventually devolved into the racist antisemitism of the nineteenth and twentieth centuries. When materialist thinking hit Europe, it hit Germany particularly hard. Many of her

30 www.hebrewcatholic.net

people committed apostasy[31] from Protestantism to Nazism. I've already covered Luther's anti-Jewish screed at length in the last chapter. Centuries later, Nazis would point to it as religious validation of their action against the Jews.

Yet supersessionism was not just misunderstood by the Protestants. A great many Catholics misunderstood it too, and this has fostered an anti-Jewish sentiment in some traditional Catholic circles. That's because there are two types of supersessionism.

The first is sometimes called "hard supersessionism" which operates on the principle of "replacement." This is the idea that the New Covenant "replaces" the old, as if to say the former no longer exists. This can easily lead to a type of *replacement ecclesiology*[32] as well, wherein the notion is put forward that God has replaced the Old Covenant people (Jews) with the New Covenant people (Christians). Historically, this has led to many cases of Jews being pressured to assimilate into the Gentile population, losing their Jewish identity entirely within a generation or two. Such was clearly the case with my own Jewish ancestors back in the early nineteenth century. The Catholic Church has rejected[33] this kind of "hard supersessionism" or *replacement ecclesiology*.

The general misunderstanding of "hard supersessionism" (replacement ecclesiology), coupled

---

[31] Apostasy = to turn away from Christianity entirely. There is nothing Christian about Nazism. To become a Nazi is to cease to be Christian. Whatever Christian terminology or images remain is just window dressing.

[32] Ecclesiology: The branch of theology that is concerned with the nature, constitution, and functions of a church. (The American Heritage Dictionary of the English Language, 5th Edition)

[33] Romans 11:29; *Lumen Gentium* 6; *Nostra Aetate* 4

with a failure by most Christians to seek clarification, is what in turn led to the overreaction (overcompensation) of Protestant Dispensationalism and Christian Zionism *letting the Jews be Jews away from us in the Holy Land.* Under Evangelical Dispensationalism, and Christian Zionism, the hostility toward Jews is eliminated, and replaced with unconditional support of the Israeli Republic, for hastening the Second Coming of Jesus Christ. All of these things are errors, and they reflect a lack of understanding of what Christianity actually teaches about the Jewish people. It also reflects a fundamental misunderstanding about the identity of the Church.

The Catholic Church's teaching on supersessionism follows along the line of what some have called "soft supersessionism" or what might better be described as *fulfillment ecclesiology*. With this understanding, Catholic supersessionism does *not* teach that the Old Covenant of Moses is *replaced by* the New Covenant in Christ, rather it teaches that the Old Covenant of Moses is *fulfilled in* the New Covenant in Christ. This may, at first, seem like a subtle nuance, but it's actually a huge difference. By saying the Old Covenant is fulfilled, rather than replaced, we are saying that the Old Covenant is (and always has been) a historical reality, albeit *incomplete* without the New Covenant in Christ. In its fulfilled state, however, it presents itself in a very different way, no longer requiring the rigorous observance it once did before its fulfillment. Thus, the New Covenant is not a replacement of the Old, but rather a fulfillment of the Old, having been fulfilled in Christ. For it was Jesus himself who said: *"Don't think that I came to destroy the law or the prophets. I didn't come to destroy, but to fulfill. For most certainly, I tell you, until heaven and earth pass away, not even one smallest letter or one tiny pen stroke shall in any way pass away from the law, until all things are accomplished"* (Matthew 5:17-18). This doesn't mean that Christians are required to follow the Law of Moses. On the contrary, Christians are required to follow the precepts of Christ's Catholic Church, which he established to reformulate the moral elements of the Law of Moses for us in a way that conforms to his own fulfillment of the Law.[34]

To help illustrate this, we could compare the Old and New Covenants to a relationship between a man and a woman. Think of the Old Covenant as an engagement, or a "betrothal" to use a Biblical term. Then, think of the New Covenant as the wedding and marriage! The two are intimately connected. Old and New Covenants can be compared to the betrothal and marriage. You can't have the second without the first. Before the wedding and marriage, there must first be the engagement or betrothal.

Western culture has its own little custom that beautifully illustrates this. Upon engagement to marry, a woman is usually given a ring by her suitor. This is her "engagement ring." It's often beautiful and elaborate. However, in numerous instances, the engagement ring itself is incomplete. The jeweler has paired it together with a wedding ring, which typically fits perfectly alongside the engagement ring. When worn together on the same finger, the two rings make a much bigger and more beautiful ring. The wedding ring is reserved for the wedding itself. It's placed on the finger during the wedding ceremony. Later, sometime after the newlywed couple has settled into their new life together, the woman usually takes her two rings to the jeweler and has them permanently fused together.

---

[34] Matthew 1:22, Matthew 5:17, Luke 24:44, Romans 10:4,

From this Western tradition, we can see an illustration of how the Old and New Covenants work in relation to each other. The Old Covenant is like the engagement ring. It's necessary and is meant to convey anticipation of something much bigger. The New Covenant is like the wedding ring, which, when worn together with the engagement ring, creates a whole new ring that looks similar to the engagement ring, in some ways, but much fuller and complete. In many ways, it looks like a whole new ring. Yet, it is really just the fusion of the two. The wedding ring custom comes from the Medieval period, and putting the engagement ring together with the wedding ring, to make a whole new ring, probably (at least on a subconscious level) grew out of the Christian understanding of marriage as related to the Old and New Covenants.

Now, consider this. When a couple is engaged, and then they are married, are they still engaged? No. The couple is no longer engaged. They are now married. Their wedding ended the engagement (or betrothal) and effectively started the marriage. So one thing (the engagement) has come to an end, and something new (the marriage) has started, but that doesn't change the historical fact that the engagement preceded the marriage, and the engagement plays a historical role in the life of the marriage. The two can never be separated. Yet, one has ended, and another has begun. The engagement has blossomed into a marriage, but the engagement is how it all began. So, as the Western tradition goes, the engagement ring is fused unto the wedding ring. The Old is fused into the New. The two are intimately connected, but what undeniably exists now is a whole new ring, which looks similar to, but very different from the first.

This is why the Apostle Paul often compared the New Covenant to a marriage.[35] Once the wedding has come, the engagement (betrothal) is over, and the marriage has begun. The two cannot coexist at the same time. The marriage fulfills and supersedes the engagement (betrothal), just like the New Covenant fulfilled and supersedes the Old Covenant,[36] yet the two remain connected through history and relation. One cannot go back to being engaged (betrothed) after having already been married. Upon being married, one can remember the engagement (betrothal), and find connections between the first relation and the second, the engagement and the marriage. Yet, one cannot go back to the first relation, and the two never exist side-by-side. Once the marriage is contracted in the wedding, the engagement is over. So, how does this relate to the relationship between Jews and Gentiles in the New Covenant?

Under the "soft supersessionism" of *fulfillment ecclesiology*, Gentiles do not replace Jews as the people of God. The physical people of God (physical Israel), which are the last two remaining tribes of the Hebrew people (i.e. Jews), are still very much the people of God. They are still very much Israel by birth, but they are not ***all*** of Israel entirely. Rather, they are only ***a part*** of the *Kingdom* of Israel, the part that is still engaged, but for whatever reason, they missed the wedding. They're still related to the King by engagement (or betrothal), but they never showed up to the wedding.[37] They can change this, by embracing Jesus as their King, thus showing up to the wedding, but until then, they only have half a ring.

---

[35] 1 Corinthians 11:1-16, Ephesians 5:22-32

[36] Galatians 3:23–25, Colossians 2:14, Hebrews 10:8-9, Hebrews 9:10, Hebrews 10:1

[37] Matthew 25:1-13

Kingdom Israel, under the New Covenant, is the Church. The government of Kingdom Israel was transferred by Israel's Messiah-King (Jesus Christ) from the Great Sanhedrin in Jerusalem, to Saint Peter and the Apostles. Think of it as a regime change. It's sort of like the way the United States transferred its system of government from the Articles of Confederation to the Constitution on March 4, 1789. Israel's government was transferred from the Great Sanhedrin to the Apostles of Jesus Christ on Pentecost Sunday in A.D. 33. This was done by the only one who had the authority to make such a change -- God himself -- in the form of Israel's divine King (Jesus of Nazareth). Only God and King could make such a change, and so God and King did just that. He just happened to be the same person.

With this change in regime, the Old Covenant of the Law of Moses was fulfilled by Jesus Christ and completed in his Catholic Church (with her teaching, disciplines and sacraments). Kingdom Israel was not destroyed or replaced. ***Rather, Kingdom Israel was expanded!*** No longer would it be limited to Jews living on a small plot of real estate in the Holy Land. Rather, it would become open to all Jews and Gentiles freely and span the whole globe. Gentiles would no longer need to convert to Judaism. These Gentiles could share in the inheritance of Kingdom Israel (the Church) fully and equally, alongside the Jews, without having to undergo circumcision, observe kosher, or the rituals of the Mosaic Law.

Stop and consider this. Jews were not replaced under the New Covenant. Rather, they were placed in a position of importance within it. Those who believed, and followed their rightful King (Jesus) went on to become the foundation of the early Church. Those who refused to believe, still remained physical Israel, but gave testimony to Kingdom Israel (the Church) negatively, by demonstrating to the world that God brought the Old Covenant system to its fulfillment. Their Temple was destroyed, and the Jews were eventually scattered. Like dead branches, they were cut from the olive tree (Kingdom Israel), but that still does not change the identity of those branches. When an olive tree's branches are cut, and cast aside, they remain olive tree branches. There may be no life in them, but their identity remains the same. They still belong in the olive tree because that is their natural home. Saint Paul refers to the olive tree as an illustration of the Church…

> *"I ask then, did God reject his people? May it never be! For I also am an Israelite, a descendant of Abraham, of the tribe of Benjamin. God didn't reject his people, whom he foreknew. Or don't you know what the Scripture says about Elijah? How he pleads with God against Israel: 'Lord, they have killed your prophets. They have broken down your altars. I am left alone, and they seek my life.' But how does God answer him? 'I have reserved for myself seven thousand men who have not bowed the knee to Baal.' Even so too at this present time also there is a remnant according to the election of grace. And if by grace, then it is no longer of works; otherwise grace is no longer grace. But if it is of works, it is no longer grace; otherwise work is no longer work.*

"What then? That which Israel seeks for, that he didn't obtain, but the chosen ones obtained it, and the rest were hardened. According as it is written, 'God gave them a spirit of stupor, eyes that they should not see, and ears that they should not hear, to this very day.'

> *"David says, 'Let their table be made a snare, a trap, a stumbling block, and a retribution to them. Let their eyes be darkened, that they may not see. Always keep their backs bent.'*

"I ask then, did they stumble that they might fall? May it never be! But by their fall salvation has come to the Gentiles, to provoke them to jealousy. Now if their fall is the riches of the world, and their loss the riches of the Gentiles, how much more their fullness!

"For I speak to you who are Gentiles. Since then as I am an apostle to Gentiles, I glorify my ministry, if by any means I may provoke to jealousy those who are my flesh, and may save some of them. For if the rejection of them is the reconciling of the world, what would their acceptance be, but life from the dead?

"If the first fruit is holy, so is the lump. If the root is holy, so are the branches. But if some of the branches were broken off,

and you, being a wild olive, were grafted in among them and became partaker with them of the root and of the richness of the olive tree, don't boast over the branches. But if you boast, remember that it is not you who support the root, but the root supports you. You will say then, 'Branches were broken off, that I might be grafted in.' True; by their unbelief they were broken off, and you stand by your faith. Don't be conceited, but fear; for if God didn't spare the natural branches, neither will he spare you. See then the goodness and severity of God. Toward those who fell, severity; but toward you, goodness, if you continue in his goodness; otherwise you also will be cut off. They also, if they don't continue in their unbelief, will be grafted in, for God is able to graft them in again. For if you were cut out of that which is by nature a wild olive tree, and were grafted contrary to nature into a good olive tree, how much more will these, which are the natural branches, be grafted into their own olive tree?

"For I don't desire you to be ignorant, brothers, of this mystery, so that you won't be wise in your own conceits, that a partial hardening has happened to Israel, until the fullness of the Gentiles has come in, and so all Israel will be saved. Even as it is written,

> *'There will come out of Zion the Deliverer, and he will turn away ungodliness from Jacob. This is my covenant with them, when I will take away their sins.'*

"Concerning the Good News, they are enemies for your sake. But concerning the election, they are beloved for the fathers' sake. For the gifts and the calling of God are irrevocable. For as you in time past were disobedient to God, but now have obtained mercy by their disobedience, even so these also have now been disobedient, that by the mercy shown to you they may also obtain mercy. For God has bound all to disobedience, that he might have mercy on all.

"Oh the depth of the riches both of the wisdom and the knowledge of God! How unsearchable are his judgments, and his ways past tracing out!

'For who has known the mind of the Lord?
Or who has been his counselor?
Or who has first given to him,
and it will be repaid to him again?'

"For of him and through him and to him are all things. To him be the glory for ever! Amen."

(Saint Paul, Romans 11)

Judaism Today

Today's form of Rabbinical Judaism was created after the fall of Mosaic Judaism, though obviously, it has its roots before that. Jesus himself was called "rabbi," as were many other Jewish leaders. It had its foundations in the Babylonian exile centuries before, but under its current form, it's not identical to the rites and rituals given by God to Moses at Mt. Sinai. It is rather a modified method of preserving Jewish identity and precepts within a Mosaic framework that does not recognize Jesus as Messiah and King, nor his Church as Kingdom Israel. This is the negative testimony affirming Christ that Saint Paul foretold. They can no longer fulfill the Mosaic Law as it was written. Instead, they must practice a modified version of it that doesn't really fulfill the sacrificial commands of the Law. Without the sacrifice of Christ, the law can't be fulfilled anymore, not in any kind of literal way.

Rabbinical Judaism, as we know it today, was crystallized after the destruction of the Second Temple in A.D. 70, which was some forty years after the crucifixion of Christ. Therefore, much to the chagrin of antisemites and Jew-haters around the world, it can rightly be said that Rabbinical Judaism is *not* responsible for the crucifixion of Jesus Christ. A religion cannot be held responsible for an event, if the event happened *before* that religion was inaugurated in its current form. The scribes, Pharisees, Sanhedrin, and Temple priests were part of a religious system that has been extinct since A.D. 70. These were the people who were materially responsible for the crucifixion of Christ, and it was just a small segment of one generation.

They are gone now. They've been gone for two millennia. It's over. The destruction of the Temple demonstrated to the world that the old Mosaic Law was fulfilled in Christ. Rabbinical Judaism is not identical to Mosaic Judaism. It is a post-Temple, and post-Christianity modification of Mosaic Judaism that retains many elements from the Mosaic period, but it's not the same thing.

Kingdom Israel

This leads me to the point of this chapter. You may have been wondering why I've spent so much time talking about Jews, Hebrew Catholics, and Rabbinical Judaism. It's because it's all interconnected with the identity of Israel, and the identity of Israel is essential to understanding the Catholic teaching on last things and the Last Days. If you get this one wrong (as the Dispensationalists have), and you fail to understand the identity of Israel, you're going to get it all wrong when it comes to understanding the Last Days. If you miss this one, you're going to be lost. It's sort of like trying to explain multiplication to somebody who doesn't understand addition. You have to teach one before the other. Likewise, when it comes to a Catholic understanding of the Apocalypse and the Last Days, the identity of Israel must be the foundation.

As I pointed out above, Father Elias wrote: *"The Church is Israel, under the New Law, as Mosaic Judaism was Israel under the Old Law."* This is verified by the new Catechism of the Catholic Church and Sacred Scripture:

> *"Likewise, it belongs to the sacramental nature of ecclesial ministry that it have a collegial character. In fact, from the*

> *beginning of his ministry, the Lord Jesus instituted the Twelve as 'the seeds of the* ***new Israel*** *and the beginning of the sacred hierarchy.'"* (Catechism of the Catholic Church, 877, emphasis mine)

> *"For* ***in Christ Jesus*** *neither is circumcision anything, nor uncircumcision, but a new creation.* ***As many as walk by this rule****, peace and mercy be on them, and on* ***God's Israel****."* (Galatians 6:15-16, emphasis mine)

As you can see from these passages, both from the Catechism and the Bible, the Church is the New Israel, or God's Israel, just as Father Elias said: *"The Church is Israel, under the New Law, as Mosaic Judaism was Israel under the Old Law."* To simplify this, I use the term ***Kingdom Israel***, to distinguish it from physical Israel (the Jewish people) and the Israeli Republic in the Middle East. I use this term to emphasize and underscore the eschatological thrust of the entire New Testament, which is that ***Jesus of Nazareth is the prophesied Messianic King of Israel***. Those who are baptized into his Name, and by extension the Name of the Holy Trinity, become his royal subjects and are incorporated into his Kingdom. Physical Israel (Jews) are the most natural subjects for this Kingdom, but not all physical Israel (Jews) have decided to come into the Kingdom yet. Many of them have chosen to remain outside the Kingdom, for the time being, still very much Israel (in a physical sense): going to synagogue, keeping elements of the Mosaic Law, and some are returning to their ancestral homeland in the Israeli Republic. They are Israel. The only thing they lack is the King of Israel and his Kingdom (the Catholic Church).

Just as Gentiles were allowed to become part of the Old Kingdom of Israel,[38] under previous kings before Jesus of Nazareth, so Gentiles are allowed to be part of this New (Fulfilled) Kingdom of Israel under King Jesus, just more so.[39]

Kingdom Israel (the Church) exists for both Jews and Gentiles. This has always been the case, as Israel was never "purely Jewish" to begin with. Even in the old Kingdom of Israel, under the old Mosaic Law, there were Gentile converts to Judaism, and within the Holy Land, non-Jewish Gentiles (those who didn't convert) were still allowed to exist within the nation and partake of some of its rituals in limited ways.

Under the New Covenant, Jews and Gentiles exist equally under Kingdom Israel, and as it happens, Gentiles actually outnumber Jews exponentially now. It's important to understand this because Catholics must realize that Kingdom Israel is the Church and the Church is Kingdom Israel. There is no separation between Jew and Gentile within the Kingdom (Church), as they both exist together as royal subjects of the King. The idea here is that Jesus, acting as Israel's divine King, brought the fulfillment of the promised Messianic Kingdom (the Church) which all Jews had been looking forward to for centuries.

Entry into the *new* Kingdom Israel is the same for everyone, whether Jew or Gentile. It is baptism in the Name of the Holy Trinity.[40] **This is why the Catholic Church considers Trinitarian**

---

[38] Exodus 22:21; Exodus 23:9; Deuteronomy 10:18; Deuteronomy 24:17; Deuteronomy 27:19; Leviticus 19:33-34; Leviticus 24:22; Numbers 9:14

[39] Acts 15

[40] Matthew 28:19, Colossians 2:11-12

baptism an informal initiation of membership into the Catholic Church, even when it is given to non-Catholics in non-Catholic communities.[41] There are two main reasons for this. The first reason is that Trinitarian baptism is the official form of Catholic baptism. Thus, all Christians who receive Trinitarian baptism, have received the first sacrament of initiation into the Catholic Church.[42] The second reason is the nature of the Catholic Church as Kingdom Israel. Under the Old Testament, male circumcision was the method of initiation into Kingdom Israel.[43] However, under the New Testament, ***baptism*** has become the method of initiation into Kingdom Israel.[44]

---

[41] This in no way violates the Catholic dogma *extra Ecclesiam nulla salus* (outside the Church there is no salvation). Membership in the Catholic Church is not always defined as formal membership on paper. There is an extended sacramental membership, through Trinitarian baptism, which can (and does) incorporate those who are not formally members of the Catholic Church. See Catechism of the Catholic Church 818, 846, 855, 866, 1226-1274.

[42] There are three sacraments of initiation into the Catholic Church: Baptism, Confirmation and Holy Eucharist. Upon receiving all three of these initiating sacraments, one becomes "fully" Catholic. Many Christians, including Evangelical Protestants, have already received the first sacrament of initiation into the Catholic Church -- Trinitarian Baptism -- and have therefore become "partial" (as opposed to "full") members of the Catholic Church. This is why the Catholic Church does not re-baptize Evangelical converts, and instructs Catholics to refer to Evangelicals (and other Protestants) as "Christian brethren."

[43] Female converts, to the Old Testament Kingdom of Israel, were only required to take a ceremonial bath. This was a foreshadowing of the Sacrament of Baptism.

[44] Colossians 2:11-12, Romans 2:29, Matthew 28:19, 1 Corinthians 12:13

From the Scriptures, we learn that the New Covenant is made with Israel.[45] Yet the Scriptures also say the New Covenant is made with the Church.[46] We learn that the people of Old Testament Israel are the children of God.[47] Yet we also learn that Christians are the children of God.[48] We learn that Old Testament Israel is the Kingdom of God,[49] but then we learn that the Church is the Kingdom of God.[50] We learn that Old Testament Israel was a kingdom of priests,[51] but then we learn that the Church is a kingdom of priests.[52] We learn that Old Testament Israelites are the people of God,[53] then we also learn that Christians are the people of God.[54] We learn that Old Testament Israel is the vineyard of God,[55] but that the Church is also the vineyard of God.[56] We learn that Old Testament Israelites were children of Abraham.[57] Yet Christians are also called the children of Abraham.[58] We learn that

---

[45] Jeremiah 31:31-33

[46] Luke 22:20, 1 Corinthians 11:25, 2 Corinthians 3:6, Hebrews 8:6-10

[47] Exodus 4:22, Deuteronomy 14:1, Isaiah 1:2,4, Isaiah 1:2,4, Isaiah 63:8, Hosea 11:1

[48] John 1:12, John 11:52, Romans 8:14-16, 2 Corinthians 6:18, Galatians 3:26, Galatians 4:5-7, Philippians 2:15, 1 John 3:1

[49] Exodus 19:6, 1 Chronicles 17:14, 1 Chronicles 28:5

[50] Romans 14:17, 1 Corinthians 4:20, Colossians 1:13, Colossians 4:11, Revelation 1:6

[51] Exodus 19:6

[52] 1 Peter 2:5-9, Revelation 1:6, Revelation 5:10

[53] Exodus 6:7, Deuteronomy 27:9, 2 Samuel 7:23, Jeremiah 11:4

[54] Romans 9:25, 2 Corinthians 6:16, Ephesians 4:12, Ephesians 5:3, 2 Thessalonians 1:10, Titus 2:14

[55] Isaiah 5:3-7, Jeremiah 12:10

[56] Luke 20:16

[57] 2 Chronicles 20:7, Psalms 105:6, Isaiah 41:8

[58] Romans 4:11-16, Galatians 3:7, Galatians 3:29, Galatians 4:23-31

Old Testament Israel was the spouse of God,[59] but then we are told that the Church is the spouse of God.[60] We are told that Jerusalem is the maternal city of Old Testament Israel,[61] but then we are told that Jerusalem is the maternal city of the Church.[62] We are told that Old Testament Israelites are the chosen people,[63] but then we are told that Christians are the chosen people.[64] We learn that Israelites are the circumcised,[65] but then we find out that Christians are also "circumcised" in a spiritual way.[66] Old Testament Israelites are called "Jews,"[67] but then Christians are called the same.[68] Old Testament Israel is called an "Olive Tree,"[69] but then we find out that Christians are grafted into that same "Olive Tree."[70] Finally, Israel is clearly defined in the Old Testament as the Hebrew people,[71] but in the New Testament, we learn that Christians are incorporated into Israel.[72] Jesus summed it up succinctly when he told his followers, the first Christians:

---

[59] Isaiah 54:5-6, Jeremiah 2:2, Ezekiel 16:32, Hosea 1:2
[60] 2 Corinthians 11:2, Ephesians 5:31-32
[61] Psalms 149:2, Isaiah 12:6, Isaiah 49:18-22, Isaiah 51:18, Lamentations 4:2
[62] Galatians 4:26, Hebrews 12:22
[63] Deuteronomy 7:7, Deuteronomy 10:15, Deuteronomy 14:2, Isaiah 43:20-21
[64] Colossians 3:12, 1 Peter 2:9
[65] Genesis 17:10, Judges 15:18
[66] Romans 2:29, Philippians 3:3, Colossians 2:11
[67] Ezra 5:1, Jeremiah 34:8-9, Zechariah 8:22-23
[68] Romans 2:29
[69] Jeremiah 11:16, Hosea 14:6
[70] Romans 11
[71] Genesis 32:38, Genesis 35:10, Exodus 3:14, Judges 20:11
[72] John 11:50-52, 1 Corinthians 10:1, Galatians 6:15-16, Ephesians 2:12-19

> *"Don't be afraid, little flock, for it is your Father's good pleasure to give you the Kingdom."* (Jesus Christ, Luke 12:32)

The overwhelming theme of the New Testament is that Israel and the Church are one and the same thing. The Kingdom of God, in this present age, is none other than the Catholic Church. Jesus did not come to take the kingdom away from Jews and give it to Gentiles. No! He came to take the kingdom's leadership away from the Sanhedrin, claim it for himself as King, and give its administration to his Apostles and their successors! (Do you understand now why the Jewish leadership hated him so much? He was a real threat to their positions of authority.) *Fulfillment ecclesiology* (soft supersessionism) means the Mosaic Law is fulfilled by Christ and the sacraments of his Church. *Fulfillment ecclesiology* means the Temple is expanded into the Church. *Fulfillment ecclesiology* means the Sanhedrin are replaced by the Apostles and their successors. *Fulfillment ecclesiology* means if you want to follow Israel's King, you must do so in Kingdom Israel (the Catholic Church) where he reigns fully and completely through the ministry of the successors of his Apostles.

Fulfillment ecclesiology (soft supersessionism) *does not* mean Jews are replaced by Gentiles or that Israel is replaced by the Church. Quite the opposite; fulfillment ecclesiology means that Kingdom Israel is the Church, and the Church is the promised Kingdom of God. Jews and Gentiles both have free access to it. For Jews, it is theirs by birthright! Because they are physically Israel. For Gentiles, it is theirs by adoption.[73] This needs to be made crystal clear.

Why is it so important? Because in the last chapter I discussed the Evangelical error of Dispensationalism, and how it leads to the modern phenomenon of Christian Zionism.

Dispensationalism is built on the false premise that Kingdom Israel and the Church are two entirely different things. Dispensationalism is built on the false premise that Kingdom Israel is for the Jews, while the Church is for Gentiles. Dispensationalism is built on the false premise that God has two chosen people (Israel and the Church), and that each group will have its own method of salvation. Dispensationalism is built on the false premise that for the Church (Gentiles), spiritual salvation comes through "faith alone" (Martin Luther's teaching), and physical salvation comes through the future Rapture of the Church (John Nelson Darby's teaching). Likewise, Dispensationalism is built on the false premise that for Israel (Jews), salvation comes through working out the Old Testament law during the Great Tribulation (the Last Days) until they finally reject Antichrist and realize that Jesus Christ is their Messiah-King.

Thus, according to Dispensationalism, Jesus returns once (secretly) to fetch his Church (Gentiles) in the Rapture, and again publicly seven-years later, to deliver Israel (Jews) from their enemies as their Messianic King. Do you see the problem? Having two separate peoples requires two separate means of salvation, and ultimately two separate comings of Christ. This is what Evangelicalism has succumbed to under Dispensationalism, which has led them into the

---

[73] Adoption: Under Jewish law, adopted children are considered the same as biological children, and entitled to the same rights, privileges, and inheritance.

phenomenon of Christian Zionism. Because by separating Israel from the Church, and putting Jews (physical Israel) into the Middle East, under the banner of a man-made republic called "Israel," the Christian Zionists can say all the conditions necessary for Christ's return have now been met, which means their Rapture will come all that much sooner.

Let me elaborate here. The error originated 500 years ago during the Protestant Revolution (Reformation) with the idea that Jews cannot exist as Jews within Christendom, and should be rejected by Christendom, and persecuted by Christians because the Church has "replaced" them entirely (hard supersessionism). Only conversion to Christianity, measured by their assimilation with Gentile culture, can save them. In other words, they must abandon all vestiges of Jewry and become Gentile Christians (according to Martin Luther).

Centuries of this mindset, compounded with the godless materialism of the 20th century, led to the Nazi Holocaust against the Jews. In response, Evangelicalism overcompensated by turning to the notion that Jews and Christians are still separate people, but God has elected them both to salvation, just in different ways (according to John Nelson Darby). Thus, the Jews are equated with Israel entirely, and the Church is just the Church. The separation of physical Israel (Jews) from the Kingdom Israel (the Church) naturally demands two separate methods of eschatological redemption. So, the Church (Christians) will see their hopes realized in the Rapture, where they will be removed from this world before the horrors of the Great Tribulation and the Antichrist begin. Meanwhile, the Jews (physical Israel) will have to endure the horrors of the Great Tribulation and the Antichrist before they realize that Jesus Christ is their

Messiah too. This realization process happens during the "hiccup" of seven years between the sixth and seventh dispensations (see Chapter 3). When that happens, Jesus will return to earth to rescue them, approximately seven years after the Rapture.

The error that Luther started was compounded by Darby, leading to where we are today. Most Evangelicals see the Church and Israel as two separate entities entirely, that require two different methods of redemption, thus two separate comings of Christ in the Last Days. The purpose of the Church, in latter times of this sixth dispensation (according to them), is to support physical Israel (the Jews) which is most clearly manifested in the Israeli Republic. Thus, according to Dispensational-Zionism, one's support for the State of Israel can be used as a gauge to determine the legitimacy of one's Christianity.

The danger for Catholics is that this Dispensational-Zionism is a real threat to our own beliefs and worldview. Already, many Catholics have embraced Dispensational ideas, such as the Rapture, and Zionism as well, manifested in the unconditional political support of the Israeli Republic and the idea that God himself backs the Republic of Israel unconditionally. As I said in the previous chapter. I have no problem with Jews moving to the Middle East, if that's where they want to go. I also have no issue with Jews living under their own government and laws.

Still, as Christians, especially as Catholic Christians, we must be welcoming. I think it is our failure to be welcoming in the past that led to the creation of Zionism in the first place. In the past, Jews were encouraged (even coerced) into assimilation within the greater Gentile population of Christendom. As a matter of fact, it was expected of them, and therein lies the Church's greatest failure in dealing with the Jewish people.

The Apostles never made such a requirement. Granted, they made it clear that salvation doesn't come from observance of the old Mosaic Law, but at the same time, they never said Hebrew Christians couldn't still be Jewish. The New Testament clearly suggests the apostles themselves kept the Mosaic Law and continued to identify as Jews, though not for salvation reasons.[74]

Jesus himself even told his apostles to follow the religious instruction of the scribes and Pharisees, though not to follow their hypocrisy.[75] Granted, observing kosher cannot be said to have any bearing on one's salvation or holiness, but if you choose to keep kosher as your own dietary habit, as a means of identification with the Hebrew people in accordance with the old Mosaic Law, that's your personal choice. Granted, celebrating the Passover Seder has no salvific quality, but if you choose to celebrate it as part of your identification with physical Israel, again that is a personal matter. This is where Christianity has failed in the past, but organizations like the AHC are making sure these mistakes are not repeated.

The greatest fear of any converting Jew is assimilation. Losing one's ethnic or cultural identity is never a pleasant prospect. In a way, it's very similar to the fear many Anglicans had (and still have) about joining the Catholic Church. Anglicans call it "absorption" but it's the same idea as “assimilation.” This is what stopped many traditional Anglicans from joining the Catholic Church for decades. There was a general fear that once brought into the Catholic

---

[74] Acts 21:20-26
[75] Matthew 23:1-3

Church, Anglicans would be told to put away their old devotions and traditions, replacing them with Roman devotions and traditions instead. The fear was that the very devotions and traditions which drew them into the Catholic Church in the first place would be discarded and replaced, thus absorbing Anglicans into Roman Catholicism so that the former ceased to be, and only the latter remained. Indeed, many Catholics still believe this is exactly how it should be. The creation of the personal ordinariates, of English Patrimony, brought an end to those fears, and now Anglican converts to Catholicism can truly say that within the ordinariates, they are "united but not absorbed." It seems only reasonable that Jewish converts, having similar fears, should be able to say the same thing, "united but not assimilated."

The Kingdom of God (Kingdom Israel) is both for Jews and Gentiles alike. It is the Church, and the Church is Kingdom Israel. This Kingdom Israel (the Church) exists with Jesus as our King in Heaven, and Mary as our Queen. (Jewish kings often named their mothers as their queens.)[76] Jews and Gentiles exist together as one people therein. This means that some are Israel by birth (Jews), or physical Israel, but most are brought into Kingdom Israel through adoption (Gentile Christians). The Catholic Church is Kingdom Israel. The nature of this Kingdom directly ties into the Last Days.

---

[76] Jewish queens were often the mother of the king. The Hebrew word for this is *Gebirah* (גְּבִירָה), meaning a female Lord (or what we would call a “Lady” according to English custom), but in the Biblical context it means queen, or more specifically a queen mother, or the mother of the king. The position of this title in ancient Israel placed the queen mother alongside the king as a very powerful ruler, second only to the king. 1 Kings 2:19-20; 2 Kings 11:3; 2 Kings 24:8,15; 2 Chronicles 22:12; Jeremiah 13:18; Jeremiah 29:2

Chapter 6
Augustinian Approach

Saint Augustine of Hippo was born on November 13 in A.D. 354 in Thagaste, or what is now modern-day Souk Ahras, Algeria. This was during the transition time of the Roman Empire, as it was moving away from Paganism and into the early stages of imperial Christianity. Several theological problems would need to be worked out in the ecumenical councils of that time, but the emperor was essentially Christian, and Christianity was, generally, protected from persecution. All of Northern Africa was under the Roman Empire at that time, and Christianity was quickly becoming the dominant religion there.[77] Augustine's mother was a devout Christian. His father was a Pagan who converted to Christianity on his deathbed. The family was Berber, part of an ethnic group native to northern Africa, but was heavily Romanized, speaking only Latin in the home. Augustine's family was also well established. As a child and young adult, Agustine went to the best schools.

His early adult life was marked by hedonism as Augustine sought the acceptance of his peers. He took a lover and eventually had a son with her. He later had a change of heart, abandoned his hedonist life, and left his lover to marry a wealthy heiress, as was common in that time (and ours) with rich families. It's likely the marriage was arranged. However, the young girl was still not old enough to marry. So while Augustine was

---

[77] Northern Africa was heavily influenced by Christianity until the late seventh century (A.D. 647-700) when it was completely overrun by Islam.

waiting to fulfill his family duties, he adopted *Manichaeism* as his religion. This put a permanent halt to his marriage plans.

Manichaeism was a major player in the religious movements of that time. Founded by the Parthian prophet Mani (A.D. 216-274), the religion was a synthesis of Mesopotamian religions and Greek Gnosticism. It revered Mani as the final prophet, following Zoroaster, Buddha, and Jesus. Manichaeism was a duelist religion, where God is not omnipotent, but rather one of two gods (one good and the other evil) in perpetual struggle. Manichaens believed the universe is the product of this struggle, and not necessarily a planned creation of the good or evil god. Mani rejected the Old Testament entirely, and only incorporated elements of the Gospel of Jesus Christ as it suited him.

Augustine was a devoted follower of Manichaeism until late August of A.D. 386, when he finally converted to Christianity at the age of thirty-one. He was baptized by Saint Ambrose, Bishop of Milan, in Italy on the Easter Vigil of A.D. 387. Augustine began his vocation as a priest in A.D. 391 after the death of both his mother and his son, preaching against the errors of Manichaeism in Northern Africa. By A.D. 395, he was made a bishop in Hippo,[78] and shortly thereafter became the head bishop.

Saint Augustine was one of the most well-documented doctors of the early Church. His recorded sermons numbered in the thousands, though only about 500 survive until now. His masterpiece was a work titled *On the City of God Against the Pagans* (Latin: *De civitate Dei contra paganos*), which is often abbreviated simply as *The City of God.* The book is a

---

[78] Hippo is the ancient name for what is now the City of Annaba in Algeria.

defense of Christianity against accusations (blame) brought by the Pagans following the sacking of Rome by the Visigoths[79] in A.D. 410. In summary, the Pagans blamed the sacking of Rome on the Christians because the gods were angry about Romans abandoning Paganism for Christianity. In other words, the gods were punishing Rome for embracing Christianity.

The City of God, completed in A.D. 426, is a twenty-two book manuscript that defends Christianity against this false accusation. In his magnificent recount of history, Augustine pointed out that Rome suffered many wars during the height of Paganism, and their false gods did nothing to spare Rome in ages past. The fall of Rome was not the result of the false Pagan gods, nor the true Christian God. It was, rather, the fault of Rome's own moral and social decadence, centuries in the making. However, in the midst of this manuscript, Augustine also went out of his way to correct errors among some Christians as well, which contributed to a different kind of hysteria in his time called *millenarianism*.

Millenarianism

Millenarianism is the Christian belief that God would set up a thousand-year age of paradise on earth just before the end of the world. The notion was based on a literal interpretation of Revelation 20:1-10 which describes a thousand-year period when Satan would be bound in chains and unable to deceive the world, while Christ would rule the world with his saints for a thousand years.

---

[79] The Visigoths were Germanic people who constituted one of the major political tribes of the Goths in the northern regions of the Roman Empire. The opposing political tribe was called the Ostrogoths.

"I saw an angel coming down out of heaven, having the key of the abyss and a great chain in his hand. He seized the dragon, the old serpent, which is the devil and Satan, who deceives the whole inhabited earth, and bound him for a thousand years, and cast him into the abyss, and shut it, and sealed it over him, that he should deceive the nations no more, until the thousand years were finished. After this, he must be freed for a short time. I saw thrones, and they sat on them, and judgment was given to them. I saw the souls of those who had been beheaded for the testimony of Jesus, and for the word of God, and such as didn't worship the beast nor his image, and didn't receive the mark on their forehead and on their hand. They lived and reigned with Christ for a thousand years. The rest of the dead didn't live until the thousand years were finished. This is the first resurrection. Blessed and holy is he who has part in the first resurrection. Over these, the second death has no power, but they will be priests of God and of Christ, and will reign with him one thousand years.

"And after the thousand years, Satan will be released from his prison, and he will come out to deceive the nations which are in the four corners of the earth, Gog and Magog, to gather them together to the war; the number of

whom is as the sand of the sea. They went up over the width of the earth, and surrounded the camp of the saints, and the beloved city. Fire came down out of heaven from God and devoured them. The devil who deceived them was thrown into the lake of fire and sulfur, where the beast and the false prophet are also. They will be tormented day and night forever and ever."

(Revelation 20:1-10)

Among the early Church Fathers, a number of them believed in a literal interpretation of this passage. This means they believed there would be a literal thousand-years between the time of the Second Coming of Christ and the Last Judgment at the end of the world. This is similar to the position held by John Darby (minus his peculiar Rapture doctrine) in Evangelical Dispensationalism.[80] However, at the same time, there were also many Church Fathers who held to a non-literal interpretation of this thousand-year period. This was mentioned by Saint Justin Martyr (A.D. 100-165), himself a believer in the literal interpretation of the millennium, who wrote in defense of his literal position: "*I signified to you that many who belong to the pure and pious faith, and are true*

---

[80] The premillennial position (literal thousand-year interpretation) held by some early Christians was similar to Darby's Dispensationalism but not identical to it. The early Christians knew nothing of a pre-tribulation rapture that precedes the coming of the Antichrist, and insisted that Christians would endure the persecution of Antichrist in the Last Days.

Christians, think otherwise."[81] From this we can clearly see that early Christianity was divided on this issue, yet both camps agreed the other was Christian.

The first camp held to the position that the millennium, mentioned in Revelation 20:1-10, was not to be taken literally. Saint Justin Martyr (whose surname describes his manner of death) mentions this camp in his *Dialogue with Trypho the Jew*, as quoted above. The second camp was the one that Justin Martyr belonged to, those who interpreted the millennium literally. It appears that while the early Christians held to two very opposing views on this particular passage of Scripture (Revelation 20:1-10), they got along with each other just fine, and it was not a source of division between them.

Some examples of Early Church Fathers who held to a non-literal interpretation of the millennium were: Clement of Alexandria,[82] Saint Hippolytus of Rome,[83] Origen,[84] Saint Cyprian,[85] Dionysius the Great,[86] Saint Ambrose of Milan,[87] Saint Athanasius the Great,[88] as well as the Church Fathers who wrote the *Didache*.

---

[81] Justin Martyr, Dialogue with Trypho the Jew, Chapter 80, written in A.D. 155-160

[82] Clement of Alexandria, Christian theologian and catechist, (A.D. 150-215)

[83] Hippolytus of Rome, One of the most important early Christian theologians, (A.D. 170-235)

[84] Origen, Christian scholar, ascetic and theologian, (A.D. 184-253)

[85] Cyprian, Bishop of Carthage, (A.D. 210-258)

[86] Dionysius the Great, Bishop and Patriarch of Alexandria from A.D. 248-264

[87] Ambrose of Milan, Bishop of Milan and theologian, (A.D. 340-396)

[88] Athanasius the Great, Bishop of Alexandria and theologian, (A.D. 296-373)

The *Didache* (Διδαχή), which means "Teaching," also known as *The Lord's Teaching Through the Twelve Apostles to the Nations* (Διδαχὴ Κυρίου διὰ τῶν δώδεκα ἀποστόλων τοῖς ἔθνεσιν), was an early constitution for the ancient church, believed to be written between A.D. 50-150. Some scholars propose that the teaching was actually a second document that came out of the Council of Jerusalem in A.D. 50 mentioned in the fifteenth chapter of the Acts of the Apostles (Acts 15). It explained basic Christian beliefs, sacraments, and procedures in early Christianity. Though it was originally written in Greek, it's easily accessible in modern English both in public libraries and on the Internet. The *Didache* makes no mention of a thousand-year span between the Antichrist and the Second Coming of Christ, the Last Judgment, and the end of the world. The *Didache* simply asserts that the Antichrist will come. He will be destroyed by the return of Christ, then comes the Last Judgment and the end of this world. There is no mention of a thousand-year interlude (millennium) between the time of Antichrist and the Last Judgment. Thus, the *Didache* would appear to be amillennial in its approach to eschatology.[89]

Augustine obviously did not invent this amillennial (non-literal) interpretation of the thousand-year period in Revelation 20:1-10, rather he crystallized it in *The City of God*. He did this in the most ingenious way, by describing all history as a tale of two cities. The city of man describes this present world and the physical universe that surrounds us. The city of God describes the heavenly realm of God, his angels, and his glorified saints. Augustine pointed out that perfection is not possible in this physical universe (the

---

[89] Didache, Chapter 16, (AD 50-150)

city of man), and the best mankind can hope for is to be incorporated into the city of God through Jesus Christ. Such incorporation into the city of God will allow some small aspects of that city to manifest in the city of man, but the full manifestation of the city of God cannot happen (in completion) until the end of this world. Thus, Augustine concluded the millennium (thousand-year period) of Revelation 20:1-10 must be interpreted figuratively as a representation of the Church Age and not literally, as if foretelling some future time of paradise on earth under the physical reign of Jesus Christ.

If we recall from the gospels, Pilate asked Jesus if he was a king...

> *"Jesus answered, 'My Kingdom is not of this world. If my Kingdom were of this world, then my servants would fight, that I wouldn't be delivered to the Jews. But now my Kingdom is not from here.'"* (John 18:36)

Augustine's approach solved a great deal of problems for Christians in his time, many struggling with one false prediction after another, concerning the return of Jesus Christ and the coming of the millennium. (It was very much like our own time.) With each passing disaster, many Christians would assume it heralded the coming of the Apocalypse, which would initiate the time of the Antichrist followed by the beginning of the millennium. A good number of Christians at that time didn't fall for this, and held to an amillennial view of Biblical prophecy. It seems that the amillennial interpretation was guarding some Christians, at that time, against the apocalyptic hysteria that was constantly besetting Christians who held to the premillennial position. Until Augustine, however, nobody had described it in such a succinct and comprehensive way. Augustine recognized Tyconius, a predecessor who was very influential on his amillennial understanding of Revelation 20. While *The City of God* was not written as a book on eschatology, it nevertheless shed insight on the topic.

Following Augustine, the Catholic Church adopted his approach to the millennium that has lasted to this very day. Even the modern Catechism forbids the teaching of a literal thousand-year millennium within Catholic churches. In just three paragraphs, the new Catechism of the Catholic Church lays out its entire teaching on the chronology of the Last Days and the Second Coming of Jesus Christ...

> *"675 Before Christ's second coming the Church must pass through a final trial that will shake the faith of many believers. [Lk 18:8; Mt 24:12] The persecution that accompanies her pilgrimage on earth [Lk 21:12; Jn 15:19-20] will unveil the 'mystery of iniquity' in the form of a religious deception offering men an apparent solution to their problems at the price of apostasy from the truth. The supreme religious deception is that of the Antichrist, a pseudo-messianism by which man glorifies himself in place of God and of his Messiah come in the flesh. [2 Thess 2:4-12; 1 Thess 5:2-3; 2 Jn 7; 1 Jn 2:18,22]*

> *"676 The Antichrist's deception already begins to take shape in the world every*

time the claim is made to realize within history that messianic hope which can only be realized beyond history through the eschatological judgment. The Church has rejected even modified forms of this falsification of the kingdom to come under the name of millenarianism, [DS 3839] especially the 'intrinsically perverse' political form of a secular messianism. [GS 20-21]

"677 The Church will enter the glory of the kingdom only through this final Passover, when she will follow her Lord in his death and Resurrection. [Rev 19:1-9] The kingdom will be fulfilled, then, not by a historic triumph of the Church through a progressive ascendancy, but only by God's victory over the final unleashing of evil, which will cause his Bride to come down from heaven. [Rev 13:8; 20:7-10; 21:2-4] God's triumph over the revolt of evil will take the form of the Last Judgment after the final cosmic upheaval of this passing world. [Rev 20:12 2 Pet 3:12-13]"

A similar understanding is true for the Eastern Orthodox Christians, as well as some older Protestant denominations. It's noteworthy to add that a few Evangelicals are beginning to return to this Augustinian approach as well, especially after multiple disappointments caused by Darby's Dispensationalism. In my own lifetime, I've experienced no less than half a dozen predictions about the Rapture, Apocalypse, and Second Coming of Jesus Christ. All of these would have likely left me disappointed and doubting my Christian faith by now, had I not left all that behind and converted to Catholicism, thus embracing the Augustinian approach to eschatology. I, personally, know dozens of Evangelicals whose faith has been shaken by the false predictions of Darby Dispensationalists. A few have lost faith completely. Augustine was dealing with similar (not identical but similar) problems in his day. *The City of God* attempted to resolve this issue in addition to absolving Christianity from the Visigoth sack of Rome.

Augustine's treatise on an amillennial interpretation of Revelation 20 comes from the twentieth book of *The City of God*. In chapter seven, he explains Saint John's use of the number one-thousand as a figurative way to describe the entire Church Age, beginning from the time of Christ's first coming, to the time of his second coming. He puts it this way...

> *"For a thousand is the cube of ten. For ten times ten makes a hundred, that is; the square on a plane superficies. But to give this superficie height, and make it a cube, the hundred is again multiplied by ten, which gives a thousand."*[90]

He then cites Matthew 19:29 and 2 Corinthians 6:10 to demonstrate that the word "hundred" cannot always be taken literally in Scripture, and then cites Psalm 105:7-8 to demonstrate that the word "thousand" cannot always be taken literally in Scripture either. In both cases, a hundred and a thousand, the interpretation is meant to be "all." So, the same could be said of the thousand-year millennium, which is

---

[90] Augustine, City of God, Book 20, Chapter 7

meant to be interpreted as "all" the years between the first and second coming of Jesus Christ.

Once we understand that the proper interpretation of Revelation 20:1-10 is figurative, it lends to a more figurative interpretation of the entire Book of Revelation (Apocalypse). Contextually, this makes sense, as the entire book is riddled with grandiose illustrations, or word-pictures, that seem to contain a more profound message. This makes sense because if we were to exclude the Book of Revelation (Apocalypse) from our thinking, and look strictly at what is taught about the Last Days in other portions of the Bible, we get a picture that is consistent with what Augustine says about the millennium. When examining these Scripture passages, excluding Revelation (Apocalypse), this is what we get.

Antichrist and the Last Days

> *"Now, brothers, concerning the coming of our Lord Jesus Christ and our gathering together to him, we ask you not to be quickly shaken in your mind, and not be troubled, either by spirit, or by word, or by letter as if from us, saying that the day of Christ has already come. Let no one deceive you in any way. For it will not be, unless the rebellion comes first, and the man of sin is revealed, the son of destruction, he who opposes and exalts himself against all that is called God or that is worshiped, so that he sits as God in the temple of God, setting himself up as God. Don't you remember that, when I was still with you, I told you*

these things? Now you know what is restraining him, to the end that he may be revealed in his own season. For the mystery of lawlessness already works. Only there is one who restrains now, until he is taken out of the way. Then the lawless one will be revealed, whom the Lord will kill with the breath of his mouth, and destroy by the manifestation of his coming; even he whose coming is according to the working of Satan with all power and signs and lying wonders, and with all deception of wickedness for those who are being lost, because they didn't receive the love of the truth, that they might be saved. Because of this, God sends them a working of error, that they should believe a lie; that they all might be judged who didn't believe the truth, but had pleasure in unrighteousness." (2 Thessalonians 2:1-12)

"Little children, these are the end times, and as you heard that the Antichrist is coming, even now many antichrists have arisen. By this we know that it is the final hour. They went out from us, but they didn't belong to us; for if they had belonged to us, they would have continued with us. But they left, that they might be revealed that none of them belong to us. You have an anointing from the Holy One, and you all have knowledge. I have not written to you because you don't know the truth, but

because you know it, and because no lie is of the truth. Who is the liar but he who denies that Jesus is the Christ? This is the Antichrist, he who denies the Father and the Son. Whoever denies the Son doesn't have the Father. He who confesses the Son has the Father also." (1 John 2:18-23)

"Beloved, don't believe every spirit, but test the spirits, whether they are of God, because many false prophets have gone out into the world. By this you know the Spirit of God: every spirit who confesses that Jesus Christ has come in the flesh is of God, and every spirit who doesn't confess that Jesus Christ has come in the flesh is not of God, and this is the spirit of the Antichrist, of whom you have heard that it comes. Now it is in the world already." (1 John 4:1-3)

"For many deceivers have gone out into the world, those who don't confess that Jesus Christ came in the flesh. This is the deceiver and the Antichrist." (2 John 1:7)

These are the only New Testament passages where Antichrist is mentioned, as well as the delusion (rebellion) concerning him. Saint John (who later penned the Book of Revelation) specifically tells us the nature of this antichrist delusion that would eventually lead to the person of Antichrist. The delusion itself is the spirit of the antichrist. It is already in the world, and has been since the time of the Apostles. It will conclude in the Last Days with a man who perpetuates the same delusion on a global scale. What is this delusion? It is simply the denial that Jesus of Nazareth is the Christ (Messiah). This is often accompanied by an attempt to replace him with another. It is a spirit of false messianism that rejects Jesus, but asserts another person as the Messiah.

In John's time, he was surrounded by this phenomenon. As far back as A.D. 6, Judas of Galilee led a Jewish rebellion against the Romans. He was hailed as the Messiah, just before he was killed. Simon bar Kokhba was also hailed as the promised Messiah when he led another Jewish revolt against the Romans in A.D. 132. These are just the big names that history remembers. There were many smaller players too. Saint John warned the Christians of his time not to be deceived by them. Their rejection of Jesus Christ, and replacing him with an alternate Messiah, was the spirit of antichrist, or the antichrist delusion. This spirit will work its way through the ages, to the Last Days, when it will culminate in one man who will do the same, with marvelous success in deceiving the whole world (minus the Church). This will be the great and final Antichrist.

There you go. It's not so complicated, is it? When we understand the word Antichrist in these terms -- the Biblical terms -- it's not such a complicated mystery. We've seen types of antichrists in our own modern period: Stalin, Hitler, Mao, etc. We've seen countless cult leaders claiming to be Christ, or some manifestation of Christ. Modern Judaism has seen a handful of messianic claimants as well. None of them amounted to much. All of them have been led to destruction, in one way or another. But that's the message, isn't it? The spirit of Antichrist is just a rejection of Jesus Christ, by replacing him with another

"Christ" (another messiah), which always leads to destruction in some form. The final Antichrist, in the Last Days, will just be a global manifestation of the same thing, that will happen to be very convincing to non-Christians, or nominally Christian people. It's the same old garbage, just bigger!

The Second Coming (Parousia)

> *"For the mystery of lawlessness already works. Only there is one who restrains now, until he is taken out of the way. Then the lawless one will be revealed, whom the Lord will kill with the breath of his mouth, and destroy by the manifestation of his coming."* (2 Thessalonians 2:7-8)

> *"When he had said these things, as they were looking, he was taken up, and a cloud received him out of their sight. While they were looking steadfastly into the sky as he went, behold, two men stood by them in white clothing, who also said, 'You men of Galilee, why do you stand looking into the sky? This Jesus, who was received up from you into the sky, will come back in the same way as you saw him going into the sky.'"* (Acts 1:9-11)

> *"But when the Son of Man comes in his glory, and all the holy angels with him, then he will sit on the throne of his glory."* (Matthew 25:31)

"Jesus said to him, 'You have said so. Nevertheless, I tell you, after this you will see the Son of Man sitting at the right hand of Power, and coming on the clouds of the sky.'" (Matthew 26:64)

"For whoever will be ashamed of me and of my words in this adulterous and sinful generation, the Son of Man also will be ashamed of him, when he comes in his Father's glory, with the holy angels." (Mark 8:38)

"But immediately after the suffering of those days, the sun will be darkened, the moon will not give its light, the stars will fall from the sky, and the powers of the heavens will be shaken; and then the sign of the Son of Man will appear in the sky. Then all the tribes of the earth will mourn, and they will see the Son of Man coming on the clouds of the sky with power and great glory. He will send out his angels with a great sound of a trumpet, and they will gather together his chosen ones from the four winds, from one end of the sky to the other… But no one knows of that day and hour, not even the angels of heaven, but my Father only." (Matthew 24:29-31, 36)

"But you watch. Behold, I have told you all things beforehand. But in those days, after that oppression, the sun will be darkened, the moon will not give its light, the stars will be falling from the

sky, and the powers that are in the heavens will be shaken. Then they will see the Son of Man coming in clouds with great power and glory. Then he will send out his angels, and will gather together his chosen ones from the four winds, from the ends of the earth to the ends of the sky… But of that day or that hour no one knows, not even the angels in heaven, nor the Son, but only the Father." (Mark 13:23-27, 32)

"Behold, I tell you a mystery. We will not all sleep, but we will all be changed, in a moment, in the twinkling of an eye, at the last trumpet. For the trumpet will sound and the dead will be raised incorruptible, and we will be changed. For this perishable body must become imperishable, and this mortal must put on immortality. But when this perishable body will have become imperishable, and this mortal will have put on immortality, then what is written will happen: 'Death is swallowed up in victory. Death, where is your sting? Hades, where is your victory?'" (1 Corinthians 15:51-55)

"For this we tell you by the word of the Lord, that we who are alive, who are left until the coming of the Lord, will in no way precede those who have fallen asleep. For the Lord himself will descend from heaven with a shout, with the voice of the archangel and with

> *God's trumpet. The dead in Christ will rise first, then we who are alive, who are left, will be caught up together with them in the clouds, to meet the Lord in the air. So we will be with the Lord forever."* (1 Thessalonians 4:15-17)

Once we remove the Book of Revelation, it all becomes pretty straightforward and easy to understand. Now, that doesn't mean we are ignoring the Book of Revelation. On the contrary, we are using the Scriptures to build our understanding of the Last Days in a basic and succinct form. Then, and only then, should we come in later with the Book of Revelation to elaborate on this understanding.

As you can see, the above passages are in literal text. There is no nuance or figurative speech here. However, the Book of Revelation is filled with nuance and figurative speech. Whenever dealing with a problem like this, we should go to the plain-spoken (literal) texts first, build our eschatology from these, then come in later with the figurative and nuanced text.

The Augustinian approach agrees with the plain-spoken (literal) references from the Bible cited above. So with Augustine, we have an eschatological system of interpretation that works, and doesn't complicate things any more than they need to be.

As an addendum to this, I should probably put a spotlight on the curious passage in 2 Thessalonians 2:7-8, where it says "*Only there is one who restrains now, until he is taken out of the way. Then the lawless one will be revealed.*" What does this mean when it says, "*one who restrains now*"? The truth is, nobody knows. Some have postulated that it refers to the pope. Some say it refers to the Roman emperor. Both theories are plausible, but neither is certain. If it is the pope, then are we to believe the Chair of Saint Peter will be vacant (*sede vacante*) at the time of Antichrist? Who knows? If it is the Roman Emperor, then your guess is as good as mine.

It should be pointed out that the Roman Empire always existed, in some form or another, until the early 19th century when the Holy Roman Empire finally ceased to be. However, we can say that vestiges of the Roman Empire still remain in the Western governments of today. So, it could just as easily be said that the "*one who restrains now*" could be the Roman Empire in a general sense, as in the Western world's willingness to continue to govern itself, using many of the principles, laws and ideals founded by Rome.

We know the "*one who restrains now*" cannot be the Holy Spirit of God because that would imply that God removes his Spirit from the world, and that cannot happen so long as there is a single Christian left on planet earth, and Jesus Christ promised the Gates of Hell would not prevail against his Church.[91]

The personal pronoun "one" or "he" (in some translations) definitely suggests this is a person, not an institution, entity, ideology or system. So, when we look at offices, occupied by real men, since the time of the Apostles until now, that really limits the possibilities. It's either the emperor of the Holy Roman Empire, an office which is dormant now, but there are a few heirs left who could retake the throne. Or else it is the papacy itself, which has never been vacant, except for brief interregnums. It's a curious passage, which Saint Paul never bothered to explain to us. It's clear the Christians in Thessalonica knew, but that knowledge was not passed down. Perhaps it's God's intention to keep it a secret for now.

---

[91] Matthew 16:18

Augustinian Eschatology

I. The millennium (thousand-year period) is not literally a thousand years, but a time period much longer, and describes all the time between the first and second coming of Jesus Christ. We are living in the millennium right now, as have all people since the First Coming of Christ two-thousand years ago.

   A. The millennium is not a time of paradise or perfection, as those things cannot be achieved in this world under the city of man.

      1. There will be wars during the millennium.
      2. There will be persecutions of Christians during the millennium,
      3. There will be natural disasters during the millennium.
      4. What makes the millennium special and glorious is the spread of the gospel throughout the world, allowing Jesus Christ to reign through the hearts of men, thus bringing glimpses of the heavenly city of God into the earthly city of man.

   B. The millennium is a time when Satan (the Devil) is "bound" or "restrained" from deceiving the entirety of humanity. He is still up to his usual mischief, but he cannot deceive the whole planet into a rebellion against God. The Church will always be out of his reach.

   C. The millennium will come to an end when Satan is released (or "loosened") for a short time, to deceive most of humanity, but not all of it. The Church will remain intact and free from his influence.

1. This period of release is known as the Great Tribulation.
2. During this time, the Antichrist will rise to world power and persecute the Church.

II. The Second Coming of Jesus Christ (Parousia) marks the end of the earthly city of man.

A. The Parousia comes at a time when nobody suspects, and cannot be predicted.

B. The Parousia is marked by the arrival of Jesus Christ in the heavens, seen and heard by all humanity at the same time.

1. Jesus Christ slays the Antichrist by the word of his mouth.
2. The dead are raised incorruptible.
3. The bodies of the living are transformed into glorious and incorruptible bodies.
4. Those who belong to Christ rise to meet him in the air.
5. Those who do not belong to Christ remain on earth for his arrival.
6. Upon arriving on earth, the Last Judgment begins, where those in Christ are rewarded with everlasting paradise, and those who are not in Christ are cast away into everlasting darkness.

7. The old heaven and earth pass away, as eternity begins.

As you can see, when compared to Chapter 3 of this book, the Augustinian approach to eschatology is much simpler than the Dispensationalist approach of John Nelson Darby, or even the Historicist approach of Martin Luther in Chapter 2. The problem with Luther and Darby is they attempted to decipher the events of the Last Days using the Book of Revelation first, then plugged in other passages of Scripture afterward, to fit their understanding of the Book of Revelation (Apocalypse). In other words, they approached the whole thing backwards. The Luther-Darby approach was to start with Revelation, then make the rest of the Bible fit. The Augustinian approach was to use the rest of the Bible first as a template, then apply the Book of Revelation afterward to see how it fits.

This makes sense when you really stop and think about it because the Book of Revelation (Apocalypse) was the last book of the Bible ever written. Some say it was written between A.D. 50 to 90. So the Apostles, and their immediate disciples (bishops of the early Church) would have already had a clear understanding of eschatology long before the Book of Revelation was written. When the Book of Revelation finally arrived between A.D. 50 to 90, it would have been read with the mindset of an eschatology already developed. That eschatology was formed by the Scripture passages I cited above in this chapter. The first-century bishops *wouldn't* have been trying to see how these above passages fit into the Book of Revelation (Apocalypse). Rather, they would be trying to see how the Book of Revelation (Apocalypse) fits into these passages.

So now, what do we do with the Book of Revelation (Apocalypse)? How do we interpret it in a way that is consistent with how most of the first-century bishops would approach it, and how Saint Augustine of Hippo approached it? Before we can do that, we need to understand the world as it appeared at the time of the Apostle John (the presumed author of the book). This requires us to take a closer look at the Gospel of John in relation to the Synoptic Gospels (Matthew, Mark and Luke), and what was going on in the late first century. I'll explore this topic further in the next chapter.

Chapter 7
Olivet Discourse

Saint John the Apostle was born in A.D. 6 at Bethsaida, a village of Galilee, a son of two devout Jewish parents, Zebedee and Salome. According to tradition, Salome was a sister of Mary, the mother of Jesus, making John one of Jesus' cousins. His father, Zebedee, was a fisherman. As was customary at that time, and in most times in history, sons followed their fathers in their working profession. Zebedee's two sons, James and John, were also fishermen, and are mentioned in Mark 3:17, where Jesus gave the pair the name *Boanerges* (Βοανεργές) meaning "sons of thunder." It likely derives from Jesus' spoken language, Aramaic, from a contraction of the words *bne* (בני) meaning "sons" and *rgas* (רגיש) meaning "tumult" or "anger" or "thunder."

So, John was a "son of thunder," along with his brother James. It was likely a reference to their religious zeal and "no compromise" attitude. It may have also been a reference to their ability to boisterously preach his gospel. Whatever the case, their relationship with Jesus was strong. They were his cousins, after all, and he brought both of them into his inner circle. Even though he gave the Keys of the Kingdom to Peter, a symbol of the highest authority a King can give, his favoritism of James and John was unmistakable. The three of them (Peter, James and John) are mentioned multiple times in the gospels as receiving privileged information from Jesus, and witnessing special miracles the others did not. John simply referred to himself as "the disciple whom Jesus loved" in his own written gospel. James went on to become the chief apostle and patriarch of Jerusalem, a key player in the early Church.

John's actual name in Hebrew was *Yochanan* (יוחנן). He was also known as John the Evangelist, John of Patmos, John the Elder and the Beloved Disciple. He was the youngest of all the disciples, outliving all of them by decades, and was the only apostle to die of natural causes. Likewise, he was the author of the Gospel of John, the epistles of First, Second and Third John, as well as the Book of Revelation. Second only to Saint Paul, he was the most prolific author of the New Testament, with Luke coming in third place. John was the only apostle present at Jesus' crucifixion. The rest of the apostles fled in fear. There, with the women beneath the cross, Jesus gave John the care of his mother, Mary, to take as his own mother. (He couldn't have done this if Jesus actually had sibling brothers, as this would be an insult to them.) John was his cousin, and therefore the closest male relative he had. In doing this, Jesus figuratively made Mary John's mother, and mother of the whole Church as well.

During the persecution of Herod Agrippa (A.D. 41-44), causing the exodus of many Christians from the Holy Land and the scattering of the Apostles throughout the Roman Empire, John took up residence in Ephesus, in Asia Minor (modern-day Turkey), where he cared for the churches founded by Saint Paul, and for Mary (Jesus' mother) until her assumption into heaven. The early Christians all unanimously believed that Mary did not die, but was assumed (translated, taken, or "raptured") into heaven at the end of her earthly life.[92]

---

92 Epiphanius, Panarion,78:23 written in A.D. 377

John then went on to endure many persecutions of the early Church, having been boiled in oil under the persecution of Emperor Domitian in A.D. 81. He miraculously survived unharmed.[93] There are those who say he was imprisoned on the island penal colony of Patmos after this failed execution. However, there are also those who say his imprisonment on Patmos was much earlier. Apringius of Beja[94] tells us this happened during the reign of Emperor Claudius (A.D. 41-54), but Saint Bede[95] tells us this imprisonment happened during the reign of Emperor Domitian (A.D. 81-96). There is no way to know for certain who is correct.

The best guess is to say the Book of Revelation (Apocalypse) was written, at the earliest, around A.D. 50, and at the latest, around A.D. 90. I tend to go with the earlier date, as this tends to make more sense when we consider the nature of the text, which is written primarily of future events proximal to A.D. 50, and also the location of Patmos within the Roman Empire.

Patmos was close to the seven churches in Asia Minor, and close to the location where John and Mary resided in Ephesus before her assumption into heaven. It makes logical sense that a Roman prisoner, like John, would be held there first, long before being taken to Rome for execution. What doesn't make much sense to me is attempting to execute a man in Rome,

---

93 Tertullian, The Prescription Against Heretics, Chapter 36, written between A.D. 197-220

94 Apringius of Beja was a sixth-century Church Father who wrote a commentary on the Book of Revelation in Latin. Only fragments of his work remain to this day.

95 Saint Bede was a Benedictine monk in England during the seventh to eighth centuries. He was a well-known author, teacher, scholar and English historian. Much of what we know about ancient English history is attributed to him.

and then sending him all the way back to his home in Asia Minor to serve out a prison sentence after the execution failed? Nobody does that. That would be the case if John was imprisoned on Patmos between A.D. 81-96, as Saint Bede claimed. It also goes against Roman traditions at the time. It was customary for the Romans to look at an execution attempt (or extreme torture) as a kind of test for political prisoners. If the prisoner survived the torture/execution, it was seen as a sign from the gods that the prisoner should be released. The Romans did this frequently with the Christians they tortured in the circus and Colosseum. If they happened to survive, they let them go. So, for this book, and to make things simpler, we'll assume that Apringius was correct, and the Book of Revelation (Apocalypse) was written around A.D. 50.

The Book of Revelation (Apocalypse) is certainly the most curious book in the entire Bible. So many books have been written about it, they could probably fill an entire library! But what is the Book of Revelation (Apocalypse)? To understand that question, we need to look at the three other gospel writers.

Synoptic Gospels

The synoptic gospels consist of Matthew, Mark and Luke. These gospels are called "synoptic" because they relate a common story, told in a nearly identical way. In fact, the narration is so similar, many scholars have surmised they all come from a common source, no longer existing, which they have named "Q." However, we know from the Church Fathers that the Gospel according to Matthew was originally written in

Aramaic, not Greek.[96] It's probable that this is the "Q" source used for the later Greek version of Matthew we have today, as well as the source text for Mark and Luke. As we read through the synoptic gospels, we find similar narration of virtually identical stories and sayings of Jesus Christ. Of particular interest to us is a section called "The Olivet Discourse," sometimes called the "Little Apocalypse," which recounts apocalyptic predictions of things to come both in the time of the Apostles, and in the Last Days.

Two Events

In the Olivet Discourse,[97] or the Little Apocalypse of Matthew, Mark and Luke, Jesus tells his disciples that the Jerusalem Temple will soon be destroyed. The disciples respond by asking Jesus a question. In Matthew 24:3 it's put this way: *"Tell us, when will these things be? What is the sign of your coming, and of the end of the age?"* In Mark 13:4 it's put this way: *"Tell us, when will these things be? What is the sign that these things are all about to be fulfilled?"* In Luke 21:7 it's put this way: *"Teacher, so when will these things be? What is the sign that these things are about to happen?"* Examine their questions closely. They're asking Jesus about the coming destruction of the Jerusalem Temple, an historical event that would happen thirty-seven years after they asked these questions. Keep this in mind. Jesus, in A.D. 33, just foretold the destruction of the Jerusalem

---

[96] Irenaeus, Against Heresies 3:1:1; Eusebius, History of the Church 3:24; Papias, Bishop of Hierapolis, Explanation of the Sayings of the Lord, as cited by Eusebius in History of the Church 3:39; Origen as cited by Eusebius in History of the Church 6:25

[97] Matthew 24; Mark 13; Luke 21

Temple (which would happen in A.D. 70), and the disciples were specifically asking him "when will this be?"

In Matthew's gospel, however, an interesting context is cited in the second question. The disciples additionally ask, *"What is the sign of your coming, and of the end of the age?"* The context is the belief of the disciples, and of most Jews at that time. They were not only expecting the Messiah (Christ) to come and institute the Kingdom of God, but they had some sense that this would be connected to the Last Days and the end of the world. The disciples equated the destruction of their Temple with the end of the world! This is actually very common among all people. People usually equate the fall of their civilizations with the end of the world. For the Jews, the Jerusalem Temple was seen as the great symbol of their people, their covenant with God, their religion and their entire worldview. The destruction of such a great edifice, in their minds, could only herald the end of the world. Today, we know this wasn't the case, but at that time in history, the disciples couldn't yet see it any other way.

Jesus then goes into a short explanation that they should expect false messiahs (antichrists), persecutions, famines, wars, earthquakes and the like, but not to worry because none of these herald the fall of the Temple or the Last Days. However, Jesus also cites a very specific sign that they were to look for, which would herald the fall of the Jerusalem Temple. In Matthew 24:15 and Mark 13:14 it's called the *"abomination of desolation"* along with a short note *"let the reader understand."*

The Gospel of Luke, however, sheds a little insight as to what this is. In Luke 21:20 the "abomination of desolation" is relayed as such: *"But when you see Jerusalem surrounded by armies, then know that its desolation is at hand."* The desolation is the coming destruction, but why is this called an abomination? The word "abomination" in the Old Testament context of the Book of Daniel[98] is typically a reference to something profane entering the Temple. This could be anything, really. It could be Pagans entering the Temple, and doing some kind of Pagan ritual. Or it could also be the destruction and theft of Temple vessels.

The Old Testament prophet, Daniel, foretold the coming of an abomination that would cause desolation of the Temple. Daniel already knew that one abomination had passed in his time; what he did not know is that his prophecy would be fulfilled not just once, but twice! At the time of Jesus, two had passed. The first was the abomination of desolation that occurred when King Nebuchadnezzar conquered Jerusalem in 587 B.C. and looted the sacred vessels from the Temple. Daniel knew about this one in his time, but he prophesied it would happen again.

The Temple was restored in 516 B.C. under the reign of Emperor Darius.[99] The second abomination of desolation occurred in 167 B.C. when Antiochus Epiphanes replaced the Temple sacrifices commanded by Moses with Pagan sacrifices. However, the Temple was restored following the Maccabean Revolt in 167-160 B.C. This is what the Feast of Dedication (Hanukkah) celebrates.[100] Jesus and the apostles celebrated this festival in John 10:22-23, so they were well aware of it, and that one of Daniel's two foretold

---

[98] Daniel 9:27; 11:31; 12:11, written in about 532 BC.
[99] Ezra 5
[100] 1st and 2nd Maccabees

abominations of desolation had already occurred. They were awaiting the second.[101]

So, the three abominations of desolation were (1) the sacking of Jerusalem by Babylon in 587 B.C., followed by (2) the profanation of the Temple by Antiochus Epiphanes in 167 B.C., and the third was yet to come in Jesus' time.

Luke's gospel, and the historical record, tell us the third and final abomination was the coming destruction of Jerusalem by the armies of Rome, which resulted once again in the sacred vessels being looted by Pagans. Luke's gospel is the giveaway. In typical physician style,[102] he explains complicated and mysterious things in plain and simple ways, so the average layperson can more easily understand. Luke would continue this process throughout The Olivet Discourse.

Jesus gave specific instructions, in all three synoptic gospels, that when his followers saw the third abomination of desolation, which is Jerusalem surrounded by Roman armies, they were to flee the city immediately, without even taking time to pack their belongings. The Christians in Jerusalem did just that, fleeing the city before the armies even had time to fully assemble. In the three and a half year siege that

---

[101] Darby-Dispensationalists often focus on the Old Testament prophets, such as Daniel for example, connecting his oracles with prophecies concerning the Last Days. However, when interpreting New Testament prophecies using the Augustinian approach (see Chapter 6), it becomes apparent that most of these Old Testament prophecies concern the times and circumstances leading up to Christ's First Coming in A.D. 1 - 33. This applies to such visions as Nebuchadnezzar's Dream (Daniel 2) , Daniel's Dream of Four Beasts (Daniel 7), and Daniel's Seventy Weeks (Daniel 9:20-27).

[102] Luke was a medical doctor.

followed, the city was reduced to rubble, the starving residents inside were slaughtered, the Temple was burned to the ground, the sacred vessels were looted, the foundation stones of the Temple were removed to retrieve the melted gold, but not a single Christian was harmed. Their obedience to Christ's prophecy saved their lives. Many fled Jerusalem to the City of Petra, in what is now Southern Jordan.

The main thrust of Christ's message in the Olivet Discourse is to beware of false messiahs (antichrists). So, he uses the opportunity of their question to explain how he can be recognized when he returns...

> *"For as the lightning flashes from the east, and is seen even to the west, so will the coming of the Son of Man be. For wherever the carcass is, that is where the vultures gather together. But immediately after the suffering of those days, the sun will be darkened, the moon will not give its light, the stars will fall from the sky, and the powers of the heavens will be shaken; and then the sign of the Son of Man will appear in the sky. Then all the tribes of the earth will mourn, and they will see the Son of Man coming on the clouds of the sky with power and great glory. He will send out his angels with a great sound of a trumpet, and they will gather together his chosen ones from the four winds, from one end of the sky to the other."*
>
> (Matthew 24:27-31)

It will be impossible to miss the Second Coming of Jesus Christ (Parousia) because as the Scriptures clearly say this will be a very public event, witnessed by all the inhabitants of the world at the same time. When Jesus Christ returns, the whole visible universe will melt away in his presence. Any so-called "messiah" who can't produce a show like that is no messiah at all. That is the main point of Jesus' monolog here. He's basically reminding them that he is the one, the only one, and to beware of any false messiahs (antichrists) who try to take his place. Here, Jesus is not necessarily giving an exact chronology of events. Rather, he is warning his friends that in his absence, many false messiahs (antichrists) will come, and this will not only lead up to the fall of the Jerusalem Temple, but these false messiahs (antichrists) will continue until the end of the world.

The synoptic accounts of this are a little more jumbled, which has led many modern Christians, especially Darby Dispensationalists, to fuse the warnings about the fall of the Temple together with the Parousia. In effect, they're making the same mistake as the disciples at the time of Christ, but from the opposite direction. The disciples had difficulty understanding a difference between these two events because they were still living before either had happened. Darby Dispensationalists have difficulty understanding the difference between these two events because of a bias in their interpretation of the text. They're assuming the entire text is a reference to the future (our future), not the past. Indeed, some text is future, particularly the apocalyptic references concerning Christ's Parousia, but some of it is past (to us), concerning the fall of the Jerusalem Temple. The problem is: The text was written in an "all future" context because it records a monolog that was given long before both events happened. Luke's synoptic account tries to make a little more sense of it all…

> *"But when you see Jerusalem surrounded by armies, then know that its desolation is at hand. Then let those who are in Judea flee to the mountains. Let those who are in the middle of her depart. Let those who are in the country not enter therein. For these are days of vengeance, that all things which are written may be fulfilled. Woe to those who are pregnant and to those who nurse infants in those days! For there will be great distress in the land, and wrath to this people. They will fall by the edge of the sword, and will be led captive into all the nations.* ***Jerusalem will be trampled down by the Gentiles, until the times of the Gentiles are fulfilled.*** *There will be signs in the sun, moon, and stars; and on the earth anxiety of nations, in perplexity for the roaring of the sea and the waves; men fainting for fear, and for expectation of the things which are coming on the world: for the powers of the heavens will be shaken. Then they will see the Son of Man coming in a cloud with power and great glory. But when these things begin to happen, look up and lift up your heads, because your redemption is near."*

(Luke 21:20-28, emphasis mine)

Luke puts things in a better chronological order for us. Everything before the line "*Jerusalem will be trampled down by the Gentiles,*" are events that were future to the apostles at the time Jesus told them, but they are in the distant past for us. These passages are a reference to the Roman siege of Jerusalem in A.D. 67-70.

The next phrase is paramount: "*until the times of the Gentiles are fulfilled.*" That means the Temple is gone. Jerusalem is no longer a Jewish city, and it will remain that way until the Last Days, when the "*times of the Gentiles are fulfilled.*" This one sentence describes the last two-thousand years of history. Jerusalem has been dominated and populated by Gentiles (non-Jews) this whole time. Even to this present day, Jerusalem is still populated by many Arab Palestinians (both Muslims and Christians), even though the city is the capital of the Republic of Israel. In the Old City, the part of Jerusalem that stood during the time of Christ, Arab Palestinians (Muslims and Christians) outnumber Jews by nearly ten to one. Clearly, according to the above passage, the "*times of the Gentiles*" are not yet complete.

Then Luke proceeds to lay out the conditions concerning the Last Days and the return of Jesus Christ (Parousia), which according to Luke, is scheduled to happen only after the *"times of the Gentiles"* are complete. That would be signaled when the Old City of Jerusalem is a Jewish majority again, and is totally under Jewish control. Currently, the vast majority of the Jewish population in Jerusalem lives outside the Old City. These annexed regions are considered part of modern Jerusalem, but they're not part of the Jerusalem that Jesus was talking about in The Olivet Discourse. Contextually speaking, he was talking about the Old City, the city he walked the streets of, not the modern annexations which would have been bare countryside in his day.

After the *"times of the Gentiles"* are complete, and the Old City of Jerusalem is a Jewish municipality once again, then and only then, will the prophecy be cleared for the Last Days to begin, culminating in the Second Coming of Jesus Christ (Parousia). At that point, Luke goes on to describe what that Second Coming will look like. These are the passages following the line: "*until the times of the Gentiles are fulfilled.*"

Luke then describes what can only be called a conflagration of nature, difficult for us to understand at this time in history, though we could possibly imagine it. What follows is the presence (Parousia) of Christ, witnessed by all people everywhere, in a way that cannot be mistaken or misunderstood. It is a supernatural arrival (advent).

Left Behind

There is also a passage in The Olivet Discourse that Darby Dispensationalists will often use as a proof text for their idea of a pre-tribulation rapture. We see it in Matthew, and it reads as follows…

> *"But no one knows of that day and hour, not even the angels of heaven, but my Father only. As the days of Noah were, so will the coming of the Son of Man be. For as in those days which were before the flood they were eating and drinking, marrying and giving in marriage, until the day that Noah entered into the ship, and they didn't know until the flood came and took them all away, so will the coming of the Son of Man be. Then two*

> *men will be in the field: one will be taken and one will be left. Two women will be grinding at the mill: one will be taken and one will be left. Watch therefore, for you don't know in what hour your Lord comes. But know this, that if the master of the house had known in what watch of the night the thief was coming, he would have watched, and would not have allowed his house to be broken into. Therefore also be ready, for in an hour that you don't expect, the Son of Man will come."*
>
> (Matthew 24:36-44)

This is *not* where the word "Rapture" comes from, but it is where the term "left behind" comes from, as well as the term "thief in the night." This passage is commonly used to describe what the Dispensationalists believe the Rapture will be like. According to them, Christians will be taken like a "thief in the night," while non-Christians will be "left behind" to suffer the reign of Antichrist during the Last Days. However, what we have in Matthew is a mashing together of two future events in Jesus' time. The first is the Fall of Jerusalem to the Romans, and the second is the Parousia. Jesus is going back and forth between the two in this account because in that account, the apostles asked him two questions: "*when will these things be? What is the sign of your coming, and of the end of the age?*" Since they asked him two questions, concerning two different events, Jesus goes back and forth between them, answering each one of their questions in a back and forth way. As for Mark's gospel account of The Olivet Discourse, he doesn't mention the question about the end of the age. So, Jesus' answer about the end of the age is not included. Luke's account, however, dispels the confusion by removing this passage from The Olivet Discourse entirely, placing it in an entirely different place in his gospel. So as not to mash the two events together like Matthew did. In Luke, the account reads as follows…

> *"Being asked by the Pharisees when God's Kingdom would come, he answered them, 'God's Kingdom doesn't come with observation; neither will they say, "Look, here!" or, "Look, there!" for behold, God's Kingdom is within you.'*
>
> *"He said to the disciples, 'The days will come when you will desire to see one of the days of the Son of Man, and you will not see it. They will tell you, "Look, here!" or "Look, there!" Don't go away or follow after them, for as the lightning, when it flashes out of one part under the sky, shines to another part under the sky; so will the Son of Man be in his day.* ***But first, he must suffer many things and be rejected by this generation.*** *As it was in the days of Noah, even so it will also be in the days of the Son of Man. They ate, they drank, they married, and they were given in marriage until the day that Noah entered into the ship, and the flood came and destroyed them all. Likewise, even as it was in the days of Lot: they ate, they drank, they bought, they sold, they planted, they built; but in the day that Lot went out from Sodom, it*

rained fire and sulfur from the sky and destroyed them all. It will be the same way in the day that the Son of Man is revealed. In that day, he who will be on the housetop and his goods in the house, let him not go down to take them away. Let him who is in the field likewise not turn back. Remember Lot's wife! Whoever seeks to save his life loses it, but whoever loses his life preserves it. I tell you, in that night there will be two people in one bed. One will be taken and the other will be left. There will be two grinding grain together. One will be taken and the other will be left.'

"They, answering, asked him, 'Where, Lord?'

"He said to them, 'Where the body is, there the vultures will also be gathered together.'"

(Luke 17:20-37, emphasis mine)

The entire passage is placed in another discourse, starting with the Pharisees, where Christ reminds them that the Kingdom of God (Kingdom Israel, or the Church) does not come like they expected, in war, power and prestige. It reigns in the hearts of Christ's followers, where the City of God shines forth in the city of man through his Church. Once that question is answered, Jesus reminds his disciples to beware of false messiahs (antichrists). Then, in typical Luke fashion, he makes a statement that clarifies the time that Jesus is talking about. After reminding them that the real Second Coming of Messiah will happen in the sky, he switches gears and reminds them that he must first be "*rejected by this generation*." After saying that, he goes into events proximal to "*this generation*," concerning the coming Fall of Jerusalem to the Romans.

Take a second look. I bolded the verse for you. Everything above that verse refers to the Second Coming of Jesus Christ (Parousia), and everything below it refers to the things related to Jesus' own generation. Namely, he's talking about the sacking of Jerusalem by the armies of Rome, and the fall of the Second Temple to the Gentiles. The language is almost identical to that used in The Olivet Discourse in Matthew and Mark.

Here's the bottom line. Once this passage is put into the context of all three synoptic gospels, the whole concept of being "taken" and "left behind" radically changes. Jesus was *not* talking about the Rapture here. He was talking about the sacking of Jerusalem by Rome. When he says "taken" here, that's not a good thing. "Taken," in this context, means killed or enslaved. Those "left behind" are those spared from the slaughter.

Just to clear up all doubt about this, Luke's gospel has the apostles ask Jesus a question. They ask where those taken will be taken to. Jesus responds with a single cryptic sentence: "*Where the body is, there the vultures will also be gathered together.*"

Some have tried to spiritualize this passage by retranslating "vultures" as "eagles," regarding the passage "*They will mount up with wings like eagles*" (Isaiah 40:31). Well, that's a nice thought, but it still doesn't explain the image of a dead body, nor does it explain the context of judgment, wrath and death.

There is no softening this passage. Jesus is talking about war here. He's talking about an assault on the Holy City of Jerusalem that would see carnage.[103] Read the passage again, and it's pretty clear to see. Those who are "taken" are taken away into carnage, death or slavery (if they were lucky). Those who are "left behind" are those who are spared.

Allow me to digress for just a moment as I recount my childhood and early adult years. The Darby-Dispensationalist eschatology taught me that this passage was all about the Rapture, and that I should seek to be "taken," while fearing the prospect of being "left behind." Now, having put these passages into their proper context, spanning all three synoptic gospels, I realize this whole picture is deeply flawed. Actually, it's upside-down. The Dispensationalist hermeneutic[104] is so bad that everything the Dispensationalists say about this passage is reversed from its actual meaning. This is a passage about war, where "taken" is bad, and "left behind" is good, and it doesn't even apply to us. It was specifically a message for the Christians and Jews living in Jerusalem in A.D. 67-70. The only thing that applies to us, is the part about Jesus warning us not to follow false messiahs

---

[103] The account of the siege of Jerusalem, by the Jewish historian Josephus, is difficult to read. The Romans were just as ruthless as the Jews were stubborn, resulting in a three and a half year catastrophe, spawning everything from starvation to cannibalism. Over a million Jews died as a result of the Roman blockade and the siege, twice as many casualties as America's Civil War. By the time it was over, almost nothing remained of the Old City. The slaughter was overwhelming, even to the Roman soldiers who executed it. See Josephus, The Jewish War, Books V & VI, published in A.D. 75

[104] Hermeneutics -- The art and science of interpreting Scripture using consistent rules of practice.

(antichrists), and that his Second Coming will be unmistakable when it happens.

John's Olivet Discourse (Apocalypse)

The Apostle John wrote his gospel in an entirely different way, having been the closest apostle to Jesus, and a member of his inner circle. He chose not to use the "Q" source, which was likely the original Gospel of Matthew written in Aramaic. Instead, he decided to work off his own memory, highlighting events not detailed in the synoptic gospels of Matthew, Mark and Luke.

Conspicuously absent from John's gospel is any mention of The Olivet Discourse. This is curious, considering this monolog by Christ was a key event toward the end of his ministry, foretelling one of his greatest prophecies concerning the siege of Jerusalem and the fall of the Temple. It's unusual that John would leave it out completely, but that is exactly what he did.

Or did he?

This Olivet Discourse was not only important to the Apostle John, but it was so important that it deserved more in-depth investigation, and this came to him during his exile on the Island of Patmos. The Book of Revelation (Apocalypse) is John's Olivet Discourse. To John, Jesus' message in The Olivet Discourse was so critical that it couldn't be contained to just one chapter in his gospel narrative. It needed more attention. It required its own book entirely. That's what the Book of Revelation (Apocalypse) is. It's the Olivet Discourse according to John.

Chapter six of John's Big Apocalypse, which introduces the outline of the whole book, even follows the exact same format as the Little Apocalypse found in the Olivet Discourse of Matthew, Mark and Luke.[105]

War
Matthew 24:6
Mark 13:7
Luke 21:9
Revelation 6:1-2

International Strife
Matthew 24:7
Mark 13:8
Luke 21:10
Revelation 6:3-4

Earthquakes
Matthew 24:7
Mark 13:8
Luke 21:11
Revelation 6:12-17

Famine
Matthew 24:7
Mark 13:8
Luke 21:11
Revelation 6:5-6

Persecution
Matthew 24:9-13
Mark 13:9-13
Luke 21:12-19
Revelation 6:9-11

---

105 As documented by R.H. Charles, A Critical and Exegetical Commentary on the Revelation of St. John, Volume 1, page 158 (Edinburgh: T&T Clark, 1920)

Conflagration

Matthew 24:15-31
Mark 13:14-27
Luke 21:20-27
Revelation 6:12-17

Most Biblical scholars agree that the Olivet Discourse (Little Apocalypse) of Matthew, Mark and Luke is a prophecy against the old Kingdom of Israel, particularly the corrupt religious system which God originally instituted, but mankind utterly perverted, so much so that God finally condemned and superseded it with the New Covenant.[106] So likewise, John's Book of Revelation (Big Apocalypse) is also a prophecy against the old Kingdom of Israel, particularly the corrupt religious system.

In the next two chapters, you'll see how the Book of Revelation (Apocalypse) fits into the same pattern of the Olivet Discourse recounted in the synoptic gospels. In the Book of Revelation (Apocalypse), Jesus again answers the apostles' two questions: "*Tell us, when will these things be? What is the sign of your coming, and of the end of the age?*" However, instead of filling just one chapter with Jesus' answer, John fills twenty-two.

---

[106] See Chapter 5

Chapter 8
Apocalypse Part I

The word Apocalypse comes from the Greek word *apokalupsis* (ἀποκάλυψις), and it literally means an unveiling, uncovering, revealing or revelation. That's why the book is often called "Revelation" in most English Bible translations today. However, when writing a commentary on the Book of Revelation, short as this one may be, I find that using the original Greek derivative of Apocalypse helps to avoid confusion. We're going to be talking about a lot of revelations in this chapter, which are part of the bigger Revelation (Apocalypse) of the book itself. So henceforth, I'll use the name Apocalypse when referring to the Book of Revelation - the last book of the Bible.

When approaching the Apocalypse, the question that most often comes up is "Where do we begin?" Most people would say we begin from the beginning, right? Well, there is a certain amount of truth to that, but we would be mistaken to think that's the full truth. In the previous chapters of this book, chapters 2 and 3, I summarized the two main Protestant approaches to the Apocalypse, which are the Historicism of Martin Luther, and the Dispensationalism of John Nelson Darby. In chapters 5, 6 and 7, I summarized the Catholic approach to the Apocalypse.

The Catholic approach is to form doctrinal beliefs about the Last Days using the gospels and epistles first. Then the Apocalypse is plugged in afterward, and must fit what we already know to be true from the gospels and epistles. The Protestant approach is almost the opposite. Under their two main approaches, Historicism and Dispensationalism, doctrinal beliefs about the Last Days are formulated from the Apocalypse first, using it as a literal timeline, either for historical or future events (depending on the school of thought). Then additional teachings from the gospels and epistles are plugged in afterward. The result has been various depictions of beliefs about the last days, of which the two most popular are Historicism (for Traditional Protestants) and Dispensationalism (for Evangelical Protestants). Both approaches have been highly unfavorable (even slanderous) to the papacy and the Catholic Church.

Catholics, who live in Protestant countries, run the risk of getting caught up in all of this, unable to answer some of the most basic questions on how to interpret the Apocalypse from a Catholic perspective. These next two chapters are not meant to be used as a comprehensive encyclopedia for that. Rather, they should be considered a primer. They should be enough to get any Catholic going in the right direction, but that's about it.

How to Interpret the Apocalypse

First things first, we have to set the context. The Apocalypse is meant to be interpreted symbolically, and that is set forth in the very first chapter. In a very real sense, the first chapter sets the "tone" for the whole book. It is not our place to flip back and forth, willy-nilly, between literal and symbolic interpretations of the text. That's what many Protestants do. The "tone" is set for us in the first chapter of the book, and we need to stick with that "tone" throughout the entire book, or we'll easily get lost.

Second things second, we have to figure out a reference point. The Apocalypse is strange and confusing. However, the author is clearly writing about things that pertain to our world, its history, and its future. So, we need to know what parts are history and what parts are future. That means we need to know where the book is about the present. For this, the Catechism of the Catholic Church gives us a big clue.

> *"The Antichrist's deception already begins to take shape in the world every time the claim is made to realize within history that messianic hope which can only be realized beyond history through the eschatological judgment. The Church has rejected even modified forms of this falsification of the kingdom to come under the name of millenarianism, especially the "intrinsically perverse" political form of a secular messianism."*[107]

To understand what the Church condemns here, we need to understand what the word "millenarianism" means. The Catholic Encyclopedia defines "millenarianism" as follows:

> *"The fundamental idea of millenarianism, as understood by Christian writers, may be set forth as follows: At the end of time Christ will return in all His splendor to gather together the just, to annihilate hostile powers, and to found a glorious kingdom* ***on earth*** *for the enjoyment of the highest spiritual and material blessings; He Himself will reign as its*

[107] Catechism of the Catholic Church, 676

> *king, and all the just, including the saints recalled to life, will participate in it. At the close of this kingdom the saints will enter heaven with Christ, while the wicked, who have also been resuscitated, will be condemned to eternal damnation. The duration of this glorious reign of Christ and His saints* ***on earth****, is frequently given as one thousand years. Hence it is commonly known as the 'millennium', while the belief in the future realization of the kingdom is called 'millenarianism.'"*[108]

So from this, we know the Catechism of the Catholic Church condemns millenarianism, or a belief in a literal millennium (one thousand years) reign of Christ on earth. What it condemns is the common belief, held by Dispensationalists today, in which Jesus Christ will reign on earth, in the future, for a literal one thousand years. As Catholics, we simply are not allowed to believe that. So, Dispensationalism is a deal-breaker for us, not only because of the problems it often has with the pope and the Catholic Church, but also because it subscribes to millenarianism, which the Catholic Church has rejected outright. This, however, brings us to the twentieth chapter of the Apocalypse, where the author writes of a thousand-year period of Christ's reign.

> *"I saw an angel coming down out of heaven, having the key of the abyss and a great chain in his hand. He seized the dragon, the old serpent, which is the*

---

108 Catholic Encyclopedia, Millennium and Millenarianism: http://www.newadvent.org/cathen/10307a.htm

devil and Satan, who deceives the whole inhabited earth, and bound him for a thousand years, and cast him into the abyss, and shut it, and sealed it over him, that he should deceive the nations no more, until the thousand years were finished. After this, he must be freed for a short time. I saw thrones, and they sat on them, and judgment was given to them. I saw the souls of those who had been beheaded for the testimony of Jesus, and for the word of God, and such as didn't worship the beast nor his image, and didn't receive the mark on their forehead and on their hand. They lived and reigned with Christ for a thousand years. The rest of the dead didn't live until the thousand years were finished. This is the first resurrection. Blessed and holy is he who has part in the first resurrection. Over these, the second death has no power, but they will be priests of God and of Christ, and will reign with him one thousand years.

"And after the thousand years, Satan will be released from his prison, and he will come out to deceive the nations which are in the four corners of the earth, Gog and Magog, to gather them together to the war; the number of whom is as the sand of the sea. They went up over the width of the earth, and surrounded the camp of the saints, and the beloved city. Fire came down out of heaven from God and devoured them.

The devil who deceived them was thrown into the lake of fire and sulfur, where the beast and the false prophet are also. They will be tormented day and night forever and ever.

"I saw a great white throne, and him who sat on it, from whose face the earth and the heaven fled away. There was found no place for them. I saw the dead, the great and the small, standing before the throne, and they opened books. Another book was opened, which is the book of life. The dead were judged out of the things which were written in the books, according to their works. The sea gave up the dead who were in it. Death and Hades gave up the dead who were in them. They were judged, each one according to his works. Death and Hades were thrown into the lake of fire. This is the second death, the lake of fire. If anyone was not found written in the book of life, he was cast into the lake of fire."

(Revelation 20)

This chapter is to be interpreted symbolically, just like the rest of the Apocalypse. Why? because the Catechism effectively says so. We can't interpret it literally. If we do, we run into millenarianism, and the Church has specifically said that we must reject that. So, what's left? The text of Revelation 20 is pretty clear. There is this long period of time in which Satan is bound. Yet, the Catechism tells us this can't be a literal one thousand years, nor can it be a literal reign of Christ on earth. Saint Victorinus[109] put it this way...

> *"Those years wherein Satan is bound are in the first advent of Christ, even to the end of the age; and they are called a thousand, according to that mode of speaking, wherein a part is signified by the whole, just as is that passage, the word which He commanded for a thousand generations, although they are not a thousand. Moreover that he says, and he cast him into the abyss, he says this, because the devil, excluded from the hearts of believers, began to take possession of the wicked, in whose hearts, blinded day by day, he is shut up as if in a profound abyss. And he shut him up, says he, and put a seal upon him, that he should not deceive the nations until the thousand years should be finished. He shut the door upon him, it is said, that is, he forbade and restrained his seducing those who belong to Christ.*
>
> *"Moreover, he put a seal upon him, because it is hidden who belongs to the side of the devil, and who to the side of Christ. For we know not of those who seem to stand whether they shall not*

---

[109] Saint Victorinus of Pettau (died in A.D. 304) was the Bishop of Poetovio (modern Ptuj in Slovenia; German: Pettau) in Pannonia. He died in the Roman persecution of Diocletian, and is known for his commentaries on various books of Scripture.

fall, and of those who are down, it is uncertain whether they may rise.

"Moreover, that he says that he is bound and shut up, that he may not seduce the nations, the nations signify the Church, seeing that of them it itself is formed, and which being seduced, he previously held until, he says, the thousand years should be completed, that is, what is left of the sixth day, to wit, of the sixth age, which subsists for a thousand years; after this he must be loosed for a little season.

"The little season signifies three years and six months, in which with all his power the devil will avenge himself under Antichrist against the Church. Finally, he says, after that the devil shall be loosed, and will seduce the nations in the whole world, and will entice war against the Church, the number of whose foes shall be as the sand of the sea…

"There are two resurrections. But the first resurrection is now of the souls that are by the faith, which does not permit men to pass over to the second death. Of this resurrection the apostle says: If you have risen with Christ, seek those things which are above…

"I do not think the reign of a thousand years is eternal; or if it is thus to be

thought of, they cease to reign when the thousand years are finished. But I will put forward what my capacity enables me to judge. The tenfold number signifies the decalogue, and the hundredfold sets forth the crown of virginity: for he who shall have kept the undertaking of virginity completely, and shall have faithfully fulfilled the precepts of the decalogue, and shall have destroyed the untrained nature or impure thoughts within the retirement of the heart, that they may not rule over him, this is the true priest of Christ, and accomplishing the millenary number thoroughly, is thought to reign with Christ; and truly in his case the devil is bound.

"But he who is entangled in the vices and the dogmas of heretics, in his case the devil is loosed. But that it says that when the thousand years are finished he is loosed, so the number of the perfect saints being completed, in whom there is the glory of virginity in body and mind, by the approaching advent of the kingdom of the hateful one, many, seduced by that love of earthly things, shall be overthrown, and together with him shall enter the lake of fire."[110]

What Saint Victorinus wrote in the late third century became the commonly accepted

---

110 Saint Victorinus, Commentary on the Apocalypse of the Blessed John 20:1-6, written in the late 3rd century

understanding of the Millennium by the time of Saint Augustine in the early fifth century, as I discussed in detail in Chapter 6 of this book. It has since remained the common understanding of the Catholic Church. The thousand-year Millennium is totally symbolic. Its beginning represents the First Coming of Christ, and the fall of the Jewish Temple in Jerusalem. Its end represents the rise of Antichrist and the Great Tribulation of the Church just before the Second Coming of Jesus Christ (Parousia). The Millennium of the Apocalypse is a symbolic representation of the interim period between the two advents (comings) of Jesus Christ. It is symbolic of the Church Age, or the "times of the Gentiles," in which the Kingdom of God is fully manifest in heaven through the reign of Christ and his Saints, while it is partially manifest on earth, through the reign of the Church.

There is nothing about these thousand years that is to be taken literally, and therein lies our historical reference point. If the Apocalypse is to be interpreted in any kind of linear fashion (which itself is debatable), then we must conclude that chapters 1 through 19 deals primarily with the ancient world proximal to the time of Saint John and his intended audience (the seven churches of Asia Minor), chapter 20 verses 1 through 7 deals with the present Church Age for the last two-thousand years, while as everything after Revelation 20:7 deals with the future events of the Last Days, leading to the Second Coming of Christ and beyond. Some people might call this mode of interpreting Preterist.[111] That would be true to a certain extent, as we would say everything before the Millennium is "pre-" as in historical, but I would assert that everything after the Millennium is future. So I

---

[111] Preterist: meaning "pre-" as in everything has is in the past.

guess you could say a Catholic approach to the book of Revelation is partial-Preterist.

Third things third, the Apocalypse doesn't just deal with history: past, present, and future. It also deals with symbolic representations of doctrine, an explanation of suffering, as well as liturgical aspects of the early Church. For example, Dr. Scott Hahn, in his book The Lamb's Supper[112] deals specifically with the liturgical aspects of the Apocalypse. So, this should always be taken into consideration too.

Now that we have three necessary foundations: (1) symbolism, (2) partial-Preterism, (3) doctrinal and liturgical aspects, we can begin to unlock the secrets of the Apocalypse from a Catholic perspective.

The following is my own short commentary on the Apocalypse (Apocalypse of Saint John), otherwise known as the Book of Revelation. The best way to approach this chapter is to have your Bible handy. Read each chapter from the Apocalypse (Revelation) first, then read my commentary on it second, progressing chapter-by-chapter through the whole book. Like all Biblical commentaries, this one reflects the views of the author, however, my views are based on the Catholic principles I described in this book. They are heavily steeped in Medieval Catholic eschatology, as developed from many of the Early Church Fathers, and a reading of the Apocalypse using Old Testament symbolism as a guide. *My views here should not be mistaken for **the** Catholic interpretation, but rather should be viewed as **a** Catholic interpretation. It is not authoritative, but I believe it is well grounded.*

---

[112] Hahn, Scott; The Lamb's Supper: The Mass as Heaven on Earth, Doubleday Publishers, a division of Random House, 1999

Apocalypse 1 - Introduction & Vision of Christ

This chapter introduces us to the Apocalypse, the author, and the nature of how the book should be interpreted. In verse 3, a general blessing is given to all who read the book. In verse 4, we are told the book is written as a letter primarily to the seven churches in Asia Minor (ancient cities in modern-day Turkey). This is important because the seven churches are named, and they were real churches in John's time. Thus, this book would mean more to them than to anyone else. Yes, it would have some general meaning to future audiences as well, people like us, but the book was primarily written to a late, first-century audience. As we can see from our second foundation above, chapters 1 through 19 pertain to the ancient world. So, the vast majority of the book is set in the ancient world, which makes sense, since it was written by an ancient author to an ancient audience.

In verse 12 we are told about seven lamp stands, reminiscent of a Hebrew menorah. Verse 16 tells us about seven stars, which correspond to the seven lamp stands. In verse 20, we learn that the seven lamp stands represent the seven named churches mentioned in verse 4, and the seven stars represent the bishops of those churches, to whom the Apocalypse is addressed. The word "angel" is sometimes used to describe a star because the Greek word used here is *aggelos* (ἄγγελος) which can mean a literal angel (spirit being), or more generally, a "messenger." The Apocalypse is addressed to the seven churches of Asia Minor, and if it is addressed to the churches, then proper Church protocol would mandate that it go through the local bishops. The same pattern is followed today. When an official document is promulgated from the pope or one of his dicasteries within the Vatican, the communication usually goes to the local bishops first, who are then responsible for disseminating it to their priests, deacons and the faithful laity under their spiritual care. So, the most reasonable explanation is that the angels represent the bishops because they are "messengers" of the gospel of Jesus Christ to the churches. Thus, they should act as "messengers" for this Apocalypse as well.

A physical description of Jesus Christ is given in this chapter, verses 13 through 16, which is very shocking. Jesus is described as having white hair, flaming eyes, skin like brass, and a voice like a waterfall. Out of his mouth proceeds a sharp double-edged sword, and his face was like the sun. From the gospels, we learn that the resurrected Christ did not look like this. His appearance was very much like a regular man. So, obviously, this description of Christ is symbolic, and this sets the "tone" for the whole Apocalypse. The white hair is symbolic of eternal wisdom. Flaming eyes and brass skin are symbolic of judgment. His voice, like a waterfall, symbolizes power. The sword from his mouth represents the word of God, which is described as a double-edged sword elsewhere in the New Testament.[113] A face like the sun is symbolic of his divine glory.

Apocalypse 2 - Message to Four Churches

In this chapter, Jesus Christ begins his exhortation to the seven churches in Asia Minor. I won't spend too much time going into the details of each church, except to say that in one sense these exhortations are to actual churches during the first century, and in another sense, they can apply to all parishes and dioceses throughout the world and in all the ages. *One thing we must be careful to avoid is the*

---

[113] Hebrews 4:12

common Protestant misinterpretations (both Historicist and Dispensationalist) that these seven churches represent seven "church-ages" throughout history. That is simply not the case. Elements from all of these churches can be found in every age of Church history, just like they were all present in the first century in which this book was written. We also must be careful to resist the temptation to assign the characteristics of one of these first-century churches to a particular church denomination in our own time. This is another common Protestant error. Characteristics of all these first-century churches can be found in all church denominations today. *You'll find **all** of these characteristics among Catholics, Orthodox, Protestants and Evangelicals.*

Verse 6 and verse 15 mention a group of people Jesus condemns. They are called the Nicolaitans. Who were they? What were they about? Darby Dispensationaists often use this passage to condemn the division between clergy and laity. They claim *Nicolaitans* (Νικολαΐτης) is a compound-Greek word meaning "to rule over the laity," which they extrapolate to mean that Jesus is condemning the clerical system. Thus, they would have us believe that Jesus condemns the very clerical system God created in the Old Testament, and the threefold Church vocations of deacon, presbyter and bishop that he (through the Holy Spirit) created in the New Testament. It's a subtle Protestant dig at the Catholic Church. As I told you earlier in this book, Protestant and Evangelical thinking about eschatology is usually accompanied by a systemic hostility toward Catholicism.

In truth, the word *Nicolaitans* (Νικολαΐτης) has been defined for us in history. Irenaeus,[114] Clement of Alexandria,[115] Tertullian,[116] Epiphanius,[117] Hippolytus[118] and Eusebius of Caesarea[119] all pretty much tell us the same thing about who the Nicolaitans were and what they practiced. They were followers of the former Church deacon, Nicolaus (one of the seven appointed by the Apostles),[120] who allegedly departed from the true Apostolic faith and embraced a form of Gnosticism that was very Epicurean[121] in nature, teaching a form of "cheap grace," similar to an extreme version of *"once saved, always saved"* eternal security, embraced by

---

114 Irenaeus (A.D. 130-202) was a Greek bishop who planted missions in what is now Southern France. He wrote extensively on Christian doctrine and against heresies. On the Nicolaitans: *Irenaeus, Against Heresies, I:26; III:11*

115 Clement of Alexandria (A.D. 150-215) was a Christian theologian and philosopher who taught at the Catechetical School of Alexandria. He was educated in classical Greek philosophy and literature. On the Nicolaitans: *Clement of Alexandria, Stromata, II:20*

116 Tertullian (A.D. 155-220) was a prolific Christian author from Carthage, Africa. He was an apologist and a polemicist against heresy, including Christian Gnosticism. On the Nicolaitans: *Tertullian, On Modesty IXX*

117 Epiphanius (A.D. 310-403) was the bishop of Salamis, Cyprus at the end of the fourth century. On the Nicolaitans: *Epiphanius, Panarion, XXV:1*

118 Hippolytus (A.D. 170-235) was a second to third century Christian theologian. On the Nicolaitans: *Hippolytus, Refutation of All Heresies VII:24*

119 Eusebius of Caesarea (A.D. 260-340) was a historian of Christianity, exegete, and Christian polemicist. He became the bishop of Caesarea Maritima in A.D. 314. On the Nicolaitans: *History of the Church III:29*

120 Acts 6:5

121 Epicurean: A Greek philosophy of self indulgence.

some Calvinists today.[122] Under the Nicolaitan version, the believer in Christ was encouraged to commit all sorts of sins of the flesh, often sexual in nature, so that the body may be disowned, and the spirit may become free to ascend to heaven. There was some debate among the Church Fathers whether Nicolaus himself subscribed to this, or just a band of Gnostics who appealed to his name for credibility. (Such a practice was common back then.) Either way, the Nicolaitans were nasty people, by Christian standards, whether Nicolaus himself led them, or had nothing to do with them.

The Venerable Bede[123] held that Deacon Nicholas allowed other men to marry his wife.[124] Saint Thomas Aquinas believed Deacon Nicholas supported polyamory (group marriage between multiple combinations of men and women). The rationale behind this heresy was complex, but centered around an abuse of Christian liberty, and the notion that Christians are freed from the Law of Moses which regulates marriage between one man and one woman. The Church historian Eusebius tells us this particular heresy was short-lived.

---

[122] "Once saved, always saved" is actually an abuse of Calvinist teaching, and John Calvin (A.D. 1509-1564) never endorsed sensual license. However, many people who embrace a superficial reading of Calvin's teachings will often adopt this position, excusing any immoral behavior that results.

[123] The Venerable Bede (672 – May 26, 735), also known as Saint Bede, was an English Benedictine monk at the monastery of Saint Peter and its companion monastery of Saint Paul in the Kingdom of Northumbria of the Angles (contemporarily Monkwearmouth–Jarrow Abbey in Tyne and Wear, England). He is known for his Biblical commentaries and history of the English people.

[124] Venerable Bede, Explanation of the Apocalypse, 2.16

The phrase "ten days," in verse 10, is a reference to a nondescript period of time. It could be a long time, or a short time, depending on how you look at it. The point is, ten is the number of completion, which is the idea that the time must be complete. The term "synagogue of Satan," in verse 9, appears again in chapter 3 verse 9. It is likely a reference specifically to events particular to that region, and at that time...

> *"In the city of Smyrna many Jews lived who encouraged the Gentiles to persecute the Christians. In this persecution many were not only robbed of their things but also crowned with martyrdom - among whom Polycarp was thrown into the fire, and when the fire did not harm him, he was struck with a sword and departed to God."*[125]

As I pointed out in Chapter 5 of this book, the relationship between Jews and Christians was considerably different in the first century. At that time, Judaism was a much larger religion than Christianity, and Christianity was considered an aberrant sect, or cult, of the Jewish faith. It was not only winning converts from among the Gentiles, but also from the Jewish synagogues as well. Because of this, the Jewish leaders considered Christianity to be a threat. Some wanted it destroyed. Not only did the Jewish leaders in first-century Palestine persecute Christians quite severely, but this pattern also continued in other parts of the Roman Empire where Judaism was well established.

---

[125] Eusebius, Church History, 4:12

Sadly, this term, "synagogue of Satan," has been used throughout history against Jewish people in general. One has to consider that the tables have turned since the first century. Christianity has since grown immeasurably larger than Judaism. The religion that was once the underdog in the first century, is now the dominant force, not only over Judaism, but also in the world. Not only are the Jews of today innocent of what happened twenty centuries ago, but even if they were somehow responsible, it would be petty for anyone to hold them accountable anymore. The battle between Christianity and Judaism is over. It ended even before the Middle Ages began. Christianity has indisputably won, and is now a dominant religion in the modern world.

In verse 14, Balaam, whose name is synonymous with Nicolaus, meaning “conqueror,” was an Old Testament prophet who was not part of the Hebrew people. He discerned the weakness of the Hebrews wandering in the wilderness under Moses. He then shared this weakness with the Pagan King Balak, who promptly exploited it to weaken the Hebrews before attacking them. What was that weakness? It was sex and idolatry. Balaam taught King Balak that if he could get the Hebrews to defile themselves with unlawful sex and idolatry, they would lose their blessing from God and become vulnerable on the battlefield. The whole thing is recorded in the Old Testament and the writings of the Jewish historian Josephus.[126]

So, here we see the teachings of the Nicolaitans linked to the Old Testament story of Balaam and Balak. As you can see, a plain sense reading of this chapter simply explains itself. The so-called

---

[126]Numbers 22-25; 31; Josephus, Antiquity of the Jews IV, 6,6 (Josephus was a Jewish historian, who wrote in the late first century A.D.)

"mystery" of the Nicolaitans is no mystery at all. (It has nothing to do with the clerical system within Christianity, which is clearly a modern Evangelical jab at Catholicism.) Rather, it has everything to do with sexual immorality and idolatry. The Nicolaitans were teaching that there is no longer any sin for Christians, and that engaging in debauchery is "good" because it debases the body, so the soul can be liberated to higher levels of knowledge (gnosis) about Christ. Here, Saint John tells us that such a teaching is not only hated by Christ, but it also leads the follower into spiritual defeat and destruction. Jesus again warns that failure to repent of this heresy, and failure of the Church to discipline those who preach it, will result in the most severe penalty, coming directly from Christ.

The key verse is verse 20: "*you tolerate your woman, Jezebel.*" This is not good. The operative word here is "*tolerate.*" Jesus is talking about compromise, specifically moral compromise. The Thyatiran Christians had compromised with the Pagan morality of the trade guilds in Thyatira, probably to stake out a living. We can imagine this was so Church members could find work in various trades. We can speculate as to how the Church leaders justified such compromise, but by now we should start to see a familiar theme unfold. First, it was the Nicolaitans. Their primary sin was sexual immorality. Then, it was Balaam and Balak, along with the Nicolaitans again, pointing to sexual immorality and idolatry. Now, we have Jezebel, once again pointing to sexual immorality ***as*** idolatry. Jesus seems to be harping on something here.

Jezebel is a reference to an Old Testament queen of Israel, who led the Jewish people into idolatry.[127] This would have been immediately

---

[127] 1 Kings 21:25-26; 2 Kings 9:22

understood by the Jewish Christians, who were the primary audience of the Apocalypse. Here, Jesus calls out sexual immorality for what it really is, especially when it's combined with compromise of the gospel. It's a form of idolatry! Why? Because Jesus is God, and Jesus does not tolerate sexual immorality. Therefore, to assert that Jesus does tolerate it, is to put forward *another* Jesus, a *different* Jesus, that is altogether different from the Jesus preached by the Apostles. It is a *fake* Jesus, a *fake* God, an idol.

Apocalypse 3 - Message to Three More Churches

Based on what I have written in Apocalypse 2, this chapter is almost self-explanatory. Apocalypse 3 continues Christ's exhortation to the seven churches of Asia Minor. A few notable phrases are as follows.

"Alive but dead," means that this church has been totally secularized in a moral sense. Its moral behaviors are indistinguishable from the Pagan world around them. They've accepted the ways of the world as their own. This exhortation could directly apply to many churches, parishes and congregations in our own time. How many churches have accepted the immoral (worldly) practices of fornication, cohabitation, abortion, homosexuality and same-sex marriage? How is their moral conduct any different from what is seen in the secular world? This is the sort of thing Jesus condemns here.

"Come upon you," is a phrase of judgment, which recalls Leviticus 26 and Deuteronomy 28. God can judge us at any time. It doesn't have to be the "Last Days" or the End of the World. We are always accessible to him and his judgment. Churches can be, and have been, judged in the past. Among Catholics,

entire parishes have evaporated on their own. Some parishes have been closed and merged with others. Bad bishops and popes have been deposed. Among the Eastern Orthodox, there have been invasions by Muslim hordes and entire nations of Christians have been lost -- converted to Islam. Among Protestants, entire denominations and movements have disappeared into the history books. Where are the Puritans today? What became of the Shakers?

Christ's judgment is not reserved solely for his people. The same can apply to nations, political unions, businesses and corporations. Nothing is outside the domain of God. He, alone, allows them to rise and fall. It doesn't need to be the End of the World for this to happen. Just because Christ says he will "come upon you" in judgment, that doesn't necessarily mean he's going to wait until the End of the World to do it. In this book, we shall soon see this very principle unfold upon the Jewish people and their civilization in the late first century.

"Worship at your feet," which is found in verse 9, indicates that those who have persecuted Christians will, either in the afterlife, and through their descendants, eventually come to understand that God is Jesus Christ, and that those who follow him are united to him. It's a reference to Isaiah 60:14.

Here we see a word *proskyneo* (προσκυνέω) which means "to prostrate oneself in homage." This speaks of "worship" in the sense of a high form of reverence (veneration) stopping short of the exclusive worship due only to God, which is the Greek word *latreía* (λατρεία) not used here. So for a Catholic, this verse vindicates the reverence we all show to Mary and the Saints, wherein the Scriptures actually translate as "worship" or "adoration" a type of respect or veneration -- *proskyneo* (προσκυνέω) -- that is permissible to show toward created things worthy of such honor.

"Keep you from the hour of testing" simply means to preserve one during trial. It is not a promise to escape trial, or be removed from the world entirely, as the Darby-Dispensationalists would have us believe. The phrase is a reference back to Jude 24. It is a reference to the trial proximal to the time in which the Apocalypse was written, the late first century, and wouldn't make sense if it referred to some kind of "Last Days" events of the twenty-first century.

That *"no man takes your crown"* in verse 11 is a reference to the crown of eternal life that awaits all Christians if they persevere to the end in faith and good works.[128] Verse 12 clearly connects Christians to the promises of ancient Israel. As I pointed out in chapter five of this book. The Church is Kingdom Israel. This stands in stark contrast to the word "lukewarm" in verse 16. Faith and zeal are commendable for the cause of Jesus Christ. Those who have become neutral and apathetic, in other words "pew warmers" as the modern saying goes, are a burden to Christ. He threatens to vomit them if they do not rediscover their zeal. Being "*lukewarm*" is another illustration of worldliness, or compromise with the world. Here, Christ is speaking of churches that are completely indistinguishable from the world around them. They have not only adopted the ways of the world, but the world has adopted them as one of their own. In the time this was written, it's clear the church of which this speaks is one that has compromised with Paganism, particularly in sexual immorality, but even cooperating with Caesar worship to some extent. Some might have

---

[128] James 2:24

said: *"I threw a pinch of incense on the altar, and said 'Caesar is Lord,' but I didn't really mean it."*

In our own time, we could compare this with churches that have adopted worldly positions on social issues, which God sees as sinful, even promoting them, or at the very least providing no meaningful opposition to them at all. In our modern vocabulary, the word *milquetoast* applies nicely here. It means a timid, meek, or unassertive person. There is no place for milquetoast in the Kingdom of God. You either stand for something, or against something, but you never just "go along to get along."

Revelation 4 - Heavenly Worship

Here in this chapter we see a symbolic view of heaven. I say "symbolic" here, only because there are no words to describe the glory of heaven. That said, the words contained in this chapter probably come pretty close. I should point out here a common error made by the Dispensationalists in verse 1. The phrase *"come up here"* is misinterpreted as a reference to the secret Rapture. This is because the voice has the sound of a trumpet, and they cross-reference this to Saint Paul's warning that the Parousia (Second Coming of Christ) will be announced with the sound of a trumpet.[129] This is accompanied by the phrase, *"things which must take place after this."* Dispensationalists then recall their misinterpretation of the seven churches, of the previous two chapters, as "seven church ages" in Christian history. So in their estimation, since this passage now says, *"after this,"* they presume the following text refers to the future Great Tribulation period.

---

[129] 1 Thessalonians 4:16

At best, this is shoddy Biblical exegesis, at worst it is eisegesis.[130] It would seem that Dispensationalists are oblivious to the fact that God uses a trumpet sound to announce many things in Scripture. If we look back to the first chapter of the Apocalypse, we can see that John already heard this trumpet-voice in his vision of Christ. Does that mean the Dispensationalist Rapture happened then too? Are there two raptures now?

Dispensationalists will double-down at this point, correctly observing that the word "church" does not appear in the Apocalypse again until the nineteenth chapter. Therefore, in their estimation, this "proves" that the Church has been removed from the world during the Great Tribulation in the Last Days, only to return to earth with Christ at his Second Coming some three and a half, to seven years, later depending on the school of thought. Of course, there is a problem with proving something from the negative. The lack of a word really doesn't prove anything. By the same token, we could say the same thing about the name Jesus, which does not appear in the Apocalypse until Chapter 12. So, does that mean all these other symbolic references to Christ are not really references to Jesus Christ at all? If we follow the Dispensationalist logic of negative proof, then we have to assume so. Thus, the image of the man we saw in Chapter 1 was really somebody else.

This is not the case, and negative proof is no proof at all. The phrases *"come up here"* and *"things which must take place after this"* are exactly what they sound like. The author is simply called to come witness the scene in heaven. It means nothing more. The

---

130 Exegesis means interpreting the text of Scripture in its original context. Eisegesis means reading into the text with a preconceived notion.

reference to time, *"after this,"* simply means after the first vision of Jesus Christ and his message to the seven types of churches on earth. Anything more is reading into the text (or eisegesis).

In verse 3, there is another symbolic representation of Christ as God in his heavenly Temple, which corresponds to the Jewish Temple of the Old Testament. In verse 4, the twenty-four elders represent the administration of Christ and his Church, both in heaven and on earth. Twenty-four, being a double multiplication of the number twelve (for the twelve apostles and the twelve-tribes of Israel), is nothing new. The ancient Jewish Temple was administered by a division of twenty-four priests and singers.[131] So as it was in ancient Israel, so it is in the Church as the new Israel of God (see Chapter 5). These elders, however, representing the priesthood of the new Israel of God (the Church) are wearing crowns, representing the royal nature of this priesthood, showing that it has superseded the priesthood of the Old Testament.

Verses 5 and 8 harken back to the presence of God in the Old Testament,[132] and tell of indescribable creatures representing the immeasurable creative nature of God. However, each creature is a representation of each one of the four gospels. The man creature represents the Gospel According to Matthew, emphasizing Christ's human nature. The lion creature represents the Gospel According to Mark, emphasizing Christ's royal nature. The calf/ox/bull creature represents the Gospel According to Luke, emphasizing Christ's sacrifice, service, and strength.

---

[131] 1 Chronicles 24, 1 Chronicles 25

[132] Exodus 19:16-19, Exodus 30:17-21, 1 Kings 7:23-26, Ezekiel 1

The eagle creature represents the Gospel According to John, emphasizing Christ's divinity.

In verse 8 we have part of the *Sanctus*, sung in every mass since the days of the early Church. Here we have a liturgical aspect of the Apocalypse. As we walk through the text, a liturgical element will gradually unfold, as if one were watching the liturgy of the mass unfold before our eyes.

Here we must pause to consider the nature of worship in general. There are basically two forms of worship, private and public. Private worship is what we do ourselves. It is that "personal relationship with Jesus Christ" the Evangelicals speak of so often. They're not wrong. Even the popes have spoken about this…

- *"It is necessary to awaken again in believers a full relationship with Christ, mankind's only Savior."* - Pope Saint John Paul II
- *"Christian faith is not only a matter of believing that certain things are true, but above all a personal relationship with Jesus Christ."* - Pope Benedict XVI
- *"Only in this personal relationship with Christ, only in this encounter with the Risen One do we truly become Christians."* - Pope Benedict XVI
- *"Being a Christian means having a living relationship with the person of Jesus; it means putting on Christ, being conformed to him."* - Pope Francis

This takes the form of personal prayer and devotion, which has many varieties that cannot be limited because it is personal and there are so many different people. Some commune with God by walking through nature while praying. Others light candles in their homes. Still others prefer more disciplined forms of devotions, such as the rosary, the daily office and Bible study. Where Evangelicals sometimes err is in thinking that's all there is. Just as there is a private (or personal) side to the worship of God, so there is a public side too, and this is where liturgy comes in.

The public worship of God is a communal thing. It's something that all Christians do together, and so in doing things together there must be some degree of order. That's what liturgy is. From the earliest days of Christianity, as in ancient Judaism, liturgy has played a key role in public worship, and this is a reflection of what we see in heaven. Christianity is both a personal relationship with Christ, and the public worship of Christ at the same time. Liturgy is how the latter plays out. We see this playing out here in the Apocalypse as well.

Revelation 5 - The Lamb & The Sealed Book

Here we have a symbolic scene of what is going on in heaven. The symbolic book (in verse 1)[133] represents the mysteries of the New Testament, or more specifically the New Covenant in Christ. The writing on both the front and back recalls the Old Testament imagery of the Ten Commandments, and also the book that was given to the Old Testament prophet Ezekiel. As for Ezekiel's book, the writing on both sides indicates God's judgment against Old Testament Israel for failing to keep the commandments (Law) of the Old Covenant.[134] Here in the Apocalypse, Saint John is developing a theme along the same line, which begins with this symbolic book. I laid this out in Chapter 5. God brings an end to the Old Covenant

---

[133] Some Bible translations call this a scroll

[134] Ezekiel 2:3-10

system entirely, and he does so by outlining a legal case against the Jewish leadership of the late first century. Think of it like a divorce proceeding. He's initiating the severance decree, not from the Jewish people, nor from the hopes and expectations of Israel in the Law or the prophets. Rather, he is using the Law and the prophets as the backbone of his case against the Jewish leadership of that time (Sanhedrin, Sadducees and Pharisees), while he sets up the governance of the new Israel (the Church) which replaces their authority over the People of God. (Again, see Chapter 5).

The symbolic book plays a central role in outlining what is about to happen in the Apocalypse (verses 2-7). As a symbol of the New Covenant itself, it is sealed and written on both sides in Old Covenant fashion. Because the book is sealed, the seals must be broken, and breaking them brings consequences. No one is worthy to open them except the Lion who is the Lamb -- Jesus Christ. The Lion is symbolic of his powerful kingship over Israel and the world. The Lamb is symbolic of the way he was enthroned as King, having been led to the cross, like a lamb to the slaughter. When he opens the book, as we shall see, each seal is announced with a trumpet, which in turn results in a bowl (cups or chalice) of wrath. These bowls (cups or chalices) are poured out on the leadership of Old Testament Israel, bringing an end to them and their system of governance upon Israel and the People of God. This, in turn, sets things up for the transference of leadership to the bishops of the Church.

Verse 8 is of particular interest to Catholics. For herein we have conclusive Biblical evidence that the Saints in heaven (capital "S") actively offer up to God the prayers of the saints on earth (small "s"). Verse 13 is also of particular interest to Catholics, for it speaks of those in heaven, earth and "under the earth" offering blessing and praise to God. This phrase "under the earth" presents a problem if we interpret this to mean those damned souls in hell. That is not likely, since the damned do not offer praise to God. This is not a reference to Purgatory either because Purgatory is essentially the front gate of purification into heaven. No, this is likely a reference to the limbo of the Patriarchs. These were the Old Testament Saints who waited in "Abraham's bosom" (Luke 16:22-24) for the salvific work of Jesus Christ to unfold. In the creed, we speak of Christ descending into hell. This is as a victorious and conquering King to proclaim that the work of salvation was completed. Those in that part of hell (Abraham's Bosom, or the limbo of the Patriarchs) were then freed to enter heaven, and this portion of hell was then closed forever. All that remains of hell now is the abyss of the damned. It is likely the phrase "under the earth" here refers to the limbo of the Patriarchs, or Abraham's Bosom, which existed before the death and resurrection of Christ, but not after.

Revelation 6 - The Seven Seals

You may have heard of the "four horsemen of the apocalypse" or the "four horses of the apocalypse." Well, here they are. This is where the phrase originates from. Verses 1 through 8 deal with this, and it is a symbolic imagery of war. Here the author of the Apocalypse is telling his readers, who are primarily the seven bishops of Asia Minor, but also all Christians of the early Church, that war is coming against Israel, which at the time was both the old Kingdom of Israel under the Old Covenant (represented by the priests, scribes and Pharisees) and the Church established by Jesus Christ. They will all suffer persecution for their faith from the imperial government of Rome. Both would suffer, each from different sources. The Old Kingdom would be conquered by the Romans, as an instrument of God's wrath. (We see this method repeated in the Old Testament when Israel was conquered by the Assyrians and Babylonians). Remember, this text was written in the middle of the first century (around A.D. 50). The Church, however, would suffer not from the wrath of God, but from the wrath of man and the devil. The former would lead to utter ruin. The latter would eventually lead to triumph and victory. The next 200 years would be filled with bloodshed for the Church, until Caesar Constantine liberated Christians with the Edict of Milan in the early fourth century. He then gave Christians financial restitution, and ultimately made Christianity the official religion of the empire. However, from the perspective of these middle first-century Christians, dark times of war against them lay ahead.

1. The white horse, and its rider, represent Jesus Christ.[135]
2. The red horse, and its rider, represent war.[136]
3. The black horse, and its rider, represent famine.[137]

---

[135] Revelation 19:11-16; Habakkuk 3:9-11; Psalm 45:3-5; Genesis 9:13-17; Ezekiel 1:26-28; Revelation 4:3; Hebrews 10:26-21; Revelation 2:20; Revelation 3:11; Revelation 4:4, Revelation 4:10; Revelation 6:2; Revelation 12:1; Revelation 14:14; Saint Irenaeus, Against Heresies, IV. XXI. 3

[136] Matthew 10:34; Matthew 24:6; Mark 13:7; Luke 21:9; Flavius Josephus, The Jewish Wars, II, XVIII, 2

[137] Ezekial 4:10; Leviticus 18:24-28; Deuteronomy 28:15-34; Isaiah 24; Psalm 104:15; James 5:14-15; 1 Corinthians 11:25

4. The pale hose, and its rider, represent death.[138]

It was vital that Christians understand the nature of the judgment that was coming upon Jerusalem at the time this was written, lest they lose hope. The entire thing was initiated by Christ himself, as the God of the Old Testament, who judges his people according to the Law of Moses. Christ, the God whom they worship, is exacting his justice upon the leaders of Jerusalem and the corrupted Old Covenant system. He uses the siege of a Pagan nation, just as he did in the Old Testament. This same Pagan nation, Rome, would exact its own wrath (not the wrath of God but its own) against the Christians of that time, but God would only use this to strengthen his Church.

Verses 9-11 are of particular interest because they give us insight into the political dynamics of the late first century. At this time, Christians were persecuted primarily by the leadership of the Jewish Temple in Jerusalem. The persecution that was coming from Rome was directed at two separate peoples, but from Rome's perspective, they were one and the same. On the one hand, Rome would conduct multiple military campaigns against the Jewish nation in Palestine, during the late first-century and early second-century. The first major military campaign followed a rebellion of Jewish Zealots in A.D. 67. This resulted in a three-year siege against the City of Jerusalem, concluding with the complete destruction of the Jewish Temple in A.D. 70. Another major siege would follow in the Bar Kochba rebellion of A.D. 132 - 135, which would result in the expulsion of the Jewish people from the land of Palestine. Rome saw Christianity as some kind of Jewish offshoot or sect that was no longer completely

---

[138] Revelation 1:18; Leviticus 26; Deuteronomy 28; Ezekiel 14:21; Ezekiel 5:17; Psalm 46:8

Jewish, but still tied to the Hebraic religion in some way. Since the Jewish leaders disowned Christians, and they were seen as a threat to the Pagan economic-political system, Rome would attempt to stomp them out as well.

Here lies the mystery of the Old Kingdom and the New -- the Old Covenant and New. The imagery here of the Christian martyrs and their blood, under the altar,[139] calls to mind the old sacrificial system of lambs offered up as sacrifice by the priests of the Old Covenant. Here we see how the sacrifices of Christians, including the ultimate sacrifice, are united to the sacrifice of Christ in a mystical way. At that time, the persecution of Christians was primarily driven by the Jewish leadership in Jerusalem.

The souls under the altar cry out for justice. They are consoled and told to wait until their number is completed. They wouldn't have to wait long. The entire Jewish nation and all of its leadership would be destroyed and scattered to the four corners of the earth in the 68-year span between A.D. 67 to 135. Pagan Rome's devastation of the Jewish state was so complete that it would not rise again until the middle twentieth-century. On the other hand, Rome would see the suicide of its emperor, and after multiple failed rulers, it would eventually be converted to Christianity in the 4th century.

Verses 12-17 are apocalyptic language. They simply cannot be taken literally. A single star is hundreds to thousands of times larger than the earth, and that's a small one. Not only is it impossible for a star to fall upon the earth, but if the earth fell into one, the whole planet would be instantly consumed in a vast ocean of nuclear fusion. Verse 13 specifically says the

---

[139] Revelation 6:9-10

stars of heaven fell to the earth. This cannot be interpreted literally. Neither can any other part of this section. The language is reminiscent of the Olivet Discourse (Matthew 24:29-34) where Jesus uses apocalyptic language to speak of the events of A.D. 67-70, when Rome surrounded the City of Jerusalem for three years before leveling it. In the Olivet Discourse, Jesus connects the destruction of Jerusalem with the "sign of his coming."[140] This is not his literal Second Coming in bodily form, but rather a coming of judgment and destruction, as Israel's God-King judges the nation and government that spent the last 40 years judging him and his followers. The judgment clearly did not end in A.D. 70, but continued to unfold until A.D. 135, when all Jews were permanently expelled from their homeland. All the synoptic gospels contain their own version of the Olivet Discourse or Little Apocalypse (Matthew 24, Mark 13 & Luke 21), but it is conspicuously absent from John's gospel. The Book of the Apocalypse itself is John's expanded Olivet Discourse.

Revelation 7 - 144,000 Jews & The New Israel of God

In this chapter, the author takes a break between the sixth and seventh seal to elaborate on the work of the Church in the midst of all this worldly chaos. It is good to pause and consider how God is using evil to bring about good, and the suffering of Christians is working to save the world.

The 144,000 Jews of verse 1-8 are highly symbolic. The exact number in actual history is not necessary. What is critical is what this number

---

[140] Matthew 24:3, 30

represents. 144,000 is 12 squared times 10 cubed (144,000 = 12^2 x 10^3). In the symbolic imagery of apocalyptic literature, numbers are important. The number 12 represents the 12 tribes of Israel and the 12 apostles. Each 12 is multiplied with 10 cubed, or a trinity of tens, equaling 1,000. This simply represents numerous people, but it's a perfect round number, meaning that it's all part of God's divine plan. These 144,000 Jews represent the very first Jewish Christians who took the gospel into the world. Their witness for Christ, along with their suffering with him in persecution, results in a great harvest of an uncountable number of Gentiles coming into the Church (verses 9-10). These symbolic 144,000 Jewish Christians would escape the great tribulation of those times because they would not take part in the rebellion against the Roman Empire, and they fled Jerusalem before the Roman legions came, just as they were warned to do by Jesus Christ himself in the Olivet Discourse.

They are "marked" or "sealed" to God on their “foreheads," which is a symbolic representation of their mind being given over to God. This is important to pause and consider. Here, the Apocalypse explicitly tells us the servants of God are “marked” on their “foreheads.” Yet nobody takes this mark literally. Are you a Christian? If so, do you have a visible “mark” on your forehead? The Apocalypse says you do. Yet, if you look in the mirror, you’ll likely see nothing there. That’s because this is apocalyptic language. It’s not meant to be taken literally. It’s symbolism. The “mark” of the servants of God is symbolic. Just as we will later see, the “mark” of the servants of the Beast is meant to be taken symbolically as well. Neither the mark of God, nor the mark of the Beast, is literal. Both are symbolic.

The remainder of this chapter chronicles the celebration in heaven at the mighty victory of the Church in the midst of her great sufferings. I should reiterate what I said above. Two wraths are at work here: the wrath of God and the wrath of man. The wrath of God results in utter annihilation. The wrath of man results in eventual triumph and victory for the servants of God. This is why God “marks" his servants. He is setting them aside, or designating them, for triumph and eventual victory.

Revelation 8 - The Seven Trumpets

The author concludes the narrative of the seven seals by opening the seven trumpets. In a sense, the seventh seal contains the seven trumpets, and these parallel the trumpets of the Olivet Discourse in Matthew 24, Mark 13 and Luke 21. The seven seals and the seven trumpets are really the same thing. There are three sets of seven judgments in the Apocalypse: seven seals, seven trumpets, and seven bowls or vials. Each reveals the same events, essentially, but from three different perspectives. The seven seals give us the heavenly perspective. While the seven trumpets give us the perspective of the Old Testament Israel, specifically the view of the Sanhedrin and the Judean leadership of the late first century.

Of particular interest to Catholics are verses 3 and 4. These give a symbolic picture of how angels deliver our prayers to God. This, combined with Revelation 5:8, gives us a nearly complete picture of the "communion of Saints" wherein angels and Saints in heaven work together in offering our prayers up to God Almighty.

The first trumpet uses apocalyptic language (not to be taken literally) to describe the effect of the Jewish-Roman wars between A.D. 67 to A.D. 135. This signals the end of the old understanding of the Kingdom of Israel. Now the Kingdom of Israel consists of Christ the King, and the new Israel of God is the Church. What is to come of the old governmental systems, hierarchy, and jurisdictions that have rejected Christ the King and his reign? These trumpets elaborate. Considering this first trumpet, and considering that apocalyptic language is not to be taken literally, we should look at what historical events actually happened. The Roman war machine actually deforested the entire area around Jerusalem for miles, cutting down trees to craft weapons, tools, and crosses for thousands of executions.

The second trumpet uses the image of a mountain cast into the sea. The mountain represents royal dynasties. All traces of Jewish royal dynasties were destroyed by the Roman occupation and war machine.

The third trumpet tells of a star named "wormwood" (verses 10-11), poisoning the waters. On the one hand, we could interpret this as a metaphor for what happens when you bury numerous dead bodies in shallow graves after warfare. I happen to live near an American Civil War battlefield, wherein typhoid fever broke out the following year after the battle in 1861, thanks to water runoff from shallow graves (rotting bodies) into a nearby creek, which served as the local water supply. That could be a viable interpretation, but there is another, more Biblical one. The word "wormwood" appears elsewhere in the Bible.

> *Therefore Yahweh of Armies says concerning the prophets:*
>
> *"Behold, I will feed them with wormwood,*

and make them drink poisoned water;
for from the prophets of Jerusalem ungodliness has gone out into all the land."

Yahweh of Armies says,

"Don't listen to the words of the prophets who prophesy to you.
They teach you vanity.
They speak a vision of their own heart,
and not out of the mouth of Yahweh.
They say continually to those who despise me,
'Yahweh has said, "You will have peace;"'
and to everyone who walks in the stubbornness of his own heart they say,
'No evil will come on you.'

(Jeremiah 23:15-17)

Remember, every word is important in apocalyptic language. The word "wormwood" is used in Revelation 8:10-11 for a reason. It is likely to call back to mind the language of the prophecy in Jeremiah 23:15-17. It is likely the bishops of the seven churches in Asia Minor were Christian Jews (Hebrew Christians), as Christians of Jewish descent would usually have the most historical and cultural understanding leading the Church in the first century, and remember, there were Jewish synagogues in every major city in the Roman Empire. If there was a Jewish synagogue, there would also be a Christian community because it was the practice of the apostles to preach in the synagogues, first to the Jews, before going to the Gentiles in the streets and markets.

The mention of wormwood here calls us back to Jeremiah, and it has to do with false prophets. God promises to give them wormwood (bitterness) to drink. It's a Hebrew idiom, sort of like the English idiom "to eat one's own words." It's a way of saying you'll get what you deserve, or you'll reap what you've sown. The Sanhedrin and all the Jewish leaders of the first century promised peace and safety, if only they would turn against Jesus Christ and hail Caesar as their only king.[141] We could say the "star" that fell from heaven is none other than the Jewish high priest. When the Roman siege against Jerusalem came, these same leaders consoled their people by promising that God would eventually deliver them from the Romans in military victory. Then again, in the Bar Kochba rebellion of A.D. 132-135, they hailed Simon Bar Kochba as the promised Messiah. In an interesting footnote to all of this; it was the Jewish sage Rabbi Akiva (A.D. 40 - 137) who indulged the possibility that Simon could be the promised Messiah, and so gave him the surname "Bar Kokhba" meaning "son of a star" in Aramaic. The connection to wormwood as a "star" in Revelation 8:10-11 seems a little more than coincidental.

The fourth angel sounds his trumpet in verses 12-13. Here we have a recap of the destruction that awaits ancient Biblical Judaism. It began with the siege of Jerusalem in A.D. 67, climaxed with the destruction of the Herodian Temple in A.D. 70, and reached its total completion with Jewish expulsion from the Holy Land in A.D. 135. The destruction of the old order was complete and total.

---

[141] John 19:15

The Judaism that would rise from the ashes, modern Rabbinical Judaism, is not the same as the Biblical Judaism of the Old Testament. Biblical Judaism was centered on the Temple. Rabbinical Judaism is centered on the synagogue. Biblical Judaism relied on the rites of the priests. Rabbinical Judaism relies on the teachings of the rabbis. Biblical Judaism had a priestly hierarchy. Rabbinical Judaism has no priesthood whatsoever. Biblical Judaism was based in a theocratic monarchy. Rabbinical Judaism has no monarchy.

The only Jewish King that remains today is King Jesus, and the only Kingdom of Israel that exists today is the Church. All other vestiges of the Old Testament realm have been obliterated. Thus, when looked at from this perspective, the apocalyptic language here makes perfect sense. For the first-century Jew, living under the old hierarchical system without Christ, it was as if the world was coming to an end. Indeed, the Biblical Jewish world did come to an end.

Revelation 9 - Trumpets of Judgment

The fifth and sixth trumpet here chronicle the method of destruction that fell upon the Old Testament hierarchy and the Jewish state in the late first century to early second century. The star is recalled, which again may be a reference to the Jewish high priesthood, or even the "son of a star," Simon Bar Kochba, toward the end of Israel's catastrophe. Perhaps the star represents all of these things and more, but falling from the sky is a bad omen. It means it has symbolically lost its place in the sky, thus having fallen from God's good graces. The locusts represent the Roman armies, and the final siege of Jerusalem under Titus, which lasted about five months.

The beast from the bottomless pit in verse 11 has a symbolic name "Abaddon" or "Apollyon" which means "destroyer." This is likely Titus, who commanded the Roman armies during the siege of Jerusalem. We will see this beast return later in the text.

Verses 13-21 describe the siege on Jerusalem itself in apocalyptic language. The number of horsemen in verse 16 is not to be taken literally. It is a description of the overwhelming force the Jewish rebels in Jerusalem would face with no hope of victory.

Revelation 10 - The Angel & Little Book

Verses 8-11 are where the word "bittersweet" comes from. The book which the author is told to eat is the book (or scroll) that was unsealed by the Lamb (Christ) in previous chapters. It is sweet to the taste because it chronicles the deliverance of Christians from the persecution of the Sanhedrin and Romans. However, it becomes bitter with the realization that their deliverance would mean the total destruction of Biblical Judaism, the hierarchy, and the Jewish state. The author of the Apocalypse is believed to be Saint John the Apostle, and he was a Jewish Christian. The book he is writing chronicles the deliverance of the Church he shepherds, and simultaneously, the destruction of his kindred people and countrymen. Imagine, if you will, what it would be like for an American Christian having to chronicle the deliverance of Christians in America, at the cost of the destruction of the American nation and everything it represents. The author is going through a similar catharsis here. The experience is sweet and bitter at the same time -- bittersweet -- provoking both tears of joy and agony.

The time period of 3 ½ years, or 42 months, or 1,260 days is a recurring theme. It recalls Daniel 9:27 and Daniel 12:11. This time period is considered a time period of judgment. We see it first unfold in the

Maccabean War in 167 - 160 B.C., after the desecration of the Temple by Antiochus Epiphanes. Jewish leaders, in the first century, promised that would be the last time the Temple was desecrated. Not so, according to the teachings of Jesus Christ, who corrected their misunderstanding of the prophecy in Matthew 24:15. It would eventually unfold twice more.

The first just before the Roman invasion of A.D. 67 - 70. This happened in A.D. 40, when Caesar Caligula ordered that a statue of himself, as Zeus (or Jupiter) incarnate, be erected in every temple throughout the empire. A great upheaval and near rebellion occurred over it in A.D. 41 as preparations were being made by Pontius Pilate to erect the statue. However, Caligula's assassination that same year brought an end to the standoff, and the statue never made it past the Temple gates. Twenty-seven years before the Roman siege of Jerusalem, it served as a powerful warning to Christians in the city that the time to escape was at hand.

By the time of the Roman siege of Jerusalem, which lasted 3 ½ years (A.D. 67-70), few Christians remained in the city, and of those few that remained, they immediately fled at the first sign of the Roman armies and their idolatrous ensigns in the distance. The prophecy was fulfilled again in A.D. 132, in the most literal way imaginable, when Caesar Hadrian attempted to install a Pagan statue of Jupiter Capitolinus on the site of the ruined Jewish Temple. This provoked the Bar Kochba rebellion, which also lasted 3 ½ years and ended in the total ruin of the Jewish nation.

Dispensationalists believe the prophecies of Daniel and Christ refer to some future event. While that is not entirely impossible, it is also entirely unnecessary. Daniel's prophecy was fulfilled multiple times already. Three times an abomination that causes desolation was erected (or nearly erected) in the Jewish Temple, and the last time it resulted in the total desolation of the Temple for thousands of years.

Revelation 11 - The Two Witnesses

The "two witnesses" of this chapter are symbolic representations of the law and prophets (Old Testament), and bodily represented as Moses and Elijah, as fulfilled in Jesus Christ and his Church. This chapter deals with the realization that the Kingdom, which the Jews were promised, was fulfilled in King Jesus and his Kingdom Church. The "two witnesses" suffer symbolic persecution and humiliation, just as Christ and his Church did, under the rule of the Jewish leaders at that time. However, their victory is assured, as they conquer through martyrdom. In turn, fire burns those who persecute them. Jerusalem was destroyed by fire in A.D. 70. The Temple, in particular, was not only burned to the ground, but all the gold and silver therein melted in between the cracks of the stone. So, the stones were pulled out, one by one, by conquering Roman troops, to retrieve the precious metals.

Verses 15-19 reveal rejoicing in heaven over this, and the heavenly Temple is described, wherein the ark of the covenant resides. The author of Revelation appears to comfort his readers here, reminding them that under the Kingdom established by Christ, the real Mosaic "Temple" is now in heaven where Christ dwells as our great high priest.

Chapter 9
Apocalypse Part II

The next four chapters serve as an interlude to the chronology of the vision, and they are probably the most important section in the Apocalypse. Here we have a recap of the gospel, as it relates to Christians of the late first century.

Revelation 12 - The Woman & The Dragon

There are three main characters (symbolic personages) that need to be identified in this chapter. The first character is the male Child in verse 5, this can only be a symbolic image of Jesus Christ the King.

The second character is the Woman. Notice that at the end of chapter 11, when the author sees an image of the heavenly Temple, his attention is immediately diverted to another sign in heaven, beginning in chapter 12. It is the woman, who is "crowned with stars," clothed in the sun, and the moon under her feet. She gives birth to a male Child. If the male Child is correctly identified as Jesus Christ the King, then the Woman can be none other than the Blessed Virgin Mary. The description of her recalls to mind the apostolic traditions that she was assumed into heaven and crowned Queen of heaven and earth.

Now, this all falls in line with Jewish traditions. Great Old Testament prophets like Enoch, Moses and Elijah were assumed into heaven. So it was with Mary too; she vanished and was taken into heaven, which is why we have no relics of her to venerate. The Church has always taught this, but the teaching was finalized in A.D. 1950 when it was declared infallible by Pope

Pius XII in the Apostolic Constitution *Munificentissimus Deus*. It defines *ex cathedra*[142], the dogma of the Assumption of the Blessed Virgin Mary. It was the first *ex cathedra* infallible statement since the official ruling on papal infallibility was made at the First Vatican Council (1869–1870). Previously, in 1854, Pope Pius IX made an infallible statement with *Ineffabilis Deus* on the Immaculate Conception of the Virgin Mary, which was a basis for this dogma on her Assumption as well.

However, her coronation as the Queen of heaven and earth is likewise a Jewish tradition. Jewish kings, especially the good ones, always crowned their mothers (not their wives) as their queens.[143] Jesus is Jewish, he is the King, and he is good. Therefore, according to Jewish custom, he would crown his mother as his Queen. This chapter gives us a symbolic representation of that in verse 1. The twelve stars of

---

142 *Ex cathedra* (Latin: "from the chair"): It is a common error that popes are always infallible. That is not what the Catholic Church teaches. Rather, the Church teaches that popes can make infallible (without error) statements, on rare occasions, when they declare that such statements are infallible in a solemn decree called *ex cathedra* (Matthew 16:19; Catechism of the Catholic Church: 881, 891). Outside of the canonization of Saints, this has only happened twice in the last two centuries. Both occasions concerned doctrinal questions about the Blessed Virgin Mary. Decrees made *ex cathedra* are one way the pope can act as an arbitrator, permanently settling doctrinal disputes within the Catholic hierarchy.

143 Jewish queens were often the mother of the king. The Hebrew word for this is *Gebirah* (גְּבִירָה), meaning a female Lord (or what we would call a "Lady" according to English custom), but in the Biblical context it means queen, or more specifically a queen mother, or the mother of the king. The position of this title in ancient Israel placed the queen mother alongside the king as a very powerful ruler, second only to the king. 1 Kings 2:19-20; 2 Kings 11:3; 2 Kings 24:8,15; 2 Chronicles 22:12; Jeremiah 13:18; Jeremiah 29:2

her crown represent the twelve tribes of Israel, as well as the twelve apostles of the Church. However, there is more to this symbolism than just that.

Mary was the first Christian, and therefore, she is the firstborn of the Church, or the Mother of the Church, depending on how you look at it. Therefore, her connection with the Church is central. This symbol of Mary is just that -- a symbol -- and because it is just a symbol it goes on to represent the Church as well, particularly Jewish Christians in Judea at the time of the Roman siege of Jerusalem. In verses 6 and 13-16, we are reminded that these Christians fled into the wilderness at the time of the Roman invasion. While, as in verse 17, we are told that Christians in other parts of the empire, the Woman's offspring, would now suffer persecution.

Here in the middle of the Apocalypse, John records a symbolic vision of Our Lady, the Blessed Virgin Mary. That's because she plays a central role not only in the gospel but also in the final eschaton, as we shall see. She is the firstborn of the Church, the very first Christian, and so she leads all Christians in faith, whether they realize it or not, following her divine Son, Jesus Christ, into suffering, redemption and salvation.

The third character is the dragon. The dragon is none other than Satan the devil, and he is identified as such in verse 9. The "stars" that his "tail" drew out of heaven represent the angels of heaven. A third of them followed Satan to become his demons.

Verse 5 tells us the child is definitely Jesus Christ. So, the woman who gave birth to him undoubtedly represents Mary. But she also represents the Church because she is the first Christian. The vision records that she flees into the wilderness for safety in verse 6. This is followed by the reference to about 3 ½ years, or "one thousand two hundred sixty days," which is significant from a historical perspective. This is exactly how long the Roman siege against Jerusalem lasted. During that time, or I should say just before the siege started, Christians fled from the city, remembering the words of Our Lord in Matthew's Gospel: *"When, therefore, you see the abomination of desolation, which was spoken of through Daniel the prophet, standing in the holy place (let the reader understand), then let those who are in Judea flee to the mountains. Let him who is on the housetop not go down to take out the things that are in his house. Let him who is in the field not return back to get his clothes."*[144] Luke's Gospel seems to clarify things for us, defining what Our Lord actually meant by this: *"But when you see Jerusalem surrounded by armies, then know that its desolation is at hand. Then let those who are in Judea flee to the mountains. Let those who are in the middle of her depart. Let those who are in the country not enter therein."*[145]

Matthew calls it the *"abomination* ***of*** *desolation,"* while Luke calls it the abomination ***that causes*** desolation, and he specifically defines it as Jerusalem surrounded by armies (plural). These armies would be Roman armies, raised from the multiple provinces of the Roman Empire, each carrying the idols of their respective regions, and all of them united under the

---

144 Matthew 24:15-18; where Jesus renewed the prophecy of Daniel in Daniel 9:27, Daniel 11:31 and Daniel 12:11. Though the prophecy seemed to have already been fulfilled during the Maccabean Revolt (1 Maccabees 1:54-49; 2 Maccabees 6:1-2), Jesus renewed it in the Olivet Discourse (Little Apocalypse of the Synoptic Gospels), saying something similar would happen again, in the near future, proximal to his time.

145 Luke 21:20-21; the entire account of the siege of Jerusalem in A.D. 70 is recorded in *Josephus, Wars of the Jews, Books 4-6*.

idol of the Roman ensigns. Upon conquering Jerusalem, after a 3 ½ year siege, the Romans set up these ensigns on the eastern gate, near the Temple location, and made sacrifices to them, in a sign of Pagan idolatry in the most visible place of the Holy City.

The Woman, a symbol of Mother Mary, now symbolizing her spiritual children (Christians in general, or the Jerusalem Church in particular), flees into the wilderness, for safety, where a place is prepared for her. Tradition tells us that the early Christians in Jerusalem fled the city when they saw the Roman armies coming, heading east toward Jordan, where they found refuge in the ancient city of Petra, a monument of catacombs, complete with an amphitheater, carved into the cliffs of the mountains there.

Verses 13-17 tell us that the devil, working through the Roman authorities, began persecuting Christians. Apparently, there was some pursuit of the Jerusalem Christians into Jordan, but based on the symbolic account in the Apocalypse, it would appear the pursuit was called off. Instead, Christians would suffer throughout the empire, intermittently, by the hands of various emperors and their local authorities. How would this happen? Enter the two beasts...

Revelation 13 - The Two Beasts

In this chapter, we are introduced to two other symbolic characters in this ongoing interlude to help the readers gain more perspective. This has to be one of the most misunderstood chapters in the entire Bible.

The first symbolic character is the Beast out of the Sea. Its grotesque description brings to mind the fourth terrible beast described by the Prophet Daniel.[146] Most Protestants have historically interpreted this great Sea Beast as the Antichrist. They are mistaken. Nowhere in this chapter, nor anywhere else in the Apocalypse, does it indicate that this Sea Beast is the final Antichrist which is to appear at the end of time. Literally, there is no context to suggest that at all. It is simply a misinterpretation passed down through the centuries and repeated by countless Protestants throughout the ages. Sadly, even some Catholics have done the same.

Rather, the Sea Beast represents the Dragon's (or Satan's) masterpiece for accomplishing his will in the world, and will now be used to make war on the Church (represented by the Woman and her offspring in Revelation 12). The sea represents the Gentile nations, and the Beast comes out of the Sea. So, this Sea Beast, maintaining the context of everything so far, is none other than the ancient Pagan Roman Empire. The ten horns, each having ten crowns, represent the ten provinces of the Roman Empire: Italy, Achaia, Asia, Syria, Egypt, Africa, Spain, Gaul, Britain and Germany. Now, we have to remember that there were actually more Roman provinces than this. The number 10 is a symbolic number representing the Gentiles. It is a number of Gentile totality. It's not meant to be taken literally, just like almost nothing else in the Book of Revelation is meant to be taken literally.

The seven heads have a double meaning. The first is the seven hills upon which Rome is built. The second is the seven Caesars of Rome, leading up to the sacking of Jerusalem in A.D. 70. Like Josephus, the Jewish historian, the author of Revelation (presumably Saint John), numbers the Roman Caesars

---

[146] Daniel 7:7-8

starting with (1) Julius, (2) Augustus, (3) Tiberius, (4) Caligula, (5) Claudius I, (6) Nero, and (7) Vespasian. It was Vespasian's son, Titus, who besieged Jerusalem and destroyed it in A.D. 70. However, Nero is the focus of the Sea Beast, and here is why. The siege of Jerusalem began under his reign in A.D. 67, while Vespasian was the Roman commander leading the siege. However, when word of Nero's death reached Vespasian in A.D. 68, his army declared him to be the next Caesar. So, he encamped them around the city, and rode to Rome to take the throne. The Roman Senate confirmed him in December of A.D. 68, and his son Titus was given charge of the troops encamped around Jerusalem. By late A.D. 70 the city was destroyed.

Nero is a key player in all of this, and it was his actions that initiated the whole chain of events. By his decision, Jerusalem would be leveled, and Christians would suffer persecution for the next two centuries. The reign of Nero was a disaster for the Roman Empire, and this is why the Sea Beast is depicted as having a wounded head. The Senate hated him, and because of his mismanagement, the empire was plagued with uprisings and civil wars, including the one in Judea which led to the destruction of the Temple, and eventually the loss of the Jewish state. In the end, everyone revolted against him, and he committed suicide.

Under Vespasian, however, the destruction of Jerusalem would be made complete, and persecution of Christians would continue. It was like a mortal wound that healed, and so the symbolic Sea Beast (Roman Empire and its war machine) continued to live. Nero's lasting legacy, however, was that of emperor worship. It was by his reign that the cult came into worldwide acceptance. The policy of the Empire was simple. You can worship whatever god or gods you want, so long as you also worship Caesar as the supreme god above them all. The author warns his readers not to fight the Sea Beast with carnal weapons, lest you face sure defeat (verse 10). Only the endurance of faith, leading even to martyrdom, can effectively fight the Sea Beast. Victory is spiritual, not physical, for the power of the Sea Beast is too great, and is given to it as a gift by the Dragon (Satan) himself.

The second symbolic character is the Land Beast with two horns. This Land Beast appears harmless, like a lamb, but speaks as a dragon. Here we see that the Land Beast is none other than the Sanhedrin, or the Jewish religious leaders, from the time of Christ, well into the early fourth century. This Land Beast empowers the Sea Beast in two main ways. The first was through alliance. The Sanhedrin were allied with the Roman procurator during the time of Christ and thereafter. The second is through rebellion, even to the point of declaring false messiahs (antichrists), thus giving Rome the excuse it needed to crush the Jewish state with its war machine. By failing to accept Jesus as their rightful King, the Sanhedrin, along with all the Judean leadership at the time, effectively led their people into ruin.

The Mark of the Beast, in verses 16-18, is again highly symbolic. Dispensationalists interpret this quite literally, insisting that it will be a literal tattoo or microchip of the future, implanted under the skin of the right hand or forehead. But again, the language of this text is highly symbolic, and is not supposed to be interpreted literally.

In an attempt to reveal the identity of the Sea Beast to a Jewish Christian audience, the author used a rabbinical numbering code for names called

Gematria (גימטריה). Under this system, a name is given a numeric value, based upon the numeric value of the letters contained therein. Remember, ancient cultures used letters for numbers. Take Rome, for example, where the number one is represented as an "I," the number five is represented as a "V," and the number ten is represented as an "X." The same applied to Hebrew, wherein certain letters had a numeric value. This was the language exclusively used by the Jewish scholars at that time. Even common Jews didn't use it. While Jesus Christ himself probably knew Hebrew, he spoke in Aramaic, which was the common street language of the Jews at that time. So only learned scholars in Hebrew would understand this, and since the audience is the seven bishops of Asia Minor (likely educated Hebrew Christians), they would have access to the means of understanding this.

According to the Hebrew spelling of Nero, as transliterated from Greek, the letters add up to 666. However, in the Hebrew transliteration of the Latin spelling of Nero, the letters add up to 616, which explains the difference in manuscripts. Some Bibles say 666, and others say 616. They both point to Nero in the Hebrew language numbering system. The difference is the source text, either Greek or Latin.

The popular translation is from the Greek, and the Greek version of the name, Nero Caesar, transliterates into Hebrew as *Nron Qsr* (נרון קסר), pronounced as *Nerōn Kaisar*, which yields a numerical value of 666, as shown below. Please keep in mind that Hebrew is read from right to left, the opposite of English...

Resh (ר)	Samekh (ס)	Qoph (ק)	Nun (נ)	Vav (ו)	Resh (ר)	Nun (נ)	Sum
200	60	100	50	6	200	50	666

Nero Caesar had his name printed on all the coins of the empire during his reign, which is to say that nobody could buy or sell without it. Those who gave assent to Caesar worship essentially put Nero's "mark" on their mind or "forehead" as well. While those who just gave lip service to it all, simply acted as if they did, taking his "mark" in their actions or "right hand." The symbolism here is reminiscent of Revelation 7:3-4, where the servants of God are marked or "sealed" on their foreheads as well.

Consider the context of the chapter. Revelation 13 begins with a vivid description of two beasts. The first comes out of the sea. It has seven heads and ten horns. The second comes up from out of the earth, and it is described as having two horns, speaking as a dragon. Are we to believe these two beasts are meant to be taken literally? Do we really think a ten-headed monster is going to come up out of the sea? Do we really believe a two-horned monster is going to climb up out of the earth? If we interpret the Book of Revelation literally, then we should! Most people, however, have enough sense to realize these are symbolic images, and not meant to be taken literally.

So if neither beast in Revelation 13 should be taken literally, why should the Mark of the Beast be taken literally? It shouldn't. To do so is to play recklessly with Biblical interpretation. One is picking and choosing, almost randomly, what to take literally and what to take figuratively. By the same token, another could say the Mark is symbolic, but the beast isn't, and we should soon expect a ten-headed Godzilla to arise from the ocean any day now.

No, we have to be consistent in our Biblical interpretation. If a particular book of the Bible, like the Apocalypse for example, calls for a symbolic interpretation from the very beginning, (just as the

Book of the Apocalypse does from the very first chapter), then we need to be consistent about that symbolic method of interpreting all the way through. So in Revelation 13, both beasts are to be interpreted symbolically, and so is the Mark of the Beast, just like the Mark of God in Revelation 7:3 and Revelation 9:4. God doesn't put literal tattoos or microchips on people, neither does the symbolic beast of Revelation 13.

Nevertheless, there is a moral we can take away from this. The imagery of the Mark of the Beast, never literal, has applications in every age, including our own. Every time a government (Caesar) demands unconditional allegiance, the kind of allegiance owed only to God, it is commanding us to wear the symbolic Mark of the Beast. When governments seek to occupy a place in our lives higher than God, that government has become Caesar, and we as Christians must resist it.

How do we resist it? Do we rise in rebellion? Do we start an insurrection? No. We simply refuse to wear the Mark of the Beast. We deny such governments unconditional allegiance that is owed only to God. Furthermore, we do this no matter the cost, even if it means forfeiting our own lives. Nothing could be sweeter than denying such a tyrannical government the satisfaction of having our unconditional allegiance, and simultaneously denying it the respect of meeting it in battle. Such a government is not worthy of our worship or our courage. It gets nothing. Killing us is empty and unsatisfying. It is a hollow victory. The Romans had to make sport of it, just to keep it interesting. Even that became a bore in time. All the while, such governments lose the respect of their subjects and the world. In the end, their fate is always the same. If they are not conquered by their enemies, they eventually collapse under their own weight. This is how the Christians of the first three centuries handled it. So, it is how Christians must handle it today.

Revelation 14 - The 144,000 & The Harvests

The chronological interlude continues with the scene in heaven, again giving us context. The vision takes us back to heaven, as Mt. Zion refers to heaven in apocalyptic literature, where we are reacquainted with the 144,000 we first met in chapter 7. Again we are reminded that these Jews have been branded with the mark of God on their foreheads. This is to remind us of the mark they received in chapter 7, and to illustrate a contrast with the Mark of the Beast in chapter 13. Again, all of this is symbolic. Unless we are to believe God marks his own with a literal tattoo or microchip, we cannot believe the Devil, using the Beast, marks his own the same way. We must understand this. We are talking about symbolic language here. The mark of God on the 144,000 is not a literal tattoo or microchip. Neither is the Mark of the Beast. If only the Mark of the Beast really were so obvious, it would be much easier to resist. (Get a tattoo or microchip and go to hell. Avoid the same tattoo or microchip and avoid hell.) No, it's so much more insidious than that. Being a symbolic thing, we have to check our lives and make sure that neither our thoughts nor our actions are beholden to the Devil, but instead are given over to God. WE must make sure our unconditional allegiance is given only to God, and not to the state or some other agent.

Again, the number 144,000 is a symbolic number that represents all the Jews who originally came into the Church from Old Testament Biblical Judaism. However, in verse 4, the author calls them "virgins" and is very specific that they were not ritually "defiled" with women. Read between the lines here, and it's clear that these 144,000 are all men as well. So, does that mean no women were saved from Biblical Judaism? No. Of course not. Again, the number is symbolic, and likewise the virginity is symbolic as well, to an extent. The author takes special care to make sure what he says about virginity is not misunderstood. There were twelve tribes of Israel. There were twelve apostles. The number one-thousand represents the fullness of quantity. In other words, it means a lot. It's not meant to be an exact number.[147]

$$12 \times 12 \times 1000 = 144{,}000$$

The three angels then make their announcement of God's judgment upon those who persecuted the Church in the first century. This is not about the final judgment at the end of time, but rather the historical judgment that came upon those who persecuted the Church at the time this book was written. Verse 13 makes it clear that this is not a reference to the last judgment at the end of time, for it references those who will die in the Lord from now on. The judgment these angels announce is coming upon "Babylon" which is a symbolic reference to another city, actually. We will explore this a little later. The third angel announces a warning to first-century Christians. If they do not resist emperor worship, they too would suffer the same fate as "Babylon." To put this into context, Christians were at this time being tempted beyond measure to give in to emperor worship. Just a pinch of incense on the Pagan altar, with the words "Caesar is Lord" would spare the Christian from any persecution by Rome, but this is exactly what the

[147] Deuteronomy 7:9; 1 Chronicles 16:15; Psalm 50:10; Psalm 84:10; Psalm 90:4; Psalm 105:8; Ecclesiastes 6:6

author is telling Christians not to do. Such action is to receive the Mark of the Beast.

Verses 14 - 20 deals with the harvest judgments. I say judgments as plural here because they are. There are two events taking place. The one like the Son of Man is a representation of Jesus Christ, who is glorified in heaven. The first sickle is given to him, and he thrusts it into the earth, reaping his harvest. This is symbolic of harvesting wheat, and it is a reference to Christ reaping the good fruit of the earth. He is harvesting his Church, meaning he is taking them as his own. During the judgment of symbolic Babylon, Christ would keep his own safe. Then a second sickle is given to him, and he thrusts it into the grapes. This is where the term "grapes of wrath" comes from. The grapes in the wine press represent blood. The second sickle represents the judgment of God upon those who have allied with symbolic Babylon.

Revelation 15 - The Church Triumphant

This short chapter gives us an interlude in which the scene goes back to heaven. It helps here to remember that the Church is the new Israel of God (see Chapter 5) because here the author refers to the Church in heaven using Old Testament imagery. The strategy of the Lamb, the Child, the Son of Man, Jesus Christ begins to unfold here.

Revelation 16 - The Wrath of God

Seven bowls, or vials, of judgment are poured out on the symbolic City of Babylon that has persecuted the Church of the first century. These judgments are very reminiscent of the judgments poured out on Egypt in the Book of Exodus. They are all highly symbolic. But the question begs to be asked,

"Why does the author of Revelation harken back to the Book of Exodus here?" It seems the only people who would understand this sequence of judgments would be Jews. Granted, the Apocalypse is written to the bishops of the seven churches in Asia Minor, who were likely Jewish-Christians shepherding mixed Jewish-Gentile congregations, but it still seems odd that God would use this particular symbolism on this symbolic City of Babylon. Again, only Jews would understand it, as they would recall these judgments annually at every Passover Seder, a meal which was supposed to be celebrated in Jerusalem. It's almost as if this sequence of judgments is custom-made for people who would understand them.

The mention of Armageddon in verse 16 is critical. The name of the place recalls one of the last battles which the Jews lost before the fall of Jerusalem to the Babylonians in 587 B.C. That led to the Jewish people being hauled off into slavery in Babylon for 70 years! The mention of this name is an ominous sign to the Jewish people. It recalls a disaster looming for Jerusalem and the Jewish nation. It's a disaster that will be elaborated upon in the next two chapters.

Revelation 17 - Mystery Babylon the Great Harlot

In this chapter, the symbolic city is revealed as a great harlot. While the actual name of the city is never mentioned, the symbolism leaves us with little doubt. The city is called "Mystery Babylon the Great" (verse 5). There are several clues which are given to help us identify the city. It's not always plain for people in modern times, but in ancient times it would be obvious, especially for certain people accustomed to Old Testament symbolism (Jews or Jewish Christians).

The woman is called a harlot, meaning she sold herself out (verses 1, 5 & 16). The imagery of prostitution is important here. What is a prostitute? It is a woman who sells her most precious intimacy (her body) for monetary gain. It is a woman who cheapens herself and gives what should rightfully belong to her husband to the highest bidder instead. She is a sellout in the worst possible way. To whom does she sell herself? She sells herself to the "kings of the earth" (verse 2), who were "made drunk" with the "wine of her fornication." But what is this "wine?" Verse 6 tells us the "wine" is symbolic of the "blood of the martyrs of Jesus." So, this city is a city that is a sellout, meaning it has given away to the "kings of the earth" what should rightfully belong to her husband. (A city that should have had a husband?) She makes these kings "drunk" with her "wine" which is really the blood of Christians. If we look to the Gospel of Matthew, we start to see a parallel unfold. Jesus said:

> *"Jerusalem, Jerusalem, who kills the prophets and stones those who are sent to her! How often I would have gathered your children together, even as a hen gathers her chicks under her wings, and you would not! Behold, your house is left to you desolate."* (Matthew 23:37-38)

The "husband" is none other than Jesus Christ. The great harlot is none other than Jerusalem. Many scholars have debated this one because some verses in this chapter seem to point to Rome, but others more clearly point to Jerusalem. The answer to this mystery becomes simple once you think about what a prostitute is. Babylon was a first-century code name for Rome. In 1st Peter 5:13 we read that Saint Peter himself referred to Rome as Babylon. However, the same imagery is employed here to make a point. Jerusalem and Rome are now one and the same thing. Why? The answer is in the Gospel of John, which records the dialogue between Pilate and the chief priests of Jerusalem over what to do with Jesus Christ:

> *"They cried out, 'Away with him! Away with him! Crucify him!' Pilate said to them, 'Shall I crucify your King?' The chief priests answered, 'We have no king but Caesar!'"*
> (John 19:15)

Jesus was Jerusalem's rightful King. He was their messianic "husband" sent to them as promised in the Old Testament prophecies. But instead, the leaders of Jerusalem sold themselves (symbolic prostitution) to Caesar, in exchange for the promise of peace and security. They had their rightful King (messianic husband) crucified instead. Then after he was resurrected, they persecuted his followers (Christians) in just about every way imaginable. In the end, the Jewish leaders convinced Rome that Christianity was not a Jewish sect, and therefore not eligible for a Jewish exemption from Caesar worship. This ignited the Roman persecution of Christians, which began under Nero (A.D. 54 - 68) and continued intermittently until Diocletian (A.D. 284 - 305). Remember, Rome was not just one kingdom. It was an empire, which consisted of many kingdoms (many kings) all serving their emperor in Rome -- Caesar! So, when Jerusalem symbolically "prostituted" herself with Rome, she was effectively prostituting herself with all the kings of the earth. The author of Revelation is telling us that Rome and Jerusalem are now one and the same. They have engaged in a "carnal union," if you will, a symbolic "sexual intimacy" based on monetary and political gain.

The confusion over the identity of "Mystery Babylon" has to do with the name Babylon itself (usually identified with Rome), and seven mountains and kings upon which the woman sits (verses 9 - 10). Ancient Rome was built on seven hills, and the seven kings are clearly a reference to the seven Caesars of Rome leading up to the fall of Jerusalem. The number of actual men who ruled as Caesar is not relevant here. Remember, this is a symbolic book. The number seven represents completion.

It's also essential here to remember that while ancient Rome was built on seven hills, so was ancient Jerusalem. The hills (or mountains) of Jerusalem include Zion, Acra, Moriah, Bezetha, Millo, Ophel, and Antonio.[148] These mirror the seven hills (or mountains) of Rome: Aventinus, Cælius, Capitolinus, Esquilinus, Palatinus, Quirinalis and Viminalis.[149] This is yet another parallel, and as I pointed out above, the religious and civil leaders of Jerusalem specifically said, *"We have no king but Caesar."* Thus, the author of Revelation appears to be suggesting, through the imagery of sexual prostitution, that Jerusalem and Rome have become one and the same entity. They have become sexually "one flesh," and that is why the

---

148 Josephus, Wars of the Jews V, 5:8

149 Note the hill upon which the Vatican is built is "Vaticanus" and is not included here. This is because Vaticanus is located across the Tiber River and apart from the ancient City of Rome. The Vatican was not built within the boundaries of the ancient City of Rome. It was rather an area outside of the city. Dispensationalists often mistakenly cite Vaticanus as one of the original seven hills of Rome. This fuels anti-Catholic and anti-papal sentiments, but this is partially due to geographical ignorance.

author of Revelation calls Jerusalem "Mystery Babylon."

Verse 3 tells us the woman rides a beast with seven heads and ten horns (See Revelation 13 above). The beast is the Roman Empire, and the woman rides atop it, benefiting from its power as she persecutes the infant Church.

Starting in verse 7 we see the fate of Mystery Babylon. She is to be destroyed. However, the instrument of her destruction is a twist of fate. Verse 16 tells us the ten kings, meaning the nations that constitute the Roman Empire, will turn against Jerusalem and "burn her with fire." In other words, the "lovers" she has prostituted herself to will destroy her. The kingdoms of Rome (the makeup of the Roman army) will destroy Jerusalem. Similar apocalyptic imagery is used in Matthew 24, Mark 13 and Luke 21. Please read them for context. The three synoptic gospels contain a version of the Olivet Discourse, but the Gospel of John does not. This Apocalypse is his expanded Olivet Discourse. The Jewish historian, Josephus, describes the horror that was the 3 ½ year siege of Jerusalem in which countless Jews died under the most horrid circumstances, some even resorting to cannibalism because there was no food left in the city during the siege. When it was all over, the Roman General Titus could no longer control his men, and they set fire to the city. The Temple was burned to the ground, and the flames grew so hot that the gold plating on the walls and vessels melted into the cracks of the stones beneath. Later the soldiers would return to pull one stone off another to get to the gold, just as Jesus prophesied would happen in Matthew 24:2, Mark 13:2 and Luke 21:6.

Another source of confusion is verse 18. It says this city reigns over the kings of the earth. Now,

Jerusalem was a Roman-occupied city. How can Revelation 17 be about Jerusalem when it says the woman (city) reigns over the kings of the earth? This has led many to believe the author is talking strictly about Rome here.

Again, we go back to the relationship between Rome and Jerusalem. It was symbolically sexual (unitive) in nature. The Scriptures describe sexual relationships as two people becoming one flesh. Again, the author puts "Mystery Babylon" (Jerusalem) in sexual union with symbolic Babylon (Rome). We have to remember that Rome indeed had a unique relationship with the Jewish nation of that time. Jews were exempt from Caesar worship. Instead of throwing a pinch of incense on the altar and worshiping Caesar upon paying their taxes, Jews were allowed to simply pay their taxes and promise to pray to the Hebrew God for Caesar instead. This goes back to a deal struck with Jerusalem long before, in which Jews would be exempt from Caesar worship, and all Pagan expectations, in exchange for the peaceful surrender of the Jewish homeland to the Roman Empire. This arrangement had its payoff. The Jewish historian, Josephus, recorded: *"The royal city Jerusalem was supreme, and presided over all neighboring countries as the head does over the body."*[150]

So, as various rebellions erupted in subsequent years, Rome could count on the Judean leadership in Jerusalem to come to its aid, and keep the people in line by religiously marginalizing the rebels. This allowed Rome to occupy that region of land, at minimal cost, which was essential to create a land bridge between the northern half of the empire in Europe and the southern half of the empire in Africa. It also

---

150 Josephus, Wars of the Jews, Book 3

provided a buffer zone for Roman troops to assemble, keeping the Parthian Empire in the east at bay. So in a very real way, the cooperation of the Jewish religious authorities in Jerusalem was helping the Romans maintain control over the kings of the earth. Rome repaid the Jewish leaders in Jerusalem generously, and the city itself became the most modern and luxurious in that region of the world.

In the end, Jewish zealots rebelled against Rome and captured Jerusalem, seizing control of their religious leaders. So, Rome had had enough, crushing Jerusalem under its feet, and taking control of the region by full military force.

Revelation 18 - Fall of Mystery Babylon

This chapter simply chronicles the final destruction of Jerusalem in A.D. 67 - 70. As I said above, the cooperation of Jerusalem's religious leaders helped make the wealth and strength of the Roman Empire possible. Now it is gone, literally up in smoke. The destruction of Jerusalem in A.D. 70 was a major turning point in Western history. While the kingdoms of the region were certainly poorer because of it, the Roman Empire ended up exhausting its coffers just to hang on to that piece of real estate. The earthly reaction to Jerusalem's fall is one of sorrow (verses 9 - 19), but ironically, there is rejoicing in heaven because of it (verses 20 - 24). Why? The answer is in verse 24, *"...for in her was found the blood of the prophets and the saints."*

We must remember here that apocalyptic language is highly symbolic, especially when it refers to military conquest and destruction. As we see in Matthew 24, Mark 13 and Luke 21, the apocalyptic language of Jesus is likewise symbolic. Both the gospels, and the author of Revelation, are conveying here an event of great upheaval. It is the same event! Symbolic language, of the whole universe in upheaval, is used to convey the gravity of this event. If you were a Jew, living in the late first century, the fall of Jerusalem really did mark the end of your world as you knew it. If you lived in Judea, or the surrounding regions, it would have been catastrophic. If you were a Jew living in Asia Minor, Egypt, Greece, Rome or Spain, the news of it would have been devastating, having profound repercussions on your life.

The fall of Jerusalem in A.D. 70 marked the end of Old Testament Israel. Never again would it rise to the importance it once had. The religion of Biblical Judaism ended there too. There hasn't been a Mosaic Temple sacrifice in over 1,900 years! The Judaism of today was reinvented after the fall of Jerusalem and is commonly called Rabbinical Judaism. It is in every sense a shadow of what once was Biblical Judaism. There are no more Jewish priests, as there were in ancient times. Jews no longer make pilgrimage to Jerusalem for the great feasts, as they once did. No Temple crowns the Temple Mount in Jerusalem anymore. What exists of Judaism today is just a remembrance of what once was.

As if this wasn't bad enough, the collapse of the Jewish nation, in total, would come sixty-six years later, when Rome crushed the Bar Kokhba revolt in A.D. 136. With that defeat, Jews would be expelled from the Holy Land entirely. They lost their religious capital, Temple, and way of life in A.D. 70. Then they lost their entire nation in A.D. 136. Jews would not return to the Holy Land in large numbers until the 20th century, some 1,800 years later! It was the longest exile in Jewish history.

Likewise, the fall of Jerusalem in A.D. 70 marked the rise to prominence of the new Israel of God

-- the Church. Once suppressed beneath the religious persecution of the Temple leadership in Jerusalem, the Church was now free to thrive, unencumbered by the meddling of Jewish leaders in Jerusalem and elsewhere. So, that is exactly what it did. It thrived, but in Rome, which would become the undisputed religious capital of Christianity by the end of the first century, despite intermittent Pagan persecutions.

Revelation 19 - The King's Victorious Wedding

The celebration in heaven continues over the fall of Mystery Babylon (ancient Jerusalem). The author then presents two images to the reader. The first is the "marriage supper of the Lamb" (verses 7-10), and the second is a "rider on the white horse" (verses 11-16, which parallels Revelation 6:2). Both are symbolic images of Christ. In the "marriage supper," Christ is depicted as the Lamb who is married to his Church. In the "rider on the white horse," Christ is depicted as a conquering King, who has come to visit judgment upon rebellious Jerusalem, just as he promised he would in Matthew 24, Mark 13 and Luke 21. Neither of these images are literal, of course. Both are symbolic. The author of Revelation wants to make sure the readers understand that Christ had fulfilled his prophetic promise, just as he said he would, within his generation.

Now, it is no help here that many Protestant Bibles list verse 11-17 as the "Second Coming of Christ." This is a gross error, but a common one. Protestant Bibles are often riddled with footnotes, margin notes, and chapter titles, which do not appear in the original Greek text. These are meant to be study tools, to help the reader better understand the text. All that would be fine and good when such tools are accurate. Unfortunately, in this case, they are not.

Frequently, such study aids are colored by the biases of the audience the publisher is attempting to market to. I have a particular "New King James Version" (NKJV) left over from my Evangelical days. I still use it from time to time. It specifically has the section title for verse 1-21 labeled as the "Second Coming of Christ," and the reader is just supposed to assume that's what these verses represent. Even though, from a symbolic interpretation of the book, this is clearly a symbolic representation of the judgment of Christ upon ancient Jerusalem and the defunct Jewish state. My Revised Standard Version (RSV), which is just a modernized version of the original American Standard Version (ASV), simply titles this section properly as "The Rider on the White Horse." Yes, Bible versions really do matter. Some are more biased than others.

Verses 17-21 present to us a very unpleasant picture. We are given an image of birds of prey feasting upon the carnage of kings, captains, mighty men, horses, great people and small people. We see the same image painted in Matthew 24:38-41 and especially Luke 17:26-37. While surely in the aftermath of Jerusalem's fall, some of this would have been literal, as is the case of any battle. However, that's not the point. The carnage includes "kings," and we know of none that died in the Fall of Jerusalem. Again, this is symbolic, which is to paint for us a bigger picture. Verse 19 elaborates that the kings of the earth were gathered against Christ. This represents the Roman persecution of Christianity.

Verse 20 tells us the beast (or sea beast) and false prophet (or land beast) are captured and thrown into the "lake of fire." This represents total destruction, never to rise again. The beast (or sea beast) is the Roman Empire, personified by Nero Caesar. The false prophet (or land beast) is the high priest of Jerusalem and the Jewish Sanhedrin in an unholy alliance with Pagan Rome. The total destruction of the false prophet is easy to see. We've just read a few chapters dedicated to it. Historically, we have a clear date -- A.D. 70 -- when Jerusalem fell. However, history tells us that wasn't quite the end. There would be a final rebellion, crushed 66 years later -- the Bar Kokhba revolt. Between these two, Biblical Judaism would never rise again. There hasn't been a Temple sacrifice in over 1,900 years!

Likewise, the fall of the beast (Nero Caesar) was most clearly seen in A.D. 68, upon his suicide. However, history tells us that "little beasts" rose after him, some enacting their own persecutions upon the Church. All of them failed, and all of them fell. The Roman Empire fell into a succession of Caesars that would eventually lead her into ruin. By A.D. 313, Christianity would be made a legal religion in the empire by Constantine the Great. By A.D. 380, Christianity would become the official state religion of the Roman Empire, demonstrating the Kingship of Christ over all the kings who originally persecuted his Church. By A.D. 500, the western Roman Empire had fallen to the Barbarian invasions. All that remained of the ancient world was the Roman Catholic Church, headquartered in Rome. With the evangelism of Northern Europe during the centuries that followed, Medieval Europe saw the supremacy of Christendom over the territories once ruled by the Roman Empire. The fall of the land beast, Jerusalem and the Jewish state, began in A.D. 70 and was complete in A.D. 136. The fall of the sea beast, the Roman Empire headed by Caesar, began in A.D. 68 and was complete by A.D. 500.

This chapter concerns itself primarily with the events of the late first century. However, as observers from the twenty-first century, we can more clearly see how these prophecies were fulfilled in their absolute completion, indeed repetition, during the following centuries. The author points this out to us in stark symbolism, to remind us that Christ made good on his word. He promised Jerusalem would fall within his generation. It did. He promised that as King, he would send judgment upon the Temple leaders and Sanhedrin. He did. Furthermore, he reminds us of this, in all its gory detail, because if Christ made good on these promises, we can count on what is to follow.

Revelation 20 - The Church Age

There is a lot to unpack here. As I outlined at the beginning of Chapter 8, the millennium described is not literal. It is a multiplied trinity of tens (10 x 10 x 10 = 1,000). Remember the ten crowns on the seven-headed dragon? The number ten has always been symbolic in Jewish imagery of the Gentile nations and peoples. In this multiplied trinity of tens, we see the imagery of God dwelling among the Gentiles. The number 1,000 is not literal, nor is it meant to be. It is simply the product of this multiplied trinity of tens. The number is given in the context of time (years), to indicate that God will dwell among the Gentiles for an undisclosed long period of time.

We, living in the twenty-first century, know this period to be at least 2,000 literal years, but there is no reason to say it ends here. The number 1,000 is frequently used in Scripture to indicate something large, but it's rarely ever taken literally. For example; in Psalm 50:10 we are told that God owns the cattle on a thousand hills. Are we to believe this limits God to just one thousand hills and no more? That's not what the verse conveys. It's symbolic, which is to say that God owns everything. Again, 1,000 cubits (1,500 feet), are used symbolically in Ezekiel 47:3-6 to describe the depth of the water flowing from the Temple. (Can you imagine how absurd that is? A river flowing 1,500 feet deep in the middle of a city? The only comparison in the world is the massive Congo River, which flows merely at a depth of 820 feet at its deepest point. The Congo would swallow the entire Temple Mount in Jerusalem.) Ezekiel's imagery is obviously symbolic. The number 1,000 is used many more times in the Old Testament to convey symbolic meaning.

Dispensationalists, of various types, often insist that this thousand-year period is literal. It has to be for them because their entire eschatology is built on it. So, let's play devil's advocate, shall we? If we must interpret Revelation 20 as literal, to come to the conclusion that the 1,000 years are literal, then we must ask ourselves the following questions. What about the bottomless pit in verse 1 and 3? Are pits really bottomless? What about the chain in verse 1, and the angels binding the devil with it in verse 2? What kind of literal chain could hold a spirit being? If we are to militantly insist that the thousand years are literal in this chapter of Revelation, then we are likewise obliged to insist that the chain and bottomless pit in the same chapter are literal too. When confronted with this, Dispensationalists usually back down a bit, conceding that the chain and bottomless pit are symbolic language, but despite that, few will admit that the thousand years are symbolic too. It's a hermeneutic[151] conundrum every Dispensationalist is faced with, but few are willing to solve. To make the thousand-year millennium literal, they have to bounce

---

[151] Hermeneutics is the art and science of interpreting Scripture.

back and forth between symbolic and literal interpretations within the same chapter, having no hermeneutic rule to follow but their own say-so.

The earliest commentary on the Apocalypse comes from Saint Victorinus of Pettau, written in A.D. 270. He is very specific about the meaning of the 1,000 years.

> *"Those years, wherein Satan is bound, are in the first advent of Christ, even to the end of the age; and they are called a thousand, according to that mode of speaking, wherein a part is signified by the whole, just as is that passage, 'the word which He commanded for a thousand generations,' although they are not a thousand."*[152]

So from the earliest period of the Church, we have a clear interpretation of the 1,000 years as symbolic. The Church historian, Eusebius, writing from the early fourth century, indicated that those who interpreted the thousand years as literal were a fringe element in the Church during his time. These also held to non-canonical teachings from Christ, as well as some apocryphal stories about Christ. They were clearly in the minority.[153]

In verse 3, we are told that after the thousand years are completed, the devil will be released for a while. The thousand years represent an undefined long period of time between the fall of Jerusalem and the beginning of the Great Tribulation, which occurs before the Second Coming of Jesus Christ at the end of time.

---

152 Saint Victorinus, Commentary on the Apocalypse, Chapter 20

153 Eusebius, History of the Church, III:39

During this symbolic thousand years, in which we currently live, the Catholic Church not only survives, but flourishes throughout the world. She would expand her reach in missionary expeditions to the ends of the earth. Her reign over the "kings of the earth" would be marked by the rise of Christian governments, Christian laws, new societal norms, and a whole new way of viewing the world. This new worldview would lead to the greatest rise in science, art, justice, and standard of living that humanity has ever seen, and as we will see in the next chapter, it's not over yet. When it is over, however, Saint Paul tells us that "he who restrains" will be removed (2 Thessalonians 2:6).

In verse 4 we are told about the thrones established for those who will rule with Christ, but these are not literal earthly thrones in an earthly royal sense. However, they are meant to convey authority.

> *"Sees or consistories of bishops and prelates, and of the prelates themselves, by whom the Church is now governed. As the judgment here given can be taken no otherwise better than that which was said by our Savior, 'Whatever you bind on earth shall be bound in heaven.'"* (Augustine, City of God, Chapter 9)

> *"He indicates that which is done in the thousand years in which Satan is bound. For the Church, which in Christ will sit on twelve thrones to judge, now sits and judges, seeing that she has obtained to*

hear from her King, 'Whatever you bind on earth shall be bound in heaven.'"[154]

"And you know what is restraining him now so that he may be revealed in his time. For the mystery of lawlessness is already at work; only ***he who now restrains*** *it will do so until* ***he is out of the way.*** *And then the lawless one will be revealed, and the Lord Jesus will slay him with the breath of his mouth and destroy him by his appearing and his coming. The coming of the lawless one by the activity of Satan will be with all power and with pretended signs and wonders, and with all wicked deception for those who are to perish, because they refused to love the truth and so be saved. Therefore God sends upon them a strong delusion, to make them believe what is false, so that all may be condemned who did not believe the truth but had pleasure in unrighteousness."*

(2 Thessalonians 2:6-12 RSVCE, emphasis mine)

The message of Revelation 20 here is that there will be an exceedingly long period of time, wherein Jesus Christ will reign on earth through his Church. This is the period we are now living in, and it is much longer than a literal 1,000 years. At the end of this time period, however long that may be, Satan will

---

154 Saint Bede on Revelation, Chapter 20, Verse 4

be released to deceive the world yet again through the final Antichrist. Saint Paul tells us that this cannot happen until he who is *"restraining him now"* be taken out of the way.

What or who is this "restrainer"? Many of the early Church Fathers suggested this mysterious restrainer is none other than the Roman emperor and his Empire, having been eventually taken over by the Catholic Church, quite literally, in the late 4th century (A.D. 380), when Paganism was dismissed, and Christianity became the official state religion of the Roman Empire. Then after the Christian Roman Empire fell in A.D. 500, it did so only in the West. It continued to reign in the East through the Byzantine Empire (the eastern half of the Roman Empire). Byzantium remained until its fall to the Ottoman Turks (Muslims) in A.D. 1453. During that time, the Roman Empire was resurrected in the West and came to be known as the Holy Roman Empire (A.D. 800 - 1806). More generally, all of Christianity, both in east and west, is known as Christendom, and even in periods without a visible emperor, its presence has been felt throughout the Christian world in law, culture, and societal norms.

While the Church has never defined this view in any kind of doctrinal way, and some prominent Saints and scholars hold to a more modified (non-specific) interpretation of this passage, the majority of the Patristic writers were in consensus on this. Jesuit priest and Saint, Robert Bellarmine (A.D. 1542-1621), absolutely insisted upon it, not as a matter of faith to be held doctrinal, but as a matter of Patristic consensus worthy of belief.

Saint Paul's reference to "he" could not in any way be a reference to the Holy Spirit, as the Dispensationalists often claim because the Apostle always wrote freely about the Holy Spirit. Yet in this passage to the Thessalonians, he wrote more covertly, almost guarding his words, and it makes sense if his reference is to the Roman emperor and the Empire. In his time the Roman Empire was still Pagan, and any suggestion that it might one day fall would be interpreted as treason, especially coming from the pen of a Christian. Hence, the reason for his careful and vague wording in this passage.

One might note that there has been no reigning emperor of the Holy Roman Empire for over 200 years now! Indeed, the Holy Roman Empire is essentially defunct, and it has been for over two centuries. This is true, but despite this, many of the political, social and legal aspects of Christendom remain. It is only in the last five to six decades that these norms have been aggressively attacked. Still yet, the consensus among many Catholic Saints, theologians and scholars, including some Church Fathers, is that there will always be a revival of the Roman Empire, in some form, to reaffirm good governance, order, and law, until the last days, when it is finally made fully defunct and essentially helpless. Thus, more than a few faithful Catholics today hold to the belief that the Holy Roman Empire will be restored soon, out of sheer necessity, at some point in the not-too-distant future.

I will explore this concept in greater detail in the next chapter, but insofar as Revelation 20 goes, we know the Church has, is, and will enjoy a prolonged period of time in which evangelization of people, cultures and laws, are possible. After that, there will be a short time in which Satan will rise again and deceive the whole world through his Antichrist.

Lastly, of course, the word "he" could simply refer to the pope himself, who assumed temporal power, in addition to his spiritual power, with the fall of the Roman Empire. The matter is open for debate. It should be noted, however, that the papacy officially renounced all temporal power (outside the Vatican City State) back in the 1960s.

We have references in verses 5-6 to the first resurrection, which implies that there will be a second. What, exactly, is meant here by this first resurrection? There is a lot of symbolism at play here. Actually, there really was a first resurrection in a historical sense. There was the physical resurrection of Christ, but Scripture records that with Christ's resurrection, select others were resurrected too, giving testimony to him in Jerusalem before they vanished.[155] In this obscure passage, we do see reference to a first resurrection which Saint Paul later elaborated on,[156] but there is so much more here than that. The first resurrection applies to all who are faithful to Christ, in that their souls are resurrected in baptism and made ready for heaven. Thus, the implied second resurrection is the final one that will occur with the Second Coming of Christ at the end of time.

Verses 7-9 describe this great deception which will occur near the end of time, presumably (if we have interpreted Paul's "restrainer" prophecy correctly), this will occur some time after all trace of the Byzantine Empire, and Holy Roman Empire, otherwise known as Christendom, has been "removed" or "taken out of the way." This could also mean the removal of the papacy as well.

Verse 8 uses the imagery of Gog and Magog which comes from Ezekiel 38 & 39. In the Old Testament, Gog was the king of the people of Magog, and as prophecy developed in the Old Testament, Gog

---

155 Matthew 27:52-53

156 1 Corinthians 15:20-23

and Magog came to be representative of all heathen people. Dispensationalists insist this is a reference to the nation of Russia. Back in the 1970s, they said it was the Soviet Union. To back this they go through elaborate, and questionable, genealogies of nations to connect Magog with Russia. However, it's all futile. There are so many ancient connections to different peoples. Some say Magog represents the Scandinavians, others say the Germans, still others name the Irish! The most common theory is the people of Asia Minor near the Black Sea. The Dispensationalists' insistence on Russia is because of Russia's historic animosity toward the modern Republic of Israel. Dispensationalists interpret Biblical Israel as this modern political entity, and so they see Russia as its natural enemy. However, that's not what Revelation 20:8 is describing here. Everything in this book is symbolic, and so is Gog and Magog. It is simply used as a representation of the future and final assault on the Church, which will be primarily spiritual in nature, but also physical, in that we know there will be many martyrs during this time. It is nonspecific to any particular race or nation of people. It's simply meant to convey those who come against the Church in the Last Days.

Verse 9 refers to the "camp of the saints" and the "beloved city" which represents the Church. It cannot mean anything else. Dispensationalists would have us believe this means the modern Republic of Israel, but even a casual reading of the text makes this impossible. The author is speaking of the Church here. Also in verse 9, we learn the destiny of Gog and Magog, which is to say those who assault the Church in the Last Days. They are destroyed by the intervention of God. We learn from the Church that this is the physical Second Coming of Christ at the end of time. In verse 10, we see the final destiny of Satan, the devil. They are cast into the Lake of Fire, which is to say Hell or eternal destruction.

Verses 11-15 simply describe the General Judgment at the end of time. This is when God will transform all the living into a glorified state, and resurrect all the dead into a glorified state. There they will all be judged and awarded their eternal destiny; some to eternal life and others to eternal damnation.

Revelation 21 - The Parousia & Eternal State

This chapter reveals the eschatological destiny of humanity, and the entire universe. We are not given any details, only that everything we know of this universe will fade away. Is this literal or symbolic? We are inclined to believe a little of both. The wording may be symbolic here, but the Scriptures elsewhere, as well as the tradition of the Church, seem to indicate there will be a "renewal" of some kind at the end of time, in which we can expect a whole "new world."

The rest of this chapter concerns the New Jerusalem. It is highly symbolic, and connects to Old Testament symbolism in just about every way. It is described as a cube measuring 12,000 furlongs (1,377 miles) in every direction. Now, anyone with an understanding of science would tell you this is impossible. If such a structure landed on the earth, its top would be well beyond the atmosphere and deep into outer space.[157] The curvature of the earth would not allow its edges to rest on the ground. In other words, it is a completely symbolic city, which represents the completion of everything. This is the symbolic representation of life in eternity!

---

[157] Outer space begins at 62 miles above sea level.

Revelation 22 - Thy Kingdom Come

Verses 1-5 finish the symbolic narrative of life in eternity. Verses 6-13 remind us of who the author is. It is Jesus Christ himself. He promises that he is coming soon, and we can count on that because as King of Israel and the Universe, he has already demonstrated that by judging his own nation. Just as he has judged ancient Israel, not sparing his own nation,[158] he will eventually judge the whole world.

In verse 14, we are given hope and encouragement if we obey the gospel. In verse 15 we are warned and reminded of the fate of those who don't. Verses 16-19 warn the bishops of the seven churches not to tamper with this Apocalypse. They are to convey it to their churches in its entirety. Verses 20-21 remind us again that he is coming soon.

---

[158] Jesus was a Jew.

Chapter 10
Be Not Afraid

Now that we have a proper understanding of Biblical prophecy, and the Church's historic teachings about the Last Days, relating to both the fall of ancient Israel in the past, and the Second Coming of Christ in the future, we can begin to better understand the times in which we live, and our place in them. In the first chapter of this book, I said we are likely facing the end of an era, and by that, I mean the end of many things. Our time marks the end of the stalemate following the Second World War, the end of democratic republics as we know them, the end of Enlightenment ideals, as well as the end of Protestantism. This may seem shocking to read, but I don't think it's really that far-fetched at all. In fact, I believe the years ahead will be marked by great upheavals on all levels, such as has not been seen in generations.

I think to deny that these times are pivotal would be foolish. Obviously, they are important, and they are going to play a defining trajectory in the history of humanity. Some are inclined to say these are the beginning of the Last Days. I disagree. I think they are obviously leading up to the Last Days, and will serve as the historical foundation upon which the Last Days will eventually take shape. However, I think it's a mistake to believe that the times of the Antichrist, followed by the Second Coming of Jesus Christ, are going to happen in the near future, namely because of what I covered in previous chapters, but also because of what I am about to cover here.

It is not beyond my ability to admit error. I could be wrong in this presumption, and I would welcome such a pleasant surprise, but I don't think I am, as there are two major clues (often overlooked by modern Christians) that lead us to believe the times of the Last Days have not yet come.

The first major clue comes from the traditions of the Early and Medieval Church, concerning the times of the Antichrist, and what we should expect. We have no way of telling which of these traditions are apostolic in nature, so we have no way of gauging their authority. What we can tell is that these traditions were widespread and believed by the majority of Christians at the time they were recorded. We should never dismiss the widespread beliefs of our Christian ancestors. If they believed something, they probably had a good reason. Indeed, the burden of proof is on anyone who would cast doubt on their commonly held beliefs. It's reasonable to conclude that some of what they wrote was at least based on Apostolic Tradition at some nominal level. Perhaps the details are off, but I think the general premise is spot on.

The second major clue comes from the unusual miracles of our time, wherein the Blessed Virgin Mary has been making appearances, and delivering messages, which seem to indicate the times in which we live are destined to be tumultuous, but not the end of history. ***I should point out here that while the Catholic Church has put its seal of approval on some of these messages, that is not the same as a note of infallibility. None of anything I write in this chapter carries the same weight as the Biblical prophecy I covered in the previous chapters.*** That has to be stressed. Nobody is obliged to believe any of the following, but at the same time, I think it would be foolish to dismiss it out of hand.

I will begin by outlining the Early Church's understanding of the Last Days at the end of history.

Ancient Writings

The most ancient writings from the Church come to us from the *Didache* (Διδαχή), meaning "teaching," an early Church constitution, written sometime between A.D. 50 to 150. To recap the understanding of the ancient Christians concerning the times before Christ's Second Coming, the *Didache* teaches...

> *"Watch for your life's sake. Let not your lamps be quenched, nor your loins unloose; but be ready, for you know not the hour in which our Lord will come. But come together often, seeking the things which are befitting to your souls: for the whole time of your faith will not profit you, if you are not made perfect in the last time. For in the last days false prophets and corrupters shall be multiplied, and the sheep shall be turned into wolves, and love shall be turned into hate; for when lawlessness increases, they shall hate and persecute and betray one another, and then shall appear the world-deceiver as Son of God, and shall do signs and wonders, and the earth shall be delivered into his hands, and he shall do iniquitous things which have never yet come to pass since the beginning. Then shall the creation of men come into the fire of trial, and many shall be made to stumble and shall perish; but those who endure in their faith shall be saved from under the curse itself. And then shall appear*

> *the signs of the truth: first, the sign of an out spreading in heaven, then the sign of the sound of the trumpet. And third, the resurrection of the dead -- yet not of all, but as it is said: "The Lord shall come and all His saints with Him." Then shall the world see the Lord coming upon the clouds of heaven."*[159]

The consensus of the ancient Christians was that the Last Days would come quickly upon the earth, and be marked clearly by the rise of Antichrist, who shall reign only a short time, before the Second Coming of Jesus Christ. As noted above, the Second Coming and the resurrection of the Church happen simultaneously, and are witnessed by the whole world. This is the teaching of the most ancient Christians and the Early Church.

However, these same Christians acknowledged that there was a time in between their time, and the coming of the Antichrist, perhaps a long period of time, and they did not hold back in proclaiming this. Most of them attributed this long period of time before Antichrist to the restraining power of the Roman Empire. Remember, Christ is King of kings, which means all worldly power is ultimately controlled by him, and nothing can happen without his permission. While many writings point to the Roman Empire as the restraining influence mentioned by Saint Paul in 2 Thessalonians 2:6-9, perhaps none is more succinct and clear as that of Saint John Chrysostom, who wrote the following in the late fourth century…

---

[159] Didache 16, written between A.D. 50 - 150

"One may naturally inquire, what is that which withholds, and after that would know why Paul expresses it so obscurely. What then is it that withholds, that is, hindering him from being revealed? Some indeed say, the grace of the Spirit, but others the Roman Empire, to whom I most of all accede. Wherefore? Because if he meant to say the Spirit, he would not have spoken obscurely, but plainly, that even now, the grace of the Spirit, that is the gifts, withhold him. And otherwise he ought to have come by now, if he was about to come when the gifts ceased; for they have long since ceased. But because he said this of the Roman Empire, he naturally glanced at it, and spoke covertly and darkly. For he did not wish to bring upon himself superfluous enmities, and useless dangers.

"And he did not say that it will be quick, although he is always saying it -- but what? 'That he may be revealed in his own season,' he says, 'For the mystery of lawlessness is already at work.' He speaks here of Nero, as if he were the type of Antichrist. For he too wished to be thought of as a god. And he has well said, 'the mystery'; that is, it does not work openly, as the other, nor without shame. For if there was found a man before that time, he means, who was not much behind Antichrist in wickedness, what wonder if there shall

now be one? But he did not also wish to point him out plainly: and this not from cowardice, but instructing us not to bring upon ourselves unnecessary enmities, when there is nothing to call for it.

"So, indeed, he also says here. 'Only there is one that restrains now, until he is taken out of the way,' that is, when the Roman Empire is taken out of the way, then he shall come. And naturally. For as long as the fear of this empire lasts, no one will willingly exit himself, but when that is dissolved, he will attack the anarchy, and endeavor to seize upon the government both of man and of God. For as the kingdoms before this were destroyed, for example, that of the Medes by the Babylonians, that of the Babylonians by the Persians, that of the Persians by the Macedonians, that of the Macedonians by the Romans: so will this also be by the Antichrist, and he by Christ, and it will no longer withhold. And these things Daniel delivered to us with great clarity."[160]

The ancients saw the Roman Empire as a "restraining force" keeping the rise of Antichrist at bay. What, however, did they mean by "Roman Empire." If we think strictly in terms of the juridical and military authority of ancient Rome, with its emperors and Roman Senate, then we would be forced to conclude

160 Saint John Chrysostom (A.D. 347-407) Doctor of the Church, Homilies on Second Thessalonians, Homily IV, 2 Thessalonians 2: 6-9

that the reign of Rome ended in A.D. 500, and the Antichrist should have arisen to power immediately thereafter. That did not happen. We know that the Roman Empire continued in the East, as the Byzantine Empire, for another thousand years before finally falling to the Ottoman Turks. We know that the Holy Roman Empire, a loose confederation of Catholic states, rose to power in A.D. 800 and lasted about a thousand years until 1806. Furthermore, we know that the Austro-Hungarian Empire carried the torch of the Holy Roman Empire until its dissolution and abdication of Emperor Karl in 1922. There are a number of possible heirs to the throne today, though none are obvious at this time.

It is apparent to see that there is more to the Roman Empire than just ancient Rome. It would appear the ancient Romans started something, which still exists, in various forms, to this very day. Perhaps we could say that when the ancient Christians said "Roman Empire" they meant the "spirit of the Roman Empire," that is to say the will of the people of Western Europe to govern themselves, and not bend the knee to Eastern forces. If this is the case, we can see elements of the Roman Empire manifested in all Western European kingdoms and even republics.

Surely, the Spanish Empire (A.D. 1492 - 1976) was an extension of this, followed by the British Empire (A.D. 1583 - 1997). What of the nations of today? There are a few European monarchies left, but ancient Rome was also a republic, as well as an imperial dictatorship. Since the end of the First World War, monarchies have been declining in Europe, all of them replaced by either republics or parliamentary (constitutional) monarchies. Is this not the spirit of the Roman Empire too, which started out as a republic and remained as one within the City of Rome, even as the rest of the world bowed to the imperial dictatorship of Caesar?

If this is the case, we could say the spirit of the Roman Empire lives on, in the European Union (EU), the British Commonwealth, and even the United States of America, its capital having a very Romanesque appearance as well. So long as the people of Western Europe, whether they live in Europe, the Americas or Oceania, have the will and ability to govern themselves (as the Roman Empire did) then the spirit and person of Antichrist is restrained. That's not to say that some literal emperor couldn't arise again in Europe. Considering Europe's extensive history with emperors, it would be foolish to dismiss it completely.

When the time shall come, that the Western world (the remnants of Christendom and the Roman Empire), shall no longer have the will to govern itself, and is willing to submit to some power from the East, then shall come Antichrist. At least, this is my understanding of the basic premise of Early and Medieval Christianity concerning the Last Days. As I have said, I am willing to admit error if proved wrong, and I've gone out of my way to brush aside the finer details of ancient predictions for conveying the broader message. It seems the most ancient Christians were in agreement that the Antichrist would come from Jerusalem (not Rome), and his arrival would follow some cataclysmic collapse of Western civilization. Writing from the early third century, Hippolytus recorded as follows...

> *"Thus, then, does the prophet set forth these things concerning the Antichrist, who shall be shameless, a war-maker, and despot, who, exalting himself above all kings and above every god, shall*

build the city of Jerusalem, and restore the sanctuary. Him the impious will worship as God, and will bend to him the knee, thinking him to be the Christ."[161]

The theme of Antichrist rebuilding the City of Jerusalem, and the Jewish Temple, is echoed many times in the writings of ancient and medieval Christians. Yet, we know that Jerusalem still stands today, a major metropolis in the Middle East, within the Israeli Republic. The Temple remains demolished, since the siege against Jerusalem by the Roman Empire in A.D. 67 through 70. However, the city itself, having been razed multiple times since then, has been rebuilt just as many times. Its current manifestation, as a modern city, stands against the notion that we are currently living in the Last Days. For it to be rebuilt by Antichrist, it must first be destroyed again. This is not likely to happen so long as the Israeli Republic remains the strongest military power in the Middle East. One could easily surmise that in order for Antichrist to rise, the Israeli Republic must fall too, alongside the entire Western world (the remnants of the Roman Empire). Cyril of Jerusalem, writing from the fourth century, supplies a little insight by telling us the Antichrist will take the power of the West (Roman Empire), after it has apparently fallen…

"But as, when formerly He was to take man's nature, and God was expected to be born of a Virgin, the devil created prejudice against this, by craftily preparing among idol worshipers fables

---

161 Hippolytus (A.D. 170 - 235), On Daniel, II, 39

of false gods, begetting and begotten of women, that, the falsehood having come first, the truth, as he supposed, might be disbelieved; so now, since the true Christ is to come a second time, the adversary, taking occasion by the expectation of the simple, and especially of them of the circumcision, brings in a certain man who is a magician, and most expert in sorceries and enchantments of beguiling craftiness; who shall seize for himself the power of the Roman Empire, and shall falsely style himself Christ; by this name of Christ deceiving the Jews, who are looking for the Anointed, and seducing those of the Gentiles by his magical illusions.

"But this aforementioned Antichrist is to come when the times of the Roman Empire shall have been fulfilled, and the end of the world is now drawing near. There shall rise together ten kings of the Romans, reigning in different parts perhaps, but all about the same time; and after these an eleventh, the Antichrist, who by his magical craft shall seize upon the Roman power; and of the kings who reigned before him, three he shall humble, and the remaining seven he shall keep in subjection to himself. At first indeed he will put on a show of mildness (as though he were a learned and discreet person), and of soberness and benevolence: and by the

lying signs and wonders of his magical deceit having beguiled the Jews, as though he were the expected Christ, he shall afterwards be characterized by all kinds of crimes of inhumanity and lawlessness, so as to outdo all unrighteous and ungodly men who have gone before him; displaying against all men, but especially against us Christians, a spirit murderous and most cruel, merciless and crafty. And after perpetrating such things for three years and six months only, he shall be destroyed by the glorious second advent from heaven of the only-begotten Son of God, our Lord and Savior Jesus, the true Christ, who shall slay Antichrist with the breath of His mouth, and shall deliver him over to the fire of hell."[162]

From these writings, we learn that both the ancient and medieval Christians firmly believed the Antichrist would come after the Roman Empire (and presumably all its Western manifestations of various types) has firmly come to an end, so that the people of the West are willing to submit themselves to a Middle Eastern king, a man who will seize the power of the West, and use it to prop himself up as the Jewish Messiah. He comes to power in Jerusalem, presumably a Jerusalem that has been rebuilt following some kind of destruction, and with this rebuilding, he will reconstruct the ancient Jewish Temple, around where the Islamic Dome of the Rock now stands. He comes at a time of kings, which is interesting since

---

[162] Cyril of Jerusalem (A.D. 313 - 386), Catechetical Lecture 15: 11, 12

much of the world is now ruled by republics. In short, the time these ancient Christians describe looks very different from our own. In fact, it looks so different that we are forced to make one of two logical conclusions. We can either dismiss these ancient writings as in error, or else we can admit that the time in which we live is not the time they describe, and therefore we are still awaiting some future date that seems very distant to us now. I tend to go with the second logical conclusion.

Along with these predictions come prophecies of a time when the Roman Empire may be restored, at some future date, in a more recognizable form, comparable to the Holy Roman Empire of ages past, but on a much larger scale. The following are excerpts from various medieval authors, concerning the widespread belief that just before the time of Antichrist, a great monarch (or emperor) will arise from France and reign over the future world, until he (or one of his successors) surrenders his kingdom (empire) in Jerusalem...

> *"Our principal doctors agree in announcing to us that toward the end of time one of the descendants of the Kings of France shall reign over all the Roman Empire and that he shall be the greatest of the French monarchs and the last of his race... After having most happily governed his Kingdom, he will go to Jerusalem and depose on Mount Olivet his Scepter and Crown. This shall be the end and conclusion of the Roman and Christian Empire."* (Blessed Rabanus Maurus, 9th Century)

"Some of our teachers say that a King of Franks will possess the entire Roman Empire. This King will be the greatest and last of all monarchs and after having prosperously governed his Kingdom, he will come in the end to Jerusalem, and he will lay down his Scepter and his Crown upon the Mount of Olives. This will be the end and consummation of the Empire of Rome, and immediately afterwards Antichrist will come." (Monk Adso, 10th Century)

"A knight shall come from the West. He shall capture Milan, Lombardy, and the Crowns. He shall then sail to Cyprus and Famagoste and the land at Jaffa, and reach Christ's grave, where he will fight. Wars and wonders shall befall till the people believe in Christ toward the end of the world." (Saint Thomas Becket, 12th Century)

"Of the blood of Emperor Charles the Great and the King of France, shall arise an Emperor named Charles, who shall rule imperially in Europe, by whom the decayed estate of the Church shall be reformed and the ancient glory of the Empire again restored." (Chronicle of Magdeburg, 12th Century)

"There shall arise in the last times a Prince sprung from the Emperor Charles, who shall recover the Land of Promise and reform the Church. He

shall be the Emperor of Europe." (Aystinger the German, 12th Century)

"By its tremendous pressure, the comet will force much out of the ocean and flood many countries, causing much want and many plagues. All coastal cities will live in fear, and many of them will be destroyed by tidal waves, and most living creatures will be killed, and even those who escape will die from horrible diseases. For in none of those cities does a person live according to the laws of God. Peace will return to the world when the White Flower again takes possession of the throne of France. During this period of peace, people will be forbidden to carry weapons, and iron will be used for making agricultural implements and tools. Also during this period, the land will be very productive, and many Jews, heathens, and heretics will join the [Catholic] *Church."* (Saint Hildegard, 12th Century)

"At that time, the pope, with the cardinals, will have to flee Rome in trying circumstances to a place where he will be unknown. He will die a cruel death in this exile. The sufferings of the Church will be much greater than at any previous time in her history… God will raise a holy pope, over whom the angels will rejoice. Enlightened by God, this man will reconstruct almost the entire

> *world through his holiness."* (Brother John of the Cleft Rock, 14th Century)

> *"Before Antichrist comes, the portals of the faith will be opened to great numbers of pagans."* (Saint Bridget of Sweden, 14th Century)

Now the gist of these prophecies, without getting too bogged down in the details, is that a time of great upheaval will come, in which those opposed to Christianity will seem to have the upper hand. However, their plans will be interrupted when a great king, aided by a holy pope, will arise and destroy these enemies. Both through war and natural catastrophe, the entire world will be turned upside-down, and Christians (previously oppressed) will quickly gain the upper hand, and retake the world in an astonishing upset to the forces of darkness. These are medieval prophecies, but we should take them with a grain of salt. We have no reason to disbelieve them, but we must also remember that they do not bear the note of infallibility. They could contain errors.

Whether an actual Christian monarch (from France) arises at some future date, to rule over all of Europe, assisted by a holy pope, is of little importance as far as we are concerned here in the early half of the twenty-first century. I say it doesn't matter whether a French king arises or not. What's important to understand is that Christian tradition tells us that hard times for the Church, and the world, do not necessarily equate to the Last Days of history. The times in which we live, wherein Christianity appears to be declining, and the enemies of Christendom appear to be on all sides closing in, does not necessarily herald the rise of the Antichrist. Great upheavals can happen. Political and social circumstances can radically change. In short order, the tables can be turned, and our situation can be reversed. None of this is beyond the scope of possibilities for Jesus Christ, the King of kings and Lord of history. How he does it is of little consequence. It only matters that he does, and that we have faith he will.

The lesson of both Scripture and Tradition is always one of militant victory. The spirit of defeat is foreign to the Christian mind. For even in death, there is victory. Christians should always be seeking to overcome, so that even when the Son of Perdition himself stands before us, we should still militantly resist him and declare his foretold destruction by the return of our Lord and King -- Jesus Christ.

This spirit of militant victory over the world should always drive our thoughts and our attitudes. Christ has overcome the world, and so shall we, if only we will remain faithful to him.

Modern Prophecies

So, now we enter into our modern era, following the horrors of two world wars, the rise of godless communism in the East, and the abandonment of Christian religion in the West. We are left wondering, are these the Last Days? Thankfully, in addition to the clues we get from Scripture, Tradition, and the writings of Christians in ages past, we are graced to be visited by prophecies and apparitions to comfort us in our present age.

When we consider the apparitions of angels and saints, both in Biblical times, and in the times since then, a common phrase is often repeated by these apparitions: “Be not afraid.”

We can go into speculation as to why heavenly beings would so often use this greeting. We have been told that the appearance of heavenly beings can be startling, even frightful, at times. Maybe so. I think, however, there is a more profound meaning to the use of this phrase. It comes down to our general attitude in life. We are frequently afraid, especially when it comes to religious matters. We're afraid to stand out. Not only that, but we're afraid to be a witness. We're afraid of being rejected, scoffed at and even persecuted. Come on, be honest. We've all had those thoughts. What if I lose my job over this? What will my family think? Will my friends want to stay with me? They're all legitimate questions, actually, and they all have the same answer. Be not afraid.

In his teleconference address to young people, from Los Angeles, on September 15, 1987, Pope Saint John Paul II said the following...

> *"I invite each of you to listen carefully to God's voice, in your heart. Listen! To his voice! DO NOT BE AFRAID. Do not be afraid. Open your hearts, open up your hearts, to Christ. The deepest joy there is in life, is the joy that comes from God. And is found in Jesus Christ, the Son of God. Jesus Christ is the hope of yours, is my hope, HE is the hope of the world!"*

His message to the youth of the United States and Canada, which he spoke in English, was "*do not be afraid*" and "*the deepest joy there is in life, is the joy that comes from God.*" I was seventeen years old when he said this. I was not Catholic at the time. In fact, I was going through a very difficult time in my life back then, following the death of my Catholic grandmother. I don't remember if I actually heard this address or not. I was a bit distracted at the time, but looking back on it now, I know it was meant for me, just as much as it was meant for you, and anyone else who heard him say it, or is now reading his words.

At this time in my life, I was deeply engrossed in the Last-Days craze of our American Evangelical culture. It caused me much anxiety. Worst of all, however, was that it was a distraction, a major distraction from the more important things in my life, most especially my walk with Jesus Christ.

This Last-Days craze, we're all living through, at this moment in history, is basically a distraction. It causes Christians to focus on things beyond their control, and pulls us away from the more essential work at hand, which is bringing the gospel to all people, and subduing our world (business, society, entertainment, government, etc.) to the gospel message. We Catholics have, at our disposal, some tremendous tools, in the form of history and tradition, to help us discern that much of this Last-Days craze is not in our best interest. We may be living through a dress rehearsal of the Last Days, but it's not likely that these are the actual Last Days before the Second Coming of Jesus Christ. Certain conditions must be met first, and to the best of our understanding, that hasn't happened yet.

Saint John Bosco

Father John Melchior Bosco, also known as Don Bosco, was an Italian priest who was born on August 16, 1815. He was an educator, writer and mystic, often associated with helping street children, juvenile delinquents, and other disadvantaged youth. It was for them he developed a new education system built on loving kindness, rather than the disciplinary systems common to education models of that time. Bosco understood that some children just cannot be reached by strong authority, fear and punishment. His model was based on the three pillars of (1) reason, (2) religion and (3) loving-kindness. It came to be called the *Salesian Preventive System* because Bosco founded the Salesians[163] congregation of men to help children.

Bosco, like many other priests of his time period, was faced with the horrors of the industrial revolution and unbridled capitalism, which took advantage of poor families, working both parents so much, they scarcely had any time for their children. Poor fathers usually died at a young age, leaving the wife to fend for the family at less than half the wages her husband earned. Children were then left to their own devices, and this resulted in all sorts of social problems in the lower economic classes. An order for religious sisters soon followed, called the *Salesian Sisters*, along with a layperson's association called the *Salesian Cooperators*.

Father John Bosco was well known not only for his corporal works of mercy, but also for his prophetic visions. Probably the most famous vision is that of the great ship and two pillars. On May 30, 1862, John Bosco recounted that he had seen an immense sea, upon which were many ships, arranged for battle against a much larger and taller ship. He also saw other smaller ships, which were defending the tall ship. This account reads as follows…

> *"In the midst of this endless sea, two solid columns, a short distance apart,*

---

[163] Salesian: named after Saint Francis DeSales

soar high into the sky. One is surmounted by a statue of the Immaculate Virgin, at whose feet a large inscription reads: 'Auxilium Christianorum' ('Help of Christians'). The other, far loftier and sturdier, supports a Host of proportionate size, and bears beneath it the inscription: 'Salus credentium' ('Salvation of believers').

"The flagship commander - the Roman Pontiff - standing at the helm, strains every muscle to steer his ship between the two columns, from whose summits hang many anchors and strong hooks linked to chains. The entire enemy fleet closes in to intercept and sink the flagship at all costs. They bombard it with everything they have: books and pamphlets, incendiary bombs, firearms, cannons. The battle rages ever more furious. Beaked prows ram the flagship again and again, but to no avail, as, unscathed and undaunted, it keeps on its course. At times, a formidable ram splinters a gaping hole in its hull, but immediately, a breeze from the two columns instantly seals the gash.

"Meanwhile, enemy cannons blow up; firearms and beaks fall to pieces; ships crack up and sink to the bottom. In blind fury, the enemy takes to hand-to-hand combat, cursing and blaspheming. Suddenly, the pope falls, seriously wounded. He is instantly helped up, but

struck a second time, dies. A shout of victory rises from the enemy, and wild rejoicing seeps to their ships. But no sooner is the pope dead than another takes his place. The captains of the auxiliary ships elected him so quickly that the news of the pope's death coincided with that of his successor's election. The enemy's self-assurance wanes.

"Breaking through all resistance, the new pope steers his ship safely between the two columns; first, to the one surmounted by the Host, and then the other, topped by the statue of the Virgin. At this point, something unexpected happens. The enemy ships panic and disperse, colliding with and scuttling each other.

"Some auxiliary ships, which had gallantly fought alongside their flagship, are the first to tie up at the two columns. Many others, which had fearfully kept far away from the fight, stood still, cautiously waiting until the wrecked enemy ships to vanish under the waves. Then they too head for the two columns, tie up at the swinging hooks, and ride safe and tranquil beside their flagship. A great calm now covers the sea."[164]

---

164 John Bosco, Memoirs, Vol. VII. Pages 107-108

The dream, of course, is highly symbolic, but it's also pretty self-explanatory. Many people believe Bosco was given a vision of the Church in the near future, meaning what would become of the Church over the next century or two. Bosco seemed to confirm this in his own interpretation of the vision. He said the trials the Church has already been through in recent memory (from the years before 1862) would be nothing compared to what is coming. With the rise of Marxism (both political and cultural) that would follow in the twentieth and twenty-first centuries, he couldn't be more correct.

The vision given to Father John Bosco conveniently came with its own interpretation. The secret to overcoming the difficult times ahead would be devotion to Mary and frequent reception of the Eucharist. These are the pillars that secure the Church in her place, and make the enemies' attacks futile.

Bosco went on to found many oratories, and missions to youth, as well as writing many books, pamphlets and journals. He died on January 31, 1888, and was canonized a Saint by Pope Pius XII on April 1, 1934.

Marian Visions & Apparitions

Throughout history, Our Lord and Our Lady have appeared to Christians, to assist them in their time of need, to deliver an important message, and to direct them in the way they should go. The Blessed Virgin Mary was assumed[165] into heaven, body and soul, between A.D. 43 - 48. Since then, she has been

---

165 Assumed; meaning taken body and soul at the end of her life. The Scriptures tell us this happened to two other people as well -- Enoch (Genesis 5:24; Sirach 44:16; Sirach 49:14; Hebrews 11:5) and Elijah (2 Kings 2:11-12).

appearing, here and there, as a messenger for Our Lord. It is fitting, that the first follower of Christ, the first Christian, and Mother of our Lord, should be the prophetess who warns and comforts the rest of those who imitate her Christian faith in their time of need. The first recorded history of a Marian apparition was by Saint Nicholas[166] (yes, the one and only "Santa Claus"), who claimed to have seen her while imprisoned in a dungeon, after striking Arius the heresiarch for blaspheming Christ and the Holy Trinity at the Council of Nicea in A.D. 325.

There have been plenty of other apparitions, and with these apparitions, we also learn from the traditions of the early Christians that at the end of time, in the Last Days, Antichrist is to appear. He will be of Jewish stock and rise to global power in Jerusalem.[167] He will subdue the world, leading the inhabitants of the earth into global apostasy (falling away), following a great Christian renaissance. Once he has seized control of the Jewish homeland, and enthroned himself (as God) in a rebuilt Jewish Temple, he shall then begin persecuting all the Christians of the world.

So... Where is this Antichrist today? We know he is to come to power in Jerusalem as a king. Yet today, the State of Israel is a republic. There is no king there. While the Israeli Republic may be the most powerful state in the Middle East, it is nothing close to a superpower. How exactly is this "king," who is to rise to power in what is currently a republic, supposed to

---

[166] Saint Nicholas was a bishop at Myra in Asia Minor (Greek: Μύρα; modern-day Demre, Turkey)

[167] Ezekiel 21:25-27; Ezekiel 28:2-10; Daniel 11:36-37; Matthew 12:43-45; John 5:43; 2 Thessalonians 2:4; Hippolytus, The Antichrist 6 [A.D. 200]; Hippolytus, Discourse on the End of the World 23-25 [A.D. 217]; Cyril of Jerusalem, Catechetical Lectures 15:12 [A.D. 350]

persecute all the Christians of the world, when this nation-state can barely defend itself from its Arab neighbors?

Clearly, the authors of the Bible, and the Fathers of the Early Church, had a radically different picture in mind about the Last Days. So, either we are to believe that they were just wrong, or else maybe it's the Last Days fanatics of today who are wrong. Which is it?

It seems to me that the most likely scenario here is that the Last Days fanatics of today are those in error. I'm far more inclined to believe the testimony of Scripture and the early Church Fathers. I believe the authors of the Bible, and the Church Fathers, were right about the identity and location of Antichrist. It seems very probable that what they were talking about was a different time, different from our own, perhaps sometime still in the distant future, even from our standpoint. When the State of Israel becomes a global superpower, and transforms from a republic into a kingdom, then I'll be inclined to say the Last Days are near, but not until then.

The Catholic Church covers what we are to expect of the Last Days in vivid detail, and I outlined this in *Chapter 6: The Augustinian Approach*. It is coming. Those days will arrive, but based on what we have seen in Chapter 6, and what we have learned here, this doesn't appear to be that time. In fact, so it would seem, we're not even that close yet.

So, what are we to make of our own time, and all the upheaval we witness around us? If this is not the Last Days, then what is it?

That is why Our Lady has come to help us. God knows that we have entered a time of great confusion and upheaval. He told Saint John Bosco as much in his vision of the ship and two pillars. Our Lady has likewise come to shed some light on the matter, and encourage us during this time.

Our Lady of Fatima

In 1917 Portugal, Our Lady (the Blessed Virgin Mary) appeared to three shepherd children while they were tending their flocks: Lucia dos Santos (age 10) and her cousins Francisco (age 9) and Jacinta Marto (age 7). As the story goes, they were tending their flocks when they began receiving multiple visions (including that of an angel who taught them how they should receive communion) preparing them for the coming visit of the Blessed Virgin Mary.

On May 13, 1917, the first visitation of Our Lady appeared to them in the countryside just outside of Fatima. *"Be not afraid. I will not harm you..."* Our Lady said to them. The children were told to meet at that place on the thirteenth day of each month, and after six months (in October) they would receive a sign to verify her visitation and the legitimacy of her message. They were then given a series of three visions, called "secrets," which Lucia would write down years later, while she was a nun in a convent.

The three children were persecuted by the Marxist leaders in Portugal. Once they were even kidnapped and threatened with death. When they would not confess to lying, even upon the threat of torture and death, they were released. Each month, a crowd of people gathered on the thirteenth day of the month, hoping to see what the children were witnessing. The crowd grew with each month, until on the thirteenth day of October, some seventy-thousand people arrived in the pouring rain to witness the sign Our Lady had promised to the three children. As the rain increased, and the children prayed, the crowd became annoyed and increasingly agitated, thinking they had been hoaxed. Then, Our Lady appeared, but only to the children. They asked for the sign, fearing the crowd would soon mob them, for they could not see the vision. Our Lady pointed toward the sun, and the children did as well.

At that moment, the rain stopped, the sun peered through the clouds and appeared to change colors, dancing around in the sky. The entire congregation of seventy-thousand people witnessed it, including the Marxist reporters from a local Communist newspaper. Then, something very startling happened. The sun appeared to grow larger in the sky, as if falling to the earth. Panic struck the onlookers, and as people began running to and fro, miracles began to happen. The blind could see, the lame could walk, and the ground, soaked in mud, instantly dried. When it was all over, the sun returned to its normal place, and everyone's clothing was dry -- seventy-thousand people in all. To this day, it is considered the largest witnessed miracle since the crossing of the Red Sea. Our Lady did not fail to deliver what she had promised.

Miracles are not designed to dazzle us. They're not for excitement or wonder. They serve a purpose. That purpose is validation. The children were given visions, or "secrets," then they were told there would be a sign. The sign was delivered, just as promised, so now we know these visions/secrets are valid. They can be trusted. The size of the miracle may simply be to gather attention, for making sure the message gets out to as many people as possible. Because of the sheer size of the miracle of the sun, the message of Our Lady of Fatima cannot be dismissed. It must be taken seriously, and it must be reported. Fatima is one of the few apparitions actually approved by the Vatican. Two of the three children, who died in the influenza pandemic of 1918, have already been canonized as

Saints. While the canonization process has already begun for the third child -- Sister Lucia -- who died in 2005.

The three visions/secrets have been revealed to the public now. The first was a vision of hell the children received, which terrified them. They were told that many souls would go there in the decades to come. The primary reason for this, it was later revealed, would be sexual immorality. The second was a promise that the Great War (World War I) would soon come to an end, but that a greater war would follow in the decades ahead (World War II), following a strange light that would illuminate the night sky.[168]

To prevent this, Our Lady asked for the consecration of Russia to her Immaculate Heart, and the establishment of the First Saturdays Devotion. If these things did not happen, Russia would begin to spread its errors all over the world,[169] causing wars and persecutions of the Church. Neither happened in a timely manner, and so Russia began spreading the

---

[168] An Aurora Borealis light storm, consisting mainly of red light, lit up the sky in Europe, North America, and much of the Northern hemisphere on the nights of January 25 and 26 in 1938.

[169] Communism is not just an economic theory. It's an all-encompassing social theory that seeks to eliminate the nuclear family, along with religion, and anything that stands in the way of its goals. According to Fredrich Engels, one of the two founders of communism, the promotion of sexual immorality is seen as essential to this end.

errors of communism and socialism[170] all over the globe. Even though the Soviet Union has fallen, the "errors of Russia" are still with us in a very persistent way.

It is here the children were assured by the promise of Our Lady that in the end, her Immaculate Heart would prevail. The consecration of the whole world, which includes Russia of course, was eventually performed by Pope Saint John Paul II in 1984, and Sister Lucia reported (twice before her death) that the consecration had been accepted in heaven. It was tardy, but it was done. It wasn't done in exactly the way Our Lady requested, but it was done in principle.

This doesn't mean the consecration of Russia can't be done again. It can. And it may have positive effects, especially if it is done in a way that is more specific to what Our Lady requested.

Pope Francis has stated his intention to consecrate Russia, by name, along with Ukraine, to Mary's immaculate Heart on March 25, 2022. *(Providentially, that is also the publication date for this book.)* This comes during the current military conflict between Russia and Ukraine, which has the real threat of spilling over into another world war. Such a consecration, during this perilous time, if accomplished as intended, would likely have a positive effect. We can only hope and pray it will. I should point out, however, that the positive effect may not be immediate. It took

---

170 Socialism and communism, as well as fascism, are all connected to the teachings of Karl Marx (Marxism). They are each manifestations of the same teaching, which centers around the concept that government is the final and absolute authority on all things (as if it were God), and that human rights (including the right to private property) are completely subject to the state. This is why the "errors of Russia" are referred to in the plural as "errors." There is more than one, but they are all connected to Karl Marx.

seven years for Pope Saint John Paul II's 1984 consecration to result in the fall of the Soviet Union.

The Soviet Union collapsed within a matter of years after the 1984 consecration, but the errors of Russia (in the form of persistent communism and cultural Marxism) remain with us until now.

The third secret of Fatima was given in a symbolic vision that is highly apocalyptic in nature…

> *"After the two parts which I have already explained, at the left of Our Lady and a little above, we saw an Angel with a flaming sword in his left hand; flashing, it gave out flames that looked as though they would set the world on fire; but they died out in contact with the splendor that Our Lady radiated towards him from her right hand: pointing to the earth with his right hand, the Angel cried out in a loud voice: 'Penance, Penance, Penance!' And we saw in an immense light that is God: 'something similar to how people appear in a mirror when they pass in front of it a Bishop dressed in White 'we had the impression that it was the Holy Father'. Other Bishops, Priests, Religious men and women going up a steep mountain, at the top of which there was a big Cross of rough-hewn trunks as of a cork-tree with the bark; before reaching there the Holy Father passed through a big city half in ruins and half trembling with halting step, afflicted with pain and sorrow, he prayed for the souls of the corpses he met on his way; having reached the top of the*

> *mountain, on his knees at the foot of the big Cross he was killed by a group of soldiers who fired bullets and arrows at him, and in the same way there died one after another the other Bishops, Priests, Religious men and women, and various lay people of different ranks and positions. Beneath the two arms of the Cross there were two Angels each with a crystal aspersorium in his hand, in which they gathered up the blood of the Martyrs and with it sprinkled the souls that were making their way to God."*[171]

While there is some controversy surrounding the nature of this third-secret of Fatima, I won't get into that here. I will only say that I think the Vatican's interpretation of this secret is very limited. It would appear to me, and others, that the meaning of the vision is far more comprehensive than what Rome has suggested.

The "*big city half in ruins*" likely represents the Church, having been ravaged by the "errors of Russia." The corpses likely represent the spiritual casualties of this ideological holocaust. Today, we see the full effects of this all around us, especially in Europe, where many of the largest cathedrals are practically museums now. Christianity is on the decline, especially in Europe, as the "errors of Russia" affect the minds of Western people.

The death of the "bishop in white" (presumably the pope) is likely symbolic as well. The nature of the attack on him suggests this (bullets and arrows), which likewise took out many of the priests, bishops and

---

171 The Message of Fátima (2000), The Congregation for the Doctrine of the Faith, The Vatican

laypeople with him. The vision seems to represent, more than anything, the loss of faith in the West, particularly in Europe, and a great spiritual martyrdom of the Catholic Church, from the pope down to the laypeople. While it cannot be a representation of the end of the Church, for Christ said the Church would be with us until the end of time,[172] it does appear to be a representation of a great spiritual holocaust unlike anything in recent history. Yes, it could always end in literal blood, but it doesn't have to. The first vision of hell reminds us there are things in the next world far worse than death in this world. The last line of this vision seems to indicate that. The blood of the martyrs acts as a witness to refresh the souls of future Christians making their way to God.

I think the Vatican's interpretation is correct, and I'm not challenging that here. Rather, I'm saying it seems incomplete. To equate the bishop in white with Pope Saint John Paul II exclusively is only part of the picture. The bishop in white could, and probably does, represent more than one pope. It may represent the papacy itself, or more specifically, the men who occupy that office in the years following the "errors of Russia." Pope Saint John Paul II suffered from physical attacks and ailments. Pope Benedict XVI suffered from betrayal within his closest ranks. As for Pope Francis, well, he seems to suffer from something, which I won't get into in this book.

When Pope Benedict XVI visited Portugal from May 11 to 14 of 2010, he explained that the interpretation of the third secret did not only refer to the attempted assassination of Pope Saint John Paul II in 1981, as the Vatican had reported. He said, rather, that the third secret...

---

172 Matthew 16:18-19

> *"Has a permanent and ongoing significance... its significance could even be extended to include the suffering the Church is going through today as a result of the recent reports of sexual abuse involving the clergy."*

The former pope may have hit the nail on the head with that analysis. On March 10, 1953, a former communist activist, Bella Dodd, testified before the U.S. Congress that while she was a communist, she orchestrated the infiltration of many Western institutions for the Soviets. With regard to the Catholic Church, her testimony before the *House Committee on Un-American Activities* (1938-1975) reads as follows...

> *"In the late 1920s and 1930s, directives were sent from Moscow to all Communist Party organizations. In order to destroy the Catholic Church from within, party members were to be planted in seminaries and within diocesan organizations... I, myself, put some 1,200 men in Catholic seminaries."*

Manning Johnson, another former official of the U.S. Communist Party, also gave the following testimony in 1953...

> *"Once the tactic of infiltration of religious organizations was set by the Kremlin... the communists discovered that the destruction of religion could proceed much faster through the infiltration of the*

> *Church by communists operating within the Church itself... The practical conclusion drawn by the Red leaders was that these institutions would make it possible for a small communist minority to influence the ideology of future clergymen in the paths conducive to communist purposes... The policy of infiltrating seminaries was successful beyond even our communist expectations."*

Further testimonies and private conversations would reveal that the communist tactic for destroying religion centered around sexual corruption, ordaining homosexual men whenever possible, preferably those with an attraction to teenage boys. Now, with all this in mind, including the words of Pope Benedict XVI, and the testimony of congressional hearings in the United States, read the third secret of Fatima again.

I don't think there is an absolute and definitive way to interpret this secret, but I do think that recent revelations concerning the communist infiltration of the Catholic Church (now indisputable) tend to shed some light on it, and give us a better idea of what Our Lady was warning us about at Fatima. Before we move on, however, we should be reminded that Our Lady of Fatima promised the three shepherd children that in the end, her Immaculate Heart would prevail. That is a promise of victory, not only for her, but also for the Catholic Church. For it is the Catholic Church, and no other, that promotes the doctrine and devotion of the Immaculate Heart of Mary.

The message of Our Lady of Fatima is twofold. The first part of the message came from the angel, who prepared the children for Mary's visit. He gave them communion and taught them how to receive it with great reverence. This was reiterated by Our Lady, wherein she requested the first Saturday devotion. This amounts to regular reception of the Eucharist no less than twice a week, once a month, for at least five months of the year. The second part of the message came from Mary herself, requesting devotion to her Immaculate Heart, which includes regular recitation of the Rosary. In this way, Christians can cope with the upheavals all around us, and be shielded from spiritual evil. Do you remember Saint John Bosco's vision of the ship and the two pillars, which pointed to regular reception of communion and devotion to Mary? Are you starting to see a pattern yet? The vision of Saint John Bosco, and the message of Our Lady of Fatima, are one and the same.

Our Lady of Akita

In 1973, Sister Agnes Katsuko Sasagawa, in the remote area in the outskirts of Akita, Japan, reported a series of visions to her from the Blessed Virgin Mary. These were accompanied by strange events. One of those events was a wooden statue of the Virgin Mary that appeared to be weeping. The phenomenon was even captured on national television.

After careful investigation, the legitimacy of the apparition and message was approved by Bishop John Shojiro Ito, of the Diocese of Niigata. The apparition and message later received a verbal approval from Cardinal Joseph Ratzinger, Prefect of the Vatican Congregation for the Doctrine of the Faith (CDF), before his election as Pope Benedict XVI. The apparition remains approved as of the date of this publication, according to the norms of the Catholic Church.

The following is a transcription of the main message given to Sister Agnes by Our Lady. It recounts much of the same message of Our Lady of Fatima, and the Vision of Saint John Bosco, with particular focus on devotion to the Holy Rosary...

> *"My dear daughter, listen well to what I have to say to you... As I told you, if men do not repent and better themselves, the Father will inflict a terrible punishment on all humanity. It will be a punishment greater than the deluge, such as one will never have seen before. Fire will fall from the sky and will wipe out a great part of humanity... the good as well as the bad, sparing neither priests nor faithful. The survivors will find themselves so desolate that they will envy the dead... Each day, recite the prayer of the rosary. With the rosary, pray for the pope, bishops and the priests. The work of the devil will infiltrate even into the Church in such a way that one will see cardinals opposing cardinals, and bishops against other bishops. The priests who venerate me will be scorned and opposed by their confreres... churches and altars sacked; the Church will be full of those who accept compromises, and the demon will press many priests and consecrated souls to leave the service of the Lord. The demon will be especially implacable against souls consecrated to God. The thought of the loss of so many souls is the cause of my sadness. If sins*

increase in number and gravity, there will be no longer pardon for them. With courage, speak to your superior... It is Bishop Ito, who directs your community. Do you still have something to ask? Today is the last time that I will speak to you in a living voice. From now on, you will obey the one sent to you and your superior... I alone am still able to save you from the calamities which approach."

The message is startling, and considering that it speaks in terms of future tense, having been given in 1973, it appears to foretell a calamitous time we have yet to fully experience. One could say that we are already beginning to experience some events of this prophecy, particularly the part about churchmen publicly opposing each other. This began in earnest under the pontificate of Pope Francis, in an ongoing way, following the publication of his Apostolic Exhortation *Amoris Laetitia* in 2016. The document appears to give permission to administer communion to divorced and remarried couples, without the need for a certificate of annulment from the Church. The public opposition between churchmen has only been getting more intense with each passing year, and with each new document or statement that comes from Rome.

From the conflict between churchmen, we can see a literal side to this prophecy. Could the whole thing be literal? Or is it more apocalyptic, like the Third Secret of Fatima? We could go either way. We have the precedence of Fatima to say the prophecy of destruction is apocalyptic (not literal), but then we have prophecies from the medieval period indicating the coming of wars and comets. Your guess is as good as mine.

In the end, it doesn't matter. The prophecy is conditional: *"if men do not repent and better themselves..."* That means the entire thing can be mitigated by our actions. There is something we can do about it. We can improve our own lives by drawing closer to Jesus Christ in the Eucharist, and his Blessed Mother in the Rosary. That's what all of these messages are about. Get closer to Jesus by going to Mass, and worthily receiving the Eucharist. That means we've got to repent of our sins by going to confession. And then we must also get closer to Mary by praying the Rosary. There really isn't anything more we can do, and that's the message Our Lady is conveying to us through all these modern apparitions.

Our Lady of Good Help

In covering the topic of Marian messages for our time, I thought it fitting to conclude with one in my own nation - the United States of America. It happened in 1859, in an area near Green Bay, Wisconsin. A Belgian immigrant, by the name of Adele Brise, was walking down a commonly used Native American trail when she saw a strange woman, clothed in brilliant white, standing between a maple tree and a hemlock tree. The woman said nothing. Adele, a bit disturbed by this, continued to walk home, quickly. However, on the third time she saw the Lady, she shouted: "*In God's name, who are you and what do you want from me?*" The woman then replied...

> "*I am the Queen of Heaven, who prays for the conversion of sinners, and I wish you to do the same. You received Holy Communion this morning, and that is*

> *well. But you must do more. Make a general confession, and offer Communion for the conversion of sinners. If they do not convert and do penance, my Son will be obliged to punish them. Blessed are they that believe without seeing. What are you doing here in idleness, while your companions are working in the vineyard of my Son? Gather the children in this wild country and teach them what they should know for salvation. Teach them their catechism, how to sign themselves with the Sign of the Cross, and how to approach the sacraments; that is what I wish you to do. Go and fear nothing. I will help you.*"[173]

Adele spent the rest of her life trying to live up to this mission. She became a Secular Franciscan, wearing a nun's habit, and offered to do all the chores of local children if their parents would give her the opportunity to teach them. Her priest said the amount of work she took on nearly killed her. She went on to found a religious school to fulfill Our Lady's request.

The takeaway from all this is the transformation this vision had in Adele's life. Notice the singular mission, the intense focus, and the unwillingness to waiver, even at the expense of her own health. Clearly, this apparition had a profound effect on this young woman (age 28), and radically changed her. There is a lesson here for all of us.

The Marian message to Adele is a message every single Catholic American should take to heart, for

---

[173] An American Apparition: Our Lady of Good Help, Marian Media, EWTN Home Videos

it applies to all of us. God's will is Our Lord's will, and Our Lord's will is Our Lady's will. What is Our Lady's will? Our Lady's will is that the United States of America should become a more Catholic nation, and this is to happen by no other means than evangelization! Take note of Our Lady's expectations of Adele: teach the catechism, how to make the sign of the cross and how to approach the sacraments. This sounds pretty Catholic to me. It seems as if Our Lady wants us to spread the Catholic Christian faith to everyone we can.

The Catholic Church is America's single largest religion at 21% of the US population, but how many of those actually practice? The United States is still very much a Protestant nation. As of the date of this publication, still 47% of Christians in the United States remain outside the Catholic Church. Then we have the growing number of 23% who maintain no religious affiliation whatsoever. The remaining 9% are members of non-Christian religions (Jewish, Hindu, Muslim, etc.) That's a pool of a whopping 79% of Americans who need some form of Catholic evangelization. Then, of course, we have to be honest with ourselves and ask how many Catholics require re-evangelization, since they no longer practice? Let that sink in. This is Our Lady's will for the United States of America. We are to evangelize no less than 79% of the American population. Our Lady gave this message to Sister Adele Brise in 1859. As of the date of this publication, that was one-hundred and sixty-three years ago. So much time has passed, and yet we still have so much work to do.

This apparition was formally approved on December 8, 2010, the Feast of the Immaculate Conception, by Bishop David L. Ricken, after much investigation, according to the norms approved by

Rome for the Catholic Church. It is called "Our Lady of Good Help," and you can visit the shrine in Champion, Wisconsin, just on the outskirts of Green Bay. As of the date of this publication, it is the only officially approved apparition site, of the Blessed Virgin Mary, in the United States. So it is fitting that it was approved on the Feast of the Immaculate Conception, as Mary is the Patron Saint of the United States, venerated under the title of the Immaculate Conception.

Conclusion

In recent years, Our Lady has visited earth to give us messages about repentance, conversion, the Eucharist and prayer. This was echoed in the vision of Saint John Bosco. However, it would appear that Our Lady has delivered an additional message to Catholics in the United States. That message is a command for us to evangelize -- aggressively! We can speculate as to why Our Lady picked the Church in our nation for this specific directive. Perhaps it is because of our religious liberties here. Perhaps it is because of our nation's wealth and sphere of influence. Perhaps it is just because it's the one thing this nation needs to survive in the future. Who knows?

I began this book telling the story about my Evangelical friend and his unusual beliefs about the Last Days. Throughout the pages of this book, I've tried to give an orthodox Catholic understanding of the Last Days from the Church's historical teachings. While it seems undoubtable to me that we are living through some kind of prophetic time period, I don't necessarily think it's the prophetic time of the Last Days. I think, rather, we could call this time period a "dress rehearsal" of the Last Days, sort of a precursor that foreshadows that time, but not necessarily the Last

Days itself. Some Catholics refer to this time as the "Minor Chastisement," which is a time of turmoil that precedes the Last Days by decades or centuries, and comes just before a time of relative peace and order in the Catholic Church, giving it one more great opportunity to evangelize the world.

Pope Saint John Paul II often referred to the "Springtime of Evangelization" and the "New Evangelization." He could not have been talking about his own time, or our time (as of the date of this publication), because since 1970 the Catholic Church has suffered the greatest decline in religious vocations, and countless members drifting away from the Church. No, he had to be speaking of the future, but he saw the seeds of that future being planted in his time and ours.

Just before he was elected pope, the Polish Cardinal Karol Wojtyla visited the United States, for the occasion of the 1976 Eucharistic Congress, in Philadelphia, which coincided with America's Bicentennial of our nation's independence. He addressed some three hundred, gathered on September 4, 1976, at the Kosciuszko Foundation in New York City. These were a combined representation of the Polish American Congress and the Polish American Clergy Association. It was here he gave this cryptic warning...

> *"We are now standing in the face of the greatest historical confrontation humanity has gone through. I do not think that wide circles of the American society or wide circles of the Christian community realize this fully. We are now facing the final confrontation between the Church and the anti-Church, of the Gospel versus the anti-Gospel. This*

> *confrontation lies within the plans of Divine Providence; it is a trial which the whole Church, and the Polish Church in particular, must take up…*
>
> *"It is a trial of not only our nation and Church, but in a sense a test of two thousand years culture and Christian civilization with all of its consequences for human dignity, individual rights, human rights and the rights of nations."*[174]

Saint John Paul II (Karol Wojtyla) was not one for sensationalism. He was not one to provoke unnecessary alarm. It should be pretty obvious what he was talking about here. It was 1976, at the height of the Cold War with the Soviet Union, but I don't think it was the Russians that concerned him so much. It was rather the spiritual poison of Marxism. He described it as anti-church, and anti-gospel. That's not to say the literal Antichrist of the Last Days, but rather an ideological system that is so incredibly toxic to Christianity, and basic human dignity, that it can only come from the devil himself. The saint saw Marxism unfolding in the world on two fronts. In the East, Political Marxism took the shape of communism in Russia, China, and various smaller nations. In the West, Cultural Marxism had made inroads deep into European and American society, in the form of academia, entertainment, and the mainstream press. Marxism isn't just an economic theory. That's only half of it. Marxism is all-encompassing social re-engineering. It involves destroying religion and the

---

[174] The Kosciuszko Foundation Newsletter XXXI, no. 2 (1976-77), page 12

nuclear family entirely. Sexual liberation is not only permitted, but even encouraged under Marxism. The institution of marriage itself is seen as an obstacle to Marxist goals. Saint John Paul II strongly chided Catholic Americans to stand strong, resist, and courageously propagate the true and authentic Catholic faith.

The Soviet Union collapsed on December 8, 1991, with the signing of the Belovezh Accords. It happened on the Feast of the Immaculate Conception on the Roman Catholic liturgical calendar, a holy day of obligation for all Catholics to attend mass. While the whole Catholic world was celebrating Mary's Immaculate Conception, the leaders of the Soviet Union were signing an agreement to bring an end to its existence. Just as she foretold at Fatima, Mary's Immaculate Heart prevailed! The Soviet Union was officially dismantled on December 25, Christmas Day, of that same year. The struggle against Marxism is nowhere near over, but the victory Our Lady attained through Christ in 1991 was both prophetic and remarkable.

Last Days eschatology can be very useful for Christian formation when it is understood in the context of faith over fear, victory over oppression, and the final assurance of our triumph over evil in Christ. If we are faithful, not even all the trials of Satan unleashed on the whole world can stop Christ from having the last word in both our personal lives and society as a whole.

The danger of Last Days eschatology is when it becomes a distraction from that message. When Christians start focusing on the details, rather than the big picture, or start worrying about who the Antichrist might be, or even worse! When they start placing all their hope in an escape hatch (Rapture) that will spare them from all suffering and having to face the evil they fear the most, they run the risk of missing the central message of the gospel. Even the greatest suffering, when offered to Christ, can produce the greatest victories of evangelism and eternal life.

The prophetic messages of Pope Saint John Paul II and Sister Adele Brise are one in the same message. They are basically two sides to the same coin. Catholics in the United States are called to resist the errors of Marxism, both outside and inside the Church, and to evangelize our fellow Americans to the best of our abilities.

Catholic Americans, we have been given our marching orders by both a canonized saint and the Queen of Heaven herself. ***Evangelize!*** It would be in our best interest to take heed and act accordingly, just as Sister Adele did.

Resources

1. Bible, World English Bible (WEB), 2000, public domain, https://ebible.org/web/
2. Bible, Douay-Rheims (DRB), American Edition, 1988
3. Bible, Revised Standard Version - Catholic Edition (RSV-CE), 1965, 1966
4. Bible, King James Version (KJV), 1611
5. Catechism of the Catholic Church, Second Edition, Doubleday Publishing, 1997
6. Baltimore Catechism No. 4, Benzinger Brothers, Baronius Press, 1921, 2015
7. Catechism of the Council of Trent, Joseph F. Wagner Inc, Baronius Press, 1962, 2018
8. New Advent, Fathers of the Church, http://www.newadvent.org/fathers/
9. New Advent, The Catholic Encyclopedia, http://www.newadvent.org/cathen/
10. Ancient Christian Commentary on Scripture, New Testament XII, Revelation, InterVasity Press, 2005
11. The Days of Vengeance: An Exposition of the Book of Revelation, Dominion Press, David Chilton, 1987, 2006, 2011
12. Wikimedia Commons, https://commons.wikimedia.org/
13. Many Religions: One Covenant, Joseph Ratzinger, Ignatius Press, 1999
14. Jewish Identity, Elias Friedman, O.C.D., Miriam Press, 1987, 2016
15. Rapture: The End Times Error That Leaves the Bible Behind, David B. Currie, Sophia Institute Press, 2003

16. Trial, Tribulation & Triumph: Before, During and After Antichrist, Desmond A. Birch, Queenship Publishing, 1996
17. The Rapture Trap, Paul Thigpen, Ascension Press, 2001
18. The Lamb's Supper: The Mass as Heaven on Earth, Scott Hahn, Crown Publishing Group, 2002
19. Are We Living In The End Times?, Tim LaHaye and Jerry B. Jenkins, Tyndale House Publishers, Inc. 1999
20. A Woman Rides the Beast, Dave Hunt, Harvest House Publishers, 1994
21. Be Not Afraid to Follow the Footprints from Heaven, John S. Carpenter, Page Publishing, Inc. 2016
22. Eusebius of Caesarea, Church History (AD 265 - 340), Translated by Arthur Cushman McGiffert. From Nicene and Post-Nicene Fathers, Second Series, Vol. 1. Edited by Philip Schaff and Henry Wace. (Buffalo, NY: Christian Literature Publishing Co., 1890.)
23. Irenaeus of Lyons, Against Heresies (AD 130 - 202), Translated by Alexander Roberts and William Rambaut. From Ante-Nicene Fathers, Vol. 1. Edited by Alexander Roberts, James Donaldson, and A. Cleveland Coxe. (Buffalo, NY: Christian Literature Publishing Co., 1885.)
24. Jerome Chronicle, translated and edited by Roger Pearse and friends, Ipswich, UK, 2005, http://www.tertullian.org/fathers/jerome_chronicle_03_part2.htm
25. Yigael Yadin, Bar-Kokhba, Random House New York 1971
26. Tertullian, On the Resurrection of the Flesh, Translated by Peter Holmes. From Ante-Nicene Fathers, Vol. 3. Edited by Alexander Roberts,

James Donaldson, and A. Cleveland Coxe. (Buffalo, NY: Christian Literature Publishing Co., 1885.)

27. Tertullian, Against Heretics, Translated by Peter Holmes. From Ante-Nicene Fathers, Vol. 3. Edited by Alexander Roberts, James Donaldson, and A. Cleveland Coxe. (Buffalo, NY: Christian Literature Publishing Co., 1885.)
28. Hippolytus, Treatise on Christ and the Antichrist, Translated by J.H. MacMahon. From Ante-Nicene Fathers, Vol. 5. Edited by Alexander Roberts, James Donaldson, and A. Cleveland Coxe. (Buffalo, NY: Christian Literature Publishing Co., 1886.)
29. Lactantius Firminianous, Divine Institutions, Translated by William Fletcher. From Ante-Nicene Fathers, Vol. 7. Edited by Alexander Roberts, James Donaldson, and A. Cleveland Coxe. (Buffalo, NY: Christian Literature Publishing Co., 1886.)
30. St. Jerome, Commentary on Daniel, transcribed by Roger Pearse, Ipswich, UK, 2004, http://www.tertullian.org/fathers/jerome_daniel_02_text.htm
31. St. Augustine of Hippo, City of God, Translated by Marcus Dods. From Nicene and Post-Nicene Fathers, First Series, Vol. 2. Edited by Philip Schaff. (Buffalo, NY: Christian Literature Publishing Co., 1887.)
32. Pius IX, Apostolic Letter Cum Catholica Ecclesia, http://www.vatican.va.
33. The Complete Works of Martin Luther, Volumes 1-8, Delmarva Publications, First edition (April 10, 2014), http://www.DelmarvaPublications.com
34. St. Victorinus, Commentary on the Apocalypse, Translated by Robert Ernest Wallis. From Ante-

Nicene Fathers, Vol. 7. Edited by Alexander Roberts, James Donaldson, and A. Cleveland Coxe. (Buffalo, NY: Christian Literature Publishing Co., 1886.)

35. Lewis Sperry Chafer, Dispensationalism (Dallas, Seminary Press, 1936)
36. Lewis Sperry Chafer, Systematic Theology (Dallas, Dallas Seminary Press, 1975)
37. Dispensational Truth [with Full Size Illustrations], or God's Plan and Purpose in the Ages, Clarence Larkin, Martino Fine Books (June 30, 2011)
38. Bede, Explanation of the Apocalypse, (Translated by the Rev. EDW. Marshall, M.A., F.S.A. Oxford and London: James Parker and Co., 1878), http://www.ecatholic2000.com/bede/untitled-31.shtml
39. Josephus, Wars of the Jews, (Translated by William Whiston, 1737), http://sacred-texts.com/jud/josephus/
40. Thomas Aquinas, Summa Theologica, (Translated by Fathers of the English Dominican Province, Second and Revised Edition, 1920)
41. Benedicti XIV. Pont. Opt. Max. opera omnia in tomos XVII. distributa: De servorum Dei beatificatione et beatorum canonizatione, Aldina, 1840
42. Three Secrets of Fátima, From Wikipedia, the free encyclopedia, https://en.wikipedia.org/wiki/Three_Secrets_of_F%C3%A1tima
43. The Apparitions of the Blessed Virgin Mary in Akita, Japan,
to Sr. Agnes Sasagawa, Eternal Word Television Network, 2011, http://www.ewtn.com/library/mary/akita.htm
44. Didache, Translated by M.B. Riddle. From Ante-Nicene Fathers, Vol. 7. Edited by Alexander Roberts, James Donaldson, and A. Cleveland

Coxe. (Buffalo, NY: Christian Literature Publishing Co., 1886.)

45. Methodius of Patara, (Pseudo-Methodius), Monumenta Patrum Orthodoxographa, Patrium Veterum Library, 1569, http://www.bibliotecapleyades.net/profecias/esp_profecia01c1a.htm
46. Dionysius of Luetzenvurg, "Life of Antichrist", published 1682
47. Corpus Christianorum, Continuo Midievalis, Brepols Publishers; Bilingual edition (December 31, 2010)

Titles by Shane Schaetzel

- The Last Days: A Catholic Analysis of the Apocalypse and the Second Coming of Jesus Christ, Regnum Dei Press, 2021
- Are Catholics Christian: A Guide to Evangelical Questions About the Catholic Church, Regnum Dei Press, 2013, 2020
- Complete Christianity: The Catholic Blog of Shane Schaetzel – Faithful to the Magisterium, http://www.complete-christianity.com

Made in the USA
Monee, IL
12 April 2022

cfc77314-33e0-4573-92e7-1a1e11cf71e4R01